Jessica Adams Gillian Anderson-Price
Victoria Aitken Eleonora Baldwin
Faith Bleasdale Vicki Arkoff
Helen Basini Janine Brown Pia Jane Bijkerk
Peter Clarke Alison Carmichael-Rulten
Pip Cummings Jane De Teliga Andreina Cordani
Lily Evans Sara Foster
Liz Challis
Alana Hunt Justin Tabari
Louise Hawson Wendy Holden
Bethea Jenner Harriet Griffey
Imogen Edwards-Jones Anna Johnson
Rachel Johnson Leonie Edwards-Jones
Emma Killick Anneli Knight
Helen Lederer Daria La Valle
Valli Little Felicity Loughrey
Karen Moline Kathryn McCusker Kris Mcintyre
Julie Moline Freya North Tyne O'connell
Rosie Mullender Justin North Rachael Oakes-Ash
Sue Ostler Jane Pirkis Rebecca Sparrow
Tamara Pitelen Tamara Sheward Noah Taylor
Julian Venables Jenny Valentish
Nia Freedman Donna Wheeler
James Williams Susan Wyndham

The holiday goddess
handbag guide

HarperCollins*Publishers*

Contents

Introduction

The Holiday Goddess Handbag Guide was born in a handbag, funnily enough. It began life as a set of scribbled notes in a diary carried by author and editor Jessica Adams and then spent the year in Melbourne, London and Paris.

As it was passed over tables from Notting Hill to Le Marais, the diary acquired more scribbles. A rough drawing of a coat of arms appeared, sketched by bestselling novelist Faith Bleasdale in a Soho club. It read: 'No Maps. No Backpacks. It's All About The Shoes'.

Other ideas for a coat of arms arrived, as the diary travelled around the world. People whose career adventures had involved everything from *Vogue* to Lonely Planet contributed at every stage – some with story ideas, others with beautiful illustrations.

What quickly became clear is that women shared the same ideas about their holidays. They didn't want to waste money on hotels they barely saw. And they *really* didn't want to waste hours online, trawling the internet for travel information from people who didn't even seem to have real names.

Everyone loved travelling, but we thought that the internet desperately required some curators – women like us, who could provide a holiday 'edit' that would save us time. And, of course, 75% off Prada shoes.

It seemed that what everybody was yearning for was a female-friendly filter, for the world's biggest and best cities. And so this book was born. Not just to inform, as so many travel books do, but to positively *inspire*.

This guide has been lovingly put together by some excellent curators – more than thirty Holiday Goddess editors with vast experience in publishing, entertainment and the media – and their friends, relatives and readers. Maybe you are one of them.

Now, welcome on board – and please stow your handbag under the seat in front of you!

Paris

We love Paris in the springtime.
But we love it any time too.

Paris is timelessly cool, which may explain why timelessly cool people have always moved there (Johnny Depp, Jarvis Cocker, Marianne Faithfull, Jim Morrison). Holiday Goddess editors who have lived or worked in the Capital of Cool are quick to point out that it's not *fashionable*, though. Parisiennes don't follow trends, they make them. Paris does not follow the rest of the world — she does her own thing, with a sexy shrug. Half the world still has royal families. Paris doesn't. Half the world is off dairy, alcohol and cigarettes. Paris says *non*. She goes her own way.

Before you go

Does anyone believe Jim Morrison spoke perfect French? *Au contraire.* The locals just worked around him. Holiday Goddess editors suspect that all Parisiennes secretly know their language is a nightmare (female words and male words, *mon dieu!*). Thus, their instinctive sympathy for visitors who rely on schoolgirl French, like us. Trust us: if you try, they will meet you halfway.

Holiday Goddess editor **Emma Killick**, who makes France her second home, thinks the much-discussed local rudeness is a myth. 'You just need to try a little French,' she says. 'Use what you find on the first two pages of a small phrasebook and say it with a smile.'

We think it's sad that many visitors to London will never go to Paris because they are terrified of the language. So what follows is our guide to French for the Fearful.

French for the Fearful

Lesson one: The important thing to do in Paris is be polite, smile and look as if you're trying. Most Parisiennes will kindly help you out by taking over the conversation in English. Almost everyone in Paris (especially those in restaurants, hotels, bars and shops) holds down a job that depends on English as a second language. Still, our French readers tell us the attempt must be made. Because, if you at least try, then Parisiennes will help to make your life simple.

Lesson two: Always say hello first. *'Bonjour.'* Pronounced Bon-Jure. Bon as in Bon Scott, the original lead singer of AC/DC. Next syllable, Jure (with a soft J) to rhyme with The Cure. 'Bon-jure.'

Lesson three: *'Parlez-vous Anglais?'* or 'Do you speak English?' We realise that just reading those words on this page could make you feel slightly nauseous.

But don't panic. 'Parr lay voo ong lay?' is easy to say. Most Parisiennes will reply 'Yes' at this point. What a relief. English discussion will follow.

Lesson four: At the end, speak French again. 'Thank you' and 'goodbye'. Myrrh sea, oh rough wah (*merci, au revoir*). Thus:

- 'Bon jure. Parr lay voo ong lay?' ('Hello. Do you speak English?')
- English discussion or sign language and pointing follows.
- Discussion ends. Phew! Now say, 'Myrrh sea. Oh rough wah.' ('Thank you. Goodbye.')

Where to stay

Don't tell too many people this, but Holiday Goddess regularly scoops up Paris deals from hotels we trust, and posts them on Twitter. These hourly deals are often for just one or two rooms – but that's how you end up paying around $120 per night.

Our other great source is Hotels Fairy. This is rather like having a real-life fairy godmother find a miracle on the internet. If you want to book The Ritz for less, then flap your wings over to *hotels-fairy.com*.

The Old Faithful: Hôtel du 7e Art, La Marais

Several Holiday Goddess editors and friends have stayed at this bargainista hotel in the hip Le Marais district of Paris. It's a five-minute walk from St Paul metro station and simple to find, thanks to the flags of all nations hanging above the entrance. It's not glamorous or luxurious, but it's comfortable, quiet and chiconomical. In the off-peak holiday season, single rooms begin from around $100, and doubles from $150. The old Hollywood film posters on the walls, granny eiderdowns and sweet shuttered windows (opening onto a small courtyard) really make the place.

There is a bargainista breakfast, too, if you like croissants and pastries. The staff all speak good English and the hotel is known to non-French speakers as The Seven Arts Hotel. Best of all, step outside and day or night you will find some of the best little shops, cafes, restaurants and bars in Paris. If you're here to see Paris, not spend your holiday looking at pricey hotel room walls, this might just be your place.

Hôtel du 7e Art
20 Rue Saint Paul, Le Marais
METRO: Saint Paul
WEBSITE: paris-hotel-7art.com

Unspeakable luxury: The Hôtel de Crillon

For some women, the thrill of a grand hotel can be as crucial to the Paris experience as a trip to Versailles. Enter the Hôtel de Crillon. The Crillon's most famous fan is Madonna, who has made repeat visits. If you see a woman in dark glasses and a tracksuit ducking down a corridor, it's probably her. We know Lily Allen is a fan too.

For the rest of us, the Crillon is a mad luxury, best saved for honeymoons, birthdays or remarkable lottery wins.

The exterior is beautiful and just a little intimidating. Inside, the Crillon is all Michelin stars, tapestries, chandeliers, marble, gold, silk tassels and exquisite linen – with possibly the largest and most sumptuous floral displays (don't call them flowers) in the world.

It also offers a five-star bespoke hotel service for cats. Yes, that's right. Kitties.

The Crillon was built in 1758 as a palace for Louis XV. Suffice to say, in *A Moveable Feast*, Ernest Hemingway wrote, 'When I had money, I went to the Crillon'. We would tell you where the nearest Metro is, but if you can afford the Crillon, we suspect you may be carried to the front door by valets on a red velvet cushion. No train for you, missus.

Hôtel de Crillon
10 Place de la Concorde
METRO: Métro – Concorde
WEBSITE: crillon.com

Your first day

Paris is a city of walkers (*flaneurs*) and exploring the area around your hotel or home-exchange is a relaxed way to spend your first day. Paris can be overwhelming – ease in! Even an unglamorous district of Paris will still have the essentials: the fresh flower stand on the corner; the supermarket with the best jam you have ever seen; and the cafe with great Bordeaux.

In many districts you will pass a blue plaque celebrating a hero of the French Resistance. The French continue to resist everything, including modern life. As you play the *flaneur*, admire the way Parisiennes have retained all the good things. In every district.

Paris for *flaneurs*

I first visited Paris in the summer of 2006. There was an exorbitant amount of daylight at that time of year, as the sun didn't set until around 10pm, and I spent the great majority of those daylight hours wandering the city's streets – reeling in all the rhythms and eccentricities and charms that give form to the city of love.

Not surprisingly it was the French, with their heightened passion for the quotidian in life, who made an art and philosophy out of wandering a city's streets without rhyme or reason, through the figure of the *flaneur*.

In the midst of the excitement and change that ran through 19th century Paris, as the urban landscape began to take shape and the growing middle class became accustomed to the concept of 'leisure', the distinctly modern sensibility of the *flaneur*, as a detached observer of modern life, was charted by Charles Baudelaire in his influential essay 'Le Peintre de la vie moderne'.

Every sojourn with the city of love should take the art of *flanerie* as a point of departure.

When you reach Paris, take off your watch. Throw away the map and GPS gadgets. Leave the camera and phone at home – along with that list of things to do. Walk. Gradually, progressively and perhaps a little obsessively browse the cityscape. Wander. Looking past all the goods on sale search for fleeting momentary experiences. Lose yourself. Speak with a stranger. Walter Benjamin once described the *flaneur* as one who 'goes botanising on the asphalt'.

Observe. Open your eyes to the corners of buildings, the colour of shoes and the shape of coffee cups. Open your ears to passing conversations, engines rumbling and the sound of an almost empty street. *Flaneur* around Paris and feel the paradoxes that run through the city of love.

Alana Hunt

The Other Paris collections

Why are all the straw-woven chairs outside Paris cafes turned outwards, like theatre seats? Because the street is like a theatre, and every day is a fashion blogger's fantasy – no internet required. Your first day in Paris is the perfect time to see the show, which usually makes Jean-Paul Gaultier look tame. Better still, you'll be in the front row, if you bag a table.

Holiday Goddess editors and readers were all surprised to discover how important the Other Paris Collections were to them. 'It's real art, or design, or style in motion,' said one. 'Unlike other cities in the world, you are encouraged to gawp as well. And I think Parisiennes actually enjoy the attention, too.' The best people-watching time is lunch, *le déjeuner*, when those employed in fashion, media and art stride across town.

Someone at the next table may be making sketches, or clicking a camera. Everyone's an artist here, just as everyone in Los Angeles is an actress.

There are some wonderful cafes to enjoy the Alternative Collections. The Quartier Latin is full of students, most of whom seem to have style embedded in their DNA.

You'll have way more fun than Anna Wintour probably has, because these are real women – not skinny teenagers. Find a cafe at Place Saint-Michel, in the Quartier Latin, and enjoy the show.

Marvel at the way someone born in 1989 is actually wearing the fashions of 1989, but with a modern twist. And don't be surprised if you see a street-look you immediately want to copy.

New day, new scarf

Who can resist at least one shopping mission on her first day? One way to keep it under control in Paris is to limit yourself to the purchase of a carefully chosen scarf.

Many Holiday Goddess fashionistas think this minimalist shopping plan on your first day is a brilliant way to tiptoe into Paris – even if you don't normally count yourself as a scarf person. 'A scarf is the most emblematic purchase of all for a Parisienne,' one said. 'And if you go on a mission for just one thing, you'll avoid the usual shopping overwhelm.'

Scarves last forever (Parisiennes have great faith in history). They can be purchased second-hand or new, and often increase in value. They fly the flag for designers but also express individuality.

Most importantly, scarves can be used as glamorous bandages, if you run so fast towards Rue Saint-Honoré that you go derriere over decolettage.

'This is scarf city,' one Holiday Goddess reader explained. 'Parisiennes really *believe* in scarves, almost like a wardrobe religion. I go backpacking with them all the time, and they pack them like other people pack T-shirts.'

Once you've found your scarf, watch how the Parisiennes use them. You'll see them applied as headscarves, belts, handbag straps and, *mon dieu*, knotted around the neck.

Chiconomical secrets

It's no secret, but the cheapest way to get to Paris is to swim from England. Even David Walliams (*Little Britain*) has done it, covered in grease.

After that, the most chiconomical way to see Paris is Eurostar. If you're staying in London, you can go for breakfast, return for dinner. No hotel required. Or grease.

If you are a shopaholic (and don't want to see museums or galleries) then take a shoulder bag and a wheelie suitcase for all that amazing bargainista French jam and mustard. Then you can trawl the foodie heaven floor at Galeries Lafayette and legally import your stash when you return to London. Plus any sale-price shoes you find on the way.

There are plenty of other reasons to take Eurostar, of course. Some of our readers like it because of the old Kylie Minogue ads on British TV. Others prefer it because it is eco-friendly. Most of all, though, Holiday Goddess editors are addicted to Eurostar because tickets cost as little as £69 return, and the journey is around two hours. 'The other reason I have a Eurostar habit,' said one convert, 'is the five minute zoom through passport and security control. You know those three annoying queues you have to go through, just to catch a plane? They don't exist when you take Eurostar.'

Eurostar is not only cheap, it connects you to the rest of Paris by train (the Metro) with French/English signs. Walk straight off, walk straight onto the Metro, down the escalator. Then buy your bargainista Metro Pass.

If you go in autumn or winter, Eurostar may have plenty of empty seats so you can have two to yourself, and relax with porridge and tea from the buffet car.

If you are on a serious budget, you'll self-cater all day, from supermarkets, and bring a breakfast lunchbox on the train (but don't go past the Eurostar coffee – it's excellent).

The fold-down tray tables on Eurostar seats are twice as large as those on aeroplanes – we have even seen French women give themselves luxurious manicures on them. Then, before too long, the miracle occurs. You're out of the tunnel and in France. Super cool Renaults and Citroëns will whiz past the train windows.

Even better, the moment that you skip into the ladies' loo at Gare du Nord railway station, you will see little dressing tables and specially lit make-up mirrors that make every woman look like Inès de la Fressange.

Thank your lucky Eurostars you came by £69 return train. For the price of a Metro Pass and a little self-catering from the supermarkets or markets, you'll be on your way to Picasso, the Seine and the Jardins des Tuileries (all free). And home in time for bed.

Galeries Lafayette

Galeries Lafayette isn't the biggest bargainista department store. But in terms of value for time and money (especially on a day trip) it beats everywhere else. I think of Galeries Lafayette like a kind and generous French aunt. She speaks English. She has 10% discount vouchers. She'll give you a free map and guide on the Eurostar, then usher you into private fashion shows, with an additional tourist tax refund of 12% if you're from outside Europe.

Galeries Lafayette is easy to get to from Gare du Nord, where the Eurostar stops. So it's no taxi and no tax, either. The sheer range means you can always find a little French something for 20 euros. And the sales are incredible.

Jessica Adams

Galeries Lafayette
40 Boulevard Haussmann

METRO: Chaussée d'Antin – La Fayette

WEBSITE: galerieslafayette.com

The best 20th century art – free

The Musée d'Art Modern de la Ville de Paris has a free permanent collection of the best in Surrealism, Fauvism and Cubism. You can read more about our obsession with Picasso (who is in here) on page 76. But this is also the place to experience (not just see) Braque, Matisse, Derain, Vlaminck, Modigliani, Matisse, Dufy, Bonnard, Breton and Riley.

The exterior of the museum is just as staggering as the interior, thanks to larger-than-life depictions of Venus and other goddesses. Stand on the steps and you'll also see that other great work of art, the Eiffel Tower.

> **Musée d'Art Modern de la Ville de Paris, 11 Avenue du Président Wilson**
>
> **METRO:** Iéna
>
> **WEBSITE:** mam.paris.fr

Monoprix: so Frenchy, so cheap

Monoprix is a combination of a supermarket and fashion/homewares store and it's so Frenchy, but also so cheap. If you are self-catering in Paris (why not, when you can eat all along the Seine?) this is the place to come for cheese, bread, salami, pâté, yoghurt and fruit. It will be about twenty times more delicious and memorable than anything you buy in another country.

And we love the Monoprix basics. Their espadrilles, cotton pyjamas, and shirts are simple, well-made and chic.

> **Monoprix**
> **21 Avenue de l'Opéra**
>
> **METRO:** Opéra
>
> **WEBSITE:** monoprix.fr

How to be a Paris bargainista

Holiday Goddess editors have enjoyed many career adventures on glossy magazines over the years, but have a special affection for French *Marie Claire*. Their Paris staff are among the best-dressed in the business, but they also produce what we think is Le Bargainista Bible: *Paris Mode L'Indispensable*, which carries 500 *meilleures* addresses (best addresses). If you are serious about going to Paris with 100 euros and returning with a wheelie case full of joy, then buy the bible, as French fashion shopping really does require a separate book. It's printed in half-French, half-English and very handbag-friendly. Find out more at *boutiquemarieclaire.com*.

La Vallée Village is a discount shopping village where last season's collections go for 30 to 60% less. Choose from Agnès B, Armani, Bally, Calvin Klein, Christian Lacroix, Comptoir des Cotonniers, Diesel, Dolce & Gabbana, Jimmy Choo, Salvatore Ferragamo, Kenzo, Mandarina Duck, Max Mara, Guess, Paul Smith, Wolford and Ralph Lauren. La Vallée Village is 30 minutes from Paris by train. For full details visit *lavalleevillage.com*.

Private Sales are the French sisters of New York's famous sample sales, but with a difference. In Paris, you pay for the privilege. An invitation costs between 10–25 euros, and if you want to be in first, you may have to pay up to 95 euros for a privilege card.

There are no changing rooms, so women try on everything between the racks – and it can be manic. Still, what's not to love about trying on the most expensive labels in the world, without sales staff hovering? For Chloé, Diane von Furstenberg and other huge names, try the private sale at Adèle Sand et Volaire. You will find the website at *adelesandetvoltaire.com*.

Are you a fan of Descamps bed linen? It seems wrong to call them sheets. Descamps pillowcases alone are enough to make your trip to **Catherine Max** worthwhile. Check the website before you go, to see what is on offer. Catherine Max also sells jewellery (De Beers) and champagne. Visit *espacemax.com*.

The secret diaries of several shopaholics

Paris is all about designers – big personalities with big labels. It's also about professional 'noses' who create the perfume we love to take home. But really, Paris is a city for every kind of shopaholic.

I travel so much that I don't keep a lot of memorabilia. There is one precious item in my trunk that is never thrown away though: Karl Lagerfeld's one-off illustration of my old *Vogue* horoscope column. And yet every time I look at it, I also kick myself – because I am reminded of the time I gave a Chanel skirt to a charity shop.

I'm sure the the Red Cross did cartwheels when the black pencil skirt with the double-linked C buttons came in. However, unlike Édith Piaf, *moi*, I now regret everything. Why couldn't I just sew the buttons back on? Why did I never stick with needlework classes? Anyway, Paris is very forgiving. Who knows what you'll find at the Marchés aux Puces? Here are my most coveted items.

Taking Paris home

Christian Dior turbans: They tried to bring the turban back recently but women said 'No, no, no'. Maybe that's why they are often so cheap – a Christian Dior turban can be had for around the price of a chain-store shirt. Just pretend you're Joan Collins. Looks great on a pile of old suitcases, at the end of your bed – or on a chandelier.

Half-empty perfume bottles: French women are given the world's most fantastic perfume for Christmas, and then what do they do? They throw it out. That is when you scoop up bottles of Guerlain, Chanel or Yves St Laurent scent (or body lotion) for a handful of euros. They look wonderful on a dressing table. Why not use them up?

French poodle scarves: In real life, French poodles can be rather yappy. Some of them also tremble, which puts me off. In fashion, French poodles ruled the streets in the 1950s and 1960s. They turn up on scarves, which make great cushion covers.

Boaters: A slew of Chanel films recently made boaters de rigeur again but, like turbans, women have mostly rejected them. They look great piled up in a straw basket though. Look for the plain black grosgrain or Petersham ribbon. Very *Gigi!*

Stained white linen: Nobody ever buys the slightly rust- or water-stained white linen at markets, and so it is bargained down ... and down. I buy it, because I know about Napisan, Australia's nappy whitener. Bleach won't do it. Napisan will.

Jessica Adams

The Queen of alternative fragrance: Olivia Giacombetti

Diptyque was one French brand that Holiday Goddess editors could not reach agreement on for inclusion as a cult local brand. We love it, but it's widely exported, and has crossed the line from cult to 'everywhere'. Still, when we thought about our most beloved Diptyques, the figgy Philoskyos fragrance and the spicy John Galliano candle, we realised there was a common factor: the uncommonly talented Parisian, Olivia Giacombetti.

Donna Wheeler is a huge fan of Giacombetti: 'Over the last decade or so, as my wrist and neck bore first L'Artisan Parfumeur's *Premier Figuier* then *Dzing!* then *Tea for Two*, and I drowned my bed sheets in *Costes*, I came to realise it wasn't similar notes that drew me in, but a sensibility. It was the artist's hand, or in fact, nose, at work. Olivia Giacombetti's creations are light but uncompromising, almost narrative, conjuring emotions that are sometimes startling, other times haunting, subtle. Charting her scented trail across Paris, including stops at Cinq Monde spas, the Costes hotels and the perfume houses of Lubin, L'Artisan Parfumeur, Diptyque, Honoré des Prés and any of the Costes hotels, makes for an amazing olfactory odyssey.'

TOP TEN
Fragrance Flagships

1. Guerlain
2. Diptyque
3. Chanel
4. Annick Goutal
5. Fragonard
6. Frederick Malle
7. L'Artisan Parfumeur
8. Hermès
9. Dior
10. Yves St Laurent

Louise Hawson is the cult '52 suburbs' blogger and photographer who explored 52 Sydney suburbs over a year, helping to reinvent the city's ideas about itself. She is also a Holiday Goddess editor – and a fan of her blogging colleague in Paris, **Pia Jane Bijerk**.

Pia Jane is a stylist, photographer and author and also has a cult following online. We love her beautiful book, *Paris: Made by Hand*, and count her as one of our favourite Parisian shopaholics. When Pia Jane began to search out the city's artisans for her book, she finally discovered the Paris that she'd always wanted to find.

Louise took the opportunity to interview Pia about her favourite, Parisian artisans. This is what she had to say:

For me, the artisans are the ones who create the buzz. It's like they're behind the scenes making Paris the dream city that we all want to see. Start in Montmartre, in the 18th Arrondissement, where artists like Van Gogh and Toulouse-Lautrec used to live and where there's still a real cluster of artisans.

If you and I were going there now, we would be armed with our little blue Arrondissement map books, and we'd exit the Metro Blanche near the Moulin Rouge and walk up the hill to Rue Durantin. This street is incredibly atmospheric, filled with jewellers, sculpture, fashion and cafes. You can even visit the fruit and veg shop and cafe that Amelie frequented.

After sticking our heads into **Yonoil**, where you can find old clocks from train stations and industrial chairs and desk lamps, we'd weave our way around the little streets until we came to **Estelle Lemaitre**. Estelle makes exquisite lampshades, using feathers and the most beautiful open-weave fabrics.

After a quick peek at the Sacré Coeur we'd jump on the metro and head to the 1st and 2nd Arrondissement in the centre of Paris to check out two of my favourite artisans. **Alexia Hollinger**, who makes these amazing fabric bags, and **Ultramod**, a haberdashery where you feel like you've gone back in time to the late 1800s. The owner of Ultramod is one of the many true characters you find in Paris – he loves his stock so much he will try and convince you not to buy it!

Finally, I think we'd end our tour in the incredibly romantic 4th Arrondissement on Rue du Pont Louis-Philippe. It's nicknamed Stationery Street because it's spilling over with stationery shops, from the older style **Melodies Graphiques** to the very modern **Papier Plus**.

SHOPAHOLIC MUSTS

18th Arrondissement:
Yonoil 28 Rue Durantin
Estelle Lemaitre 69 Rue Lepic

1st Arrondissement:
Alexia Hollinger 3 Rue Therese
Ultramod 2–3 Rue de Choiseul

4th Arrondissement:
Melodies Graphiques 10 Rue du Pont Louis-Philippe
Papier Plus 9 Rue du Pont Louis-Philippe
Kanea 4 Rue du Pont Louis-Philippe

French fashion investments

New or second-hand, French labels are investments. Not only can your future grandchildren or godchildren sell them on eBay, your purchase (from a market or a boutique) pays off in short-term joy. Every time you open the wardrobe door you'll feel the love. Many of these labels live in the vast department stores Galeries Lafayette (see page 21) and Printemps. The rest can be found at flea markets.

A.P.C. Holiday Goddess editor Donna Wheeler is a fan of this no-fuss favourite (see page 55). The flagships on the Right and Left Bank are kept deliberately plain and simple, like the clothes.

Agnès B Easy, simple, clothes. Not snooty or fussy and never extreme. It helps to be small and thin if you shop at Agnès B, but the crisp cotton separates in navy, white, cream and black last for years. Her cardigans are a lesson in minimalist chic.

Balenciaga An elite fashion house favoured by Sienna Miller and Charlotte Gainsbourg. Can you imagine being Jean-Paul Gaultier's work-experience boy? Nicolas Ghesquière did it, and is now creative director. The bags are extraordinary.

Vanessa Bruno Worn by Kirsten Dunst and Charlotte Rampling, Bruno's mother was a model. Her father was one of the names behind Cacharel, too, so fashion is in her DNA. The old canvas bags with sequins are highly collectable.

Balmain Pierre Balmain died in the eighties and has been replaced by Christophe Decarnin. Gertrude Stein loved Balmain in the good old days and christened it the 'Nouveau Style Français'. New designs are worn by Sofia Coppola.

Catherine Malandrino A favourite of Holiday Goddess reader and editor of *The Knot*, Alicia Richardson. Maldandrino is also worn by Madonna. Alicia calls Malandrino's clothes and accessories 'heroes for my wardrobe'. We have to agree.

Céline Founded by Céline and Richard Vipiana in 1945, this has been revived via the brilliant Phoebe Philo, who caters for urban types working and living in inner-city Paris who need a look-to-go. The trench coats are for life.

Chanel If you are going to take a deep breath and commit to Chanel, you may as well go for the classic. The quilted bag with chain strap (the 2.55) or the two-tone shoe. This is beige with a black toe, created to shrink feet and lengthen legs. Clever.

Chloé Created in 1952 by Gaby Aghion and Jacques Lenoir, Chloé welcomed Karl Lagerfeld in 1966 and has evolved ever since. This is super-feminine, soft and luxurious fashion and has a second line – See by Chloé – for daywear.

Christian Lacroix Immortalised in *Absolutely Fabulous* (Lacroix, sweetie, Lacroix). This is best purchased second-hand and vintage, when it hit the dramatic, theatrical heights in a very supermodelly way. Just a lucky charm pendant will do for us.

Comme des Garçons This is a Japanese label, translated into French. Rei Kawakubo is the anti-hem, pro-asymmetry designer. Rei has been knighted by the French for her influence on everything from furniture to fashion. Oh so minimalist.

Christian Dior used to sketch his ideas in the bath, or in bed. After he died, Yves Saint Laurent became chief designer. Don't miss the historic flagship store.

Givenchy Hubert de Givenchy said in 1952: 'All a woman needs to be chic is a raincoat, two suits, a pair of trousers and a cashmere sweater'. Audrey Hepburn was his muse. The late Alexander McQueen took on the legend. And became one.

Hermès History tells us that Hermès is one of the few labels favoured by both Princess Grace Kelly and HM The Queen. Home of the Kelly bag and the iconic silk scarf. Set up in 1837 to sell harnesses, it still leans on equestrian themes.

Jean-Paul Gaultier is nearly 60 years old, believe it or not. Born in 1952, he is the father of the conical corset and skirts for men. He put Madonna in bondage-inspired fashion for her Blond Ambition tour.

Joseph The flagship is at Rue de Passy, but Joseph rules in London too. Old Joseph never dies, it just keeps on making you look sleeker. The softly-softly knitwear and sharply cut pants in monochrome colours are still hard to resist.

Lanvin was Jeanne Lanvin's label, loved by Marlene Dietrich. She died in 1946. The flagship on Rue du Faubourg Saint-Honoré is the best place to find the ballerina pumps and patent-leather Mary Janes but you will also find Lanvin in vintage stores.

Louis Vuitton has been ripped off around the world for 20 years but the real thing (rebooted by Marc Jacobs back in 1996) still has the impeccable stitching and printing that your grandmother knew. The luggage is still the thing to own (vintage).

Nina Ricci Reese Witherspoon and Renée Zellweger are both fans of Ricci and L'Air du Temps is probably still your aunt's favourite fragrance. The House of Nina Ricci opened in 1932, up against rivals Chanel and Schiaparelli. It's still going strong.

Sonia Rykiel Black, black, black! Rykiel made her name with Saint-Germain-des-Prés style (the Left Bank look) and she popularised chic knitwear. You can spot one of her sweaters at ten paces and she's another stalwart of the second-hand stores.

The Kooples En masse billboard and magazine advertising announced The Kooples to the world in 2011, leading one Holiday Goddess reader to remark: 'Who the hell are the Kooples?' Hipster designers is the answer, with fashionista parents!

Yves St Laurent Super cool, super sexy, super seventies YSL will forever be linked with that era – except his sleek suits also dominated boardrooms in the corporate 1980s. If you find a sharp-cut jacket second-hand, remember: no top, no bra.

It's all about the shoes

When Holiday Goddess was first dreamed up, the coat of arms bore the proud motto: 'No maps. No backpacks. It's All About The Shoes'. Well it's certainly all about the shoes in Paris. The *chaussures*! Come to Paris and you will see shoes you never imagined existed. Go to the flagships below for the latest and greatest designs.

Castañer at 86 Avenue Paul-Doumer. The first wedge-heel espadrille in the history of fashion was ordered from Castañer by Yves Saint Laurent. The label goes back to 1776 when the first espadrille was produced. *castaner.com*

Christian Louboutin at 68 Rue du Faubourg Saint-Honoré. Louboutin began by drawing for the dancers at the Folies Bergère. After that he worked for Charles Jourdan. You can't walk in them, but you can whip them out of your handbag for lunch at the last minute. *christianlouboutin.fr*

Jimmy Choo at 34 Avenue Montaigne. Holiday Goddess editor Faith Bleasdale is such a fan of Jimmy Choo that she titled one of her novels *Rubber Gloves or Jimmy Choos?* Choo's partner is former British *Vogue* accessory expert Tamara Mellon. *jimmychoo.com*

Manolo Blahnik at Boutique Maria-Luisa, 7 Rue Rouget-de-Lisle. Immortalised in *Sex and the City*, Blahnik is king of the impossible ten-centimetre heel. The shoes are so light you can hardly feel them in your hand. At sale time, you may well have to be carried out on a stretcher. *manoloblahnik.com*

Michel Perry at 243 Rue Saint-Honoré. Perry is just a little bit punk rock, and a little bit glam rock. He worked alongside Vivienne Westwood in a previous life. *michelperry.com*

Repetto at 24 Rue de Châteaudun. Brigitte Bardot's discovery. Serge Gainsbourg also loved them – and we do too. Unbelievably soft, light and comfortable ballet shoes with brilliant and original detail. The only thing to wear in spring and summer. *repetto.com*

Roger Vivier at 29 Rue de Faubourg Saint-Honoré. The wonderful Inès de la Fressange is Vivier's biggest fan. They draw on retro European cinema for inspiration and their shoes usually have a large buckle, which is the label's signature. *rogervivier.com*

And for goddesses who want to save their francs, you can buy old collections or end-of-line shoes at huge discounts at:
Mi-Prix at 27 Boulevard Victor. Metro: Balard.
MODA at 45 Rue Saint-Placide. Metro: Saint-Placide.

Coco Chanel's Paris

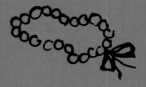

Justine Picardie is the only Chanel biographer to have been given full access to her archives by Karl Lagerfeld. When researching Coco Chanel's life and times, she came to know her Paris extremely well. This is her guide.

It is 40 years since Coco Chanel died at The Ritz in Paris, but her presence is still palpable in the surrounding streets, not least because her name remains within the famous interlocked double-C logo that denotes her empire. Its heart is the **House of Chanel** at **31 Rue Cambon**, just across the road from the side entrance to The Ritz through which Mademoiselle slipped out every morning, on her way to the work that she continued until her death in January 1971.

Legend has it that as she left The Ritz, a doorman would ring ahead with the message, 'Mademoiselle is on her way', whereupon one of her employees would spray the entrance and staircase with her favourite scent, Chanel No. 5.

You can still smell No. 5 – or as Chanel herself described it, 'the scent of a woman' – when you walk into the boutique at 31 Rue Cambon. It is a mirrored, magical place, worth visiting for the atmosphere even if you don't have a penny to spend.

If you do have the funds, this is the place to buy a Chanel classic – whether a handbag or a pair of ballet flats or the latest limited edition nail varnish or lipstick. But only the couture clients can ascend the spiral staircase to the hushed salon on the first floor; beyond that remains a private realm, just as it was when Mademoiselle Chanel reigned here. Her own apartment is hidden behind glass doors on the second floor, and still preserved as it was when she left it: antique Coromandel screens, book-lined walls, a pack of tarot cards on her desk, the crystal chandelier of her own design, with its wrought iron clues to her iconography (the double C, the number 5, and – at the very top, almost out of sight – the G for her real name, Gabrielle).

I was fortunate to be allowed to spend time within Chanel's apartment whilst researching her life and writing her biography; and readers of my book, *Coco Chanel*, often ask if they too can visit there. Unfortunately, the answer is no, but there are other places in Paris where you can walk in Chanel's footsteps.

Indeed, you could begin on the street that was her starting point in Paris, at 160 Boulevard Malesherbes (in the 17ème arrondissement), where she set up as a milliner in 1909, in the ground floor apartment that had been lent to her by her first lover, Étienne Balsan (a wealthy cavalry officer who she had met as a seamstress in Moulins). By the time Chanel reached Paris, she was already involved with one of Balsan's friends, an English polo-player and industrialist named Arthur 'Boy' Capel, who provided the initial capital for her to go into business, and to open her own dress-making premises in January 1910, at 21 Rue Cambon. As her success grew, so too did her territory on Rue Cambon – in 1918 she acquired number 31, and expanded further along the street in the 1920s.

Paris is a city made for strolling, and there is pleasure to be had in exploring the streets beyond Rue Cambon that are associated with Chanel: Avenue Gabriel, for example, where she lived with Boy Capel. For it was here that Chanel first bobbed her hair, in 1917, which was as radical an act as her designs that cut away corsets. Her account of this haircut gives some indication of the independence that she aspired to, and the freedom with which she remade herself, thereafter becoming her own best model.

She was in the apartment at Avenue Gabriel (or so she was to tell a friend in later life), dressing for an evening at the opera: 'I had a white dress made by my own modistes. My hair, which came down below my waist, was done up round my head in three braids.' But as she fiddled with the pilot light of the gas heater in the bathroom, the whole contraption exploded, scorching her hair and covering her white dress with soot. Undaunted, she simply washed her face, took her scissors to her plaits, and declaring herself liberated as she changed for the opera. 'I slipped on a black dress I had ... what a marvellous thing, youth ...'

Chanel's little black dress was to be indelibly associated with the Jazz Age, but remains equally chic today, so there is much to be said for window-shopping for a contemporary version of this timeless classic, perhaps as you stroll back from Avenue Gabriel, and then along Rue Saint-Honoré. If so, don't miss the cult fashion boutique Colette at number 213 (it wasn't there in Coco Chanel's day, but Karl Lagerfeld is a fan); but I always try to keep walking, onwards to 29 Faubourg Saint-Honoré. This grand 18th century mansion was where Chanel was living by 1932, and here that she staged an exhibition of diamond jewellery, a constellation of stars and moons and comets, some of which can now be seen at the Chanel Fine Jewellery boutique in Place Vendome. By this point, you'll need something to eat and drink, and fortunately, there are several places for Chanel aficionados to do as she once did. First, Angelina, the belle époque café at 226 Rue de Rivoli, which dates back to 1903, and still serves the richest and most velvety hot chocolate in Paris. Then, just a few steps along is Hôtel Le Meurice, as chic as it is luxurious, where Chanel entertained and also spent time with her closest female friend, Misia Sert, whose suite of rooms was the gathering place for the most celebrated musicians and artists of the era. It was here that Chanel celebrated the successes of the Ballet Russes with Diaghilev and Stravinsky, and the marriage of her friend Picasso to the Russian ballerina Olga Khokhlova.

Finally, no trip to Chanel's Paris would be complete without a drink at The Ritz, the hotel most closely associated with her. The Coco Chanel suite is as grand as ever at the front of the hotel, overlooking Place Vendome, but her bedroom from the Second World War until her death was a more modest one on the sixth floor of the Rue Cambon side, overlooking the rooftops and the sky. On a clear day, the view is as magical as it ever was, while the veil between the past and the present seems momentarily translucent ...

Justine Picardie

Paris in books and film

'The Paris in my head' is how Holiday Goddess editor **Jane de Teliga** describes the city she knows from books and films. Jane has worked for many magazines and styled covers for many of the most famous names of our age, including Nicole Kidman. She co-created the personal styling and shopping service *styleoncall.co.uk*, based in London. Jane tells us that as a little girl, she wished new shoes would appear at the end of her bed by morning, and as a teenager sitting on the station on her way to school, she wished she could run away to Paris. Now she has.

The trouble with Paris is this: it *is* the most beautiful and thus the most documented city in the world. Before you have even set one foot on a Parisian cobblestone, you have been there a million times in your head.

In childhood, full of longing, I was *Madeline*, the little French schoolgirl in the beribboned boater. I hurried along down those cobbled streets past Notre Dame, in a gaggle of girls guarded by the formidable Miss Clavel. I've floated through the streets of Paris and across the chimneyed rooftops following the *Red Balloon*.

In adolescence, full of tortured artistic sensibilities, Ernest Hemingway and I starved in a garret together in *A Moveable Feast*. I was an artist's muse in Montmartre, possibly Modigliani's tragic long-necked girlfriend Jeanne, although I drew the line at throwing myself out the window after he died. After just one visit to Picasso's studio in Paris and an instant *coup de foudre*, I was one of his many beautiful women, squeezed somewhere between Françoise and Jacqueline in the line-up. Just in time for some serious chateau living in the south of France. And there's been a lot of hanging out with the existentialists dressed in black, you know, with my pals Jean-Paul and Simone, at La Coupole.

At university I sit in a darkened movie house, a dreamy respite from dreary lectures, and I am absolutely, irrevocably Audrey Hepburn in *Funny Face*, muse to Fred Astaire's Dick Avery, modelled directly on iconic photographer Richard Avedon. Yes, I am that skinny bookish girl turned fashion model waltzing around in French couture. Although I do think Fred, divine dancer though he may be, is way too old for me.

I'm Avedon's model Dovima posing with an elephant, or I'm sizzling Suzy Parker wearing Christian Dior's sensational new look in the post-war streets and bars of Paris. Catherine Deneuve and I are definitely chatting to each other in the front row at Yves Saint Laurent.

I'm dancing with Gene Kelly along the Seine in *An American in Paris* while wishing for legs like Cyd Charisse. I'm a smouldering Greta Garbo in the 1930s, the Bolshevik *Ninotchka* being corrupted by silk stockings in The Ritz.

Paris plays *Pygmalion* to my Audrey Hepburn. So after a Parisian cooking school stint, I metamorphose from a gangling chauffeur's daughter into a couture-clad, poodle-carrying minx, and capture Humphrey Bogart's millionaire heart in *Sabrina*. My life is in danger in some very chic Givenchy coats, Audrey Hepburn again in *Charade*, trapped in a creaky Parisian elevator waiting for Cary Grant. Cary in Paris *oh la la quelle* combination!

I smoulder like the gorgeous Anouk Aimée in *A Man and a Woman*, while that theme music drums compulsively in my head. I'm not sure that's me doing something shocking with Marlon Brando and a pat of butter in *Last Tango in Paris*.

Sobbing on a railway station during the war, I'm often Linda, clad in a fur coat without a penny to her name, in *The Pursuit of Love*, rescued by the dashing aristocrat Fabrice, to begin a Parisian life that her creator Nancy Mitford lived until her death.

Lo and behold, I finally go to Paris and so begins my bittersweet three decades long love affair with the city of my dreams. The Paris of my imagination becomes real. The *prêt-à-porter* becomes, twice a year, my somewhat painful playground and my actual workplace. I come to be tortured by the French PRs who have the power to say 'oui' or 'non' to my entreaties for coveted tickets to the *prêt-à-porter* designer shows.

I do get to sit in little gold chairs and watch exquisite couture creations waft by. In the midst of mannequins modelled to the exact measurements of some of the world's most famous women, I marvel at the exquisite handwork in the couture studios of Christian Dior.

I visit, by special invitation, Coco Chanel's own apartment in Rue Cambon above the store. So perfectly preserved is it that I feel she will be back soon with a baguette tucked under the arm of her very chic tweed suit.

I've walked a million miles through the shimmering streets, or slogged exhausted through the metro, fragrant with pee. I've hung out in the marvellous Place des Vosges with the Easton Pearson girls, shopped the hip streets of the Marais, eaten macaroons in Ladurée, sat often in Les Deux Magots cafe, once with an elusive man I loved. I've cried quietly at the beauty of a sung mass in Saint Julien le Pauvre, the oldest church in Paris.

I've swooned to breathtaking theatrical shows at Christian Dior, and marvelled at the crazy beautiful couture of Christian Lacroix. I've sipped the thickest hot chocolate at Angelina's at an early Collette Dinnigan parade and made some major purchases in the Parisian atelier of Martin Grant in the Marais. I've had drinks at the bar at Hôtel le Meurice, afternoon tea at Hôtel Le Bristol and dinner at Hôtel le Crillon.

I've stayed often with my painter sister Sarah in her artist studio home, once that of artist Giacometti. With her I've walked through the Luxembourg gardens in the depths of winter, the bronze horse' manes dripping with icicles, and watched from her window as the Eiffel Tower glitters on dark velvety summer nights.

And for a year not so long ago, I lived in Paris in a tiny bijou apartment and the city of light was by turns exquisitely beautiful, exhilarating, maddening melancholic, glorious, uplifting, soul destroying and joyful. It was everything and nothing like I imagined.

Jane de Teliga

Eat, love, eat more

Faux French food and wine exists all over the world. In London we are faced with supermarket cheese pretending to be brie. In Sydney we are fobbed off with white, plasticky triangles of what purports to be Camembert. In New York the delicatessens sell us croissants which are really just Twinkies bent out of shape. One of our Paris insiders put it this way: 'If you've never been to Paris then you'll never know what you're actually missing. But once you get here, you'll never buy faux French food again. It's like dating for years, then finding love. You can never go back.'

Holiday Goddess editors agree that the only non-French versions of champagne they really love are from Tasmania, Australia or Sussex, England. Otherwise, they can accept no substitutes. French champagne, even from the lowest shelf in the *supermarche*, is usually great.

'The first time I ever walked into a French supermarket I spent all my time photographing it,' one of our confidantes confessed. 'It was very embarrassing, as I crouched down on the floor like a loony, snapping this pyramid of oysters. If you're used to British supermarkets with all their sterile packaging, you can understand why a mountain of grubby oysters looked so exotic to me. And it was in the fruit and vegetable section!'

One frequent visitor to France (over a fifty-year span) told us that she believed the French have turned their food into fantasy, because they were so deprived during the war. Whatever the reason, this is the only city in the world where cats' tongues have inspired wafer-thin, delicate chocolates. Or where even the tiniest little cake comes with a blue satin ribbon. 'Even their jam labels are beautiful,' one Holiday Goddess editor said. 'Gingham print lids, and beautiful handwritten descriptions on the front. No jam manufacturer in the rest of the world would even *bother!*'

The OMG floor at Galeries Lafayette

The OMG (Oh My Goddess!) floor at Galeries Lafayette is what the British call a Food Hall. Parisiennes call it *Les Halles des Gourmands*. Expect snails in tins so beautiful you could put flowers in them. And chocolates from Fauchon in shiny hot pink love-heart tins. Then there's the dainty rosebud tea, made from real pink roses. Half the fun is that you will never, ever see this stuff outside Paris. It's a parallel pantry universe.

Are you an Absolute Paris Beginner? If you're arriving on Eurostar, here's the easy way to reach the OMG floor at Galeries Lafayette: once you arrive from London at Gare du Nord station, look for the signs taking you to the orange train line. There are two to choose from. Select the one that ends up in Place d'Italie. Once you've caught that train, get off at Gare de l'Est station. Now, switch to the girlie pink train line (the one that ends up at Villejuif). Soon you'll arrive at a station that ends with the magic word Lafayette. Exit, walk up the stairs and there it is – Galeries Lafayette. (For more on this store see page 21). Now, take the escalator to the OMG Floor.

Angelina, one of Coco Chanel's favourite haunts, has produced a range of chocolate indulgences to take home – all given pride of place on the OMG floor. There are also bars of chocolate on Galeries Lafayette's OMG floor that should be framed, not eaten.

The champagne section is the size of a bedroom. We defy any red-blooded woman to walk in here and not scoop up a dear little mini-bottle (insert straw and go) or to invest in some lovely vintage, for a future celebration.

Very few foreign brands are permitted into the hallowed halls of the OMG floor at Galeries Lafayette, which may explain why many think all Parisiennes are snooty/fussy. Well, they are. But you will benefit, as any import has to please the French, and they just don't *do* ordinary.

Galeries Lafayette
40 Boulevard Haussmann

METRO: Chaussée d'Antin – Lafayette

WEBSITE: galerieslafayette.com

Ladurée: cult macaroons

The queues are always long for Ladurée, no matter if you want to take the red macaroons home, or dine in at their flagship tea room. Holiday Goddess editors agree that they go quite mad in Paris, and eat substances they would never touch at home – thus, their fetish for the lightweight, sugary, paint-coloured macaroons. The packaging is the thing. There – we said it. Ladurée is way too sweet for many of us, but to leave Paris without an exquisite pale green and gold box seems quite wrong.

Where to find Ladurée

Printemps, 64 Boulevard Haussmann

Ladurée, 75 Champs Elysées

Ladurée, 16 Rue Royale

Ladurée, Charles de Gaulle Airport

Ladurée, Versailles

Eat like the French

To eat (and drink) like the French, start and finish at La Grande Épicerie at Le Bon Marché. To describe this as a supermarket is an insult. It's really a beautiful old building, packed with excellent foodstuffs and wine for rich French housekeepers, and mad cult treats for eccentric Parisiennes. Model Ines de la Fressange, who is a sexy fiftysomething, apparently gets her baked beans, chocolate spoons and jelly beans there.

Their lunchtime takeaway rolls have the freshest seafood, the richest butter and the fluffiest bread. They also have collectable designer water.

Le Grand Epiceries
Le Bon Marche

METRO: Sevres Babylone

WEBSITE: lebonmarche.com

Eating like Elizabeth David

Elizabeth David was the Nigella Lawson of her day. She was a Conservative MP's daughter who famously introduced olive oil and garlic to British cooks and is, in the opinion of many critics, the greatest food writer of all time.

At the age of 17 she went to Paris, to live with a French family and study at the Sorbonne. She was so well-loved by her fans that after her death, her colander was auctioned at Sotheby's for £320.

Elizabeth David was famous for her love of French food, but also for her passionate love affairs. Her classic book *An Omelette and a Glass of Wine* is in many Holiday Goddess handbags. It has made a huge difference to our experience of Paris.

The title of David's classic book comes from her 1963 essay on French culinary secrets: 'Cherished in our dreams,' she wrote, 'held close to our hearts in deathless legend is the humble French restaurant, the unpretentious *petit coin pas cher*, where one may drop in at any time and be sure always of a friendly welcome, a well-cooked omelette, a good salad, a glass of honest wine.'

By *petit coin pas cher*, David meant cheap – but the wonderful thing about Paris is the chiconomical places with the checked tablecloths and cheerfully grubby menus are still there.

And yes, you may order an omelette and a glass of wine.

Here are Elizabeth David's other classic choices for lunch – so simple, so Frenchy, so cheap, so chic.

Petit pois à la française: small, fresh peas cooked with lettuce
Potage de légumes: vegetable soup
Sole meunière: whole sole cooked with butter
Quiche lorraine: made with bacon, eggs and cream in a tin
Moules marinière: mussels in delicious sauce, in a pot
Terrine de campagne: pork belly pâté

For more on Elizabeth David and for the secrets of five of her most famous recipes see *holidaygoddess.com*.

Boulangerie

Perfect Paris picnics

Holiday Goddess editor **Alison Carmichael-Rulten** and *delicious.* magazine food director **Valli Little** both agree that Paris is the best place in the world to have a picnic.

As Valli says: 'For a perfect picnic I would start with an early morning visit to the Polâine Bakery at **8 Rue de Cherche-Midi** for a loaf of their famous bread but be warned. As these loaves are hand crafted and can weigh up to two kilos you might want to take a friend along to carry it for you.'

Valli's next stop is Le Grand Épicerie at **38 Rue de Sèvres**, where, as we've seen, Ines de la Fressange buys her jelly beans. 'This shop truly is a mecca for food lovers and for a picnic, I would select from cured meats, pâtés terrines and accompaniments – followed by a visit to their cave, where the experienced cellar staff recommend wines to match your choices. On a Paris picnic, finish with cheese or something sweet.'

'My favourite cheeses come from Androuet at **37 Rue de Verneuil**– for me this is the best cheese store in the world, because the heady perfume of old and aged specimens that greets you when you walk in is truly intoxicating.

'For something sweet the celebrated shop of Pierre Hermé at **72 Rue Bonaparte** would be my choice. His famous macaroons, exquisitely packaged, come in a multitude of flavours – my favorite Le Mogador is an unusual mixture of chocolate and passion fruit (but in winter I like to try the black truffle macaroon).'

Where to picnic in Paris

With your picnic shopping complete, the only choice left is the location. For Valli it would have to be Jardin des Tuileries by the side of the Louvre. It is a place to watch Paris pass by as you indulge in what will probably be the best picnic you will ever have. *Bon appétit!*

Holiday Goddess editors suggest preparing for the pilgrimage to the Louvre next door by having a breakfast picnic in Jardin des Tuileries first. Then take a deep breath and begin your mission. It's one way of beating the crowds and starting the day in a beautiful way.

A travel editor's favourites

Donna Wheeler is a stylish Lonely Planet guidebook author who has been visiting Paris for over twenty years. These are two of her favourites for eating out, or dining in.

Marché des Enfants Rouges

While it might be almost 400 years old, this covered market's evocative name harks back even further, to when it was the site of an orphanage whose little charges were clad in red. Haut-Marais locals do pop in for their flowers and produce, but Enfants Rouges really hits its straps for an impromptu lunch, with a fascinating, diverse range of stalls. I head to the Afro-Antilleans for spicily sauced curries and creole *boudin*, or to the Moroccans for a groaning spread of tajines, couscous and sweets. Properly made Illy espresso (a rarity in France) from, naturally, the Italians, is also always on my list.

**Marché des Enfants Rouges,
39 Rue de Bretagne**

Rose Bakery: Let them eat (carrot) cake

Rose Carrarini's book *Breafast, Lunch, Tea* is one of the best baking books I know. Her three ever-heaving cafes, the original up the hill in the 9th arrondissement, the others in the Haut-Marais and the 3rd, dish up super-fresh, seasonal, organic and – *quelle horreur!* – classically English cooking that has enchanted often stuck-in-their-ways Parisians. Nutty granola or creamy porridge for Saturday breakfast, trout and leek tarts and lentil salads for weekday lunches, carrot cake or scones any time. In fact, the best cure for a rosé hangover might just be a Rose Bakery crumble (with a magic jug of custard on the side).

Rose Bakery, 46 Rue de Martyrs

The world's most beautiful salt

The French aren't frightened of salt. It goes into most menu favourites in fat, generous pinches. The world's most beautiful salt (yours to take home) can be found in any supermarket here, and most gourmet food temples. It is called Baleine, and decorated with a splendid etching of a whale. This is *sel de mer* – sea salt – and a firm chefs' favourite.

It's crazy cheap. It's also the present for friends and family that really lasts the distance. They use it to the last speck, then request more, every trip.

Baleine – Le sel des Grands Espaces
WEBSITE: labaleine.com

Made in Paris: Cult local brands

Let's face it. Every French perfume that's not in a duty-free shop is a cult local brand. Thus, Parisian scent deserves a book to itself. Even if you have been loyal to a big-name, mainstream perfume all your life, the moment you sniff a bottle of L'Ambre by Roger Vivier, or the costly Frederic Malle's Editions de Parfums, you will be lost to corporate scent forever. We believe in feeling like a goddess for less, though – so begin with Estéban incense and home perfume from Durance.

Estéban

Some women love incense. And some loathe it. Those who love it are Estéban converts and cram 20 packets into their bags to take home. Those who loathe incense because they think it is too studenty or hippie, become instant converts when they see the beautiful Estéban packaging – and breathe in the delicate fragrance. This is not your ex-boyfriend's Nag Champa! This is an exquisite collection of bamboo sticks, fragranced with water lily, late summer fig, thyme and wild fig, lavender flowers and tomato leaves. There are dozens of delicious scents to choose from.

Each long, slender packet is decorated with one-off prints of herbs and flowers, and costs 5 euros.

That's why Holiday Goddess editors cram 20 packets into their bags – then hand them out, like Paris Santa, to grateful friends, sisters, aunts and mothers. And of course, to men in touch with their feminine side.

Estéban invented the global passion for home scent. Their tiny bottles of home fragrance oil are the French householder's choice for refreshing pot pourri – but you can throw a few drops in an aromatherapy burner too. Or drop into a lightbulb burner to transform a room.

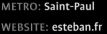

Estéban
20 Rue de Francs-Bourgeois
METRO: **Saint-Paul**
WEBSITE: **esteban.fr**

Durance & Côté Bastide

Why are Parisiennes such dedicated fans of incense, fragrance oil and scented candles? Some readers suggested it was because their homes are shrines to Roquefort cheese, and thus smell less than fabulous. One Holiday Goddess editor thought the Parisian obsession with home fragrance was down to their equal obsession with strong cigarettes, like Gitanes. Perhaps some or all of this is true, but you don't have to be local to love Durance.

This is another household word brand in Paris, and you'll often find a small brown glass bottle of their concentrated home perfume in local apartments. Glampackers love it, because it weighs nothing, costs very little, and instantly changes the atmosphere of any drab hostel room, or communal campsite shower block.

A tiny bottle of Durance Tea Leaf oil (*Extrait de Parfum d'Ambiance*) does, in fact, alter the ambience.

Here's an old French glampacking trick: if your cheap hostel room has a sink, and most will, fill it with hot water, then sprinkle a few drops of Durance home perfume on the surface. Instant Paris!

Our other favourite cult local brand is Côté Bastide. Their candles in plain white signature boxes, with old-fashioned scrawled lettering on the front, always fill the last gap in our bags.

Durance Raris IV
37 Rue St Louis en l'Isle
METRO: Pont Marie
WEBSITE: durance.fr

Côté Bastide
4 Rue de Poissy
METRO: Maubert – Mutualité
WEBSITE: cotebastide.com

Fragonard

Fragonard is the first shop I visit in Paris, and I sometimes double back there at the end, because I love it so much. Where shall I begin? Is it the tiny pots of solid, waxy perfume they sell, illustrated with pictures of the Arc de Triomphe, love hearts and lucky horseshoes? Or is it the beautiful drawstring cotton bags, embroidered with everything from pictures of shoes, to your zodiac sign characteristics? (In French!)

Those drawstring bags are brilliant for travellers, because they organise a suitcase instantly and weigh nothing. Fragonard is the place to find them. Even though it is famous as a parfumeur, I think their flagship store in Le Marais is a kind of drawstring-bag temple.

I've never purchased here, or even online, without some small, free surprise at the end. On the last two occasions I shopped, I was given a complimentary cotton tote bag. I don't know who their painters, illustrators and designers are, as each bag is unsigned – but *j'adore*.

Jessica Adams

Fragonard
51 Rue des Francs Bourgeois
WEBSITE: fragonard.com

A.P.C.

Holiday Goddess editor **Donna Wheeler** loves sexy, rebellious A.P.C. We know women who make the pilgrimage here, purely for the stiff, dark denim jeans. 'With T-shirts declaring "fashion is for losers" and jeans murmuring "fuck 'em" from an arse cheek, there's no doubting A.P.C.'s anti-fashion stance. Tunisian-born, erstwhile left-wing intellectual and musician Jean Touitou's label (an acronym for the appropriately anti-ego *Atelier Production et Création,* or Production and Design Workshop) may be nearing a quarter century, but the rebellious posturing and brainy sexiness is little tempered.

Wardrobe staples are gently reinvented each season and rarely date; beautiful, unusual fabrics resist constant wear. I could happily wear nothing but A.P.C. smocks, knits and jeans. The surplus shop, tucked away below Sacré Coeur, is always my first stop in town.'

A.P.C.
20 Rue Andre del Sarte
WEBSITE: **apc.fr**

TOP TEN
Cult Brand Boutiques

1. A.P.C.
2. Agnès B
3. Joseph
4. Comptoir des Cotonniers
5. Christian Louboutin
6. Jamin Puech
7. Antoine et Lili
8. The Kooples
9. COS
10. Robert Clergerie

Christophe Robin

For **Donna Wheeler**, Christophe Robin provides the Local Colour in Paris: 'His salon lies in the Hôtel Le Meurice salon and Catherine Deneuve, Madame Sarkozy and Kristin Scott-Thomas are among the faithful (I don't use the term 'salon' lightly). My mouse-brown mane sadly is yet to know the patrician beige or dirty blonde highlights Robin might bestow – at €600 a visit, I've still not made it in for a visit – but it's still reaping the benefit of his deep respect for hair.

Marionnaud branches throughout Paris stock his remarkable products, designed to maintain vibrancy in coloured locks, but also perfect if you dislike SLS detergents and silicones. His lemon hair cream gives my hair back child-like softness and a natural, old-fashioned shine.

Salon Christophe Robin
Le Meurice, Suite 128–129,
228 Rue de Rivoli
WEBSITE: **christophe-robin.com**

G. Lalo

Holiday Goddess editors live online, but regret the passing of the letter. Still, there is hope for future historians – beautiful writing paper is making a steady comeback. It can also be wickedly expensive, but the French have come up with their own answer to Smythson of London. They write their love notes and thank-you letters on creamy, heavy stock from the legendary G. Lalo. For something that takes up very little room in your bag (and costs around $10) a packet of Lalo *cartes* is the gift that goes on giving.

Of course, you may want to gift this to yourself. Unless you print out all your old e-mails (or heaven forfend, your Facebook posts and tweets), Lalo is the best way to document life.

G. Lalo, Galeries Lafayette
40 Boulevard Haussmann

METRO: Chaussée Antin – Lafayette

WEBSITE: g-lalo.fr

Cire Trudon stink bombs

Cire Trudon have been in business since 1643, and today sell candles (and their unique stink bombs) to women from all over the world. And – we note – quite a few metrosexuals. The stink bombs are precious little glass phials designed to be thrown on your Parisian balcony. The small candles are good for hotel rooms. A bland hotel room designed for a suit can instantly become a boudoir once you light a candle, turn on the lamp and make some tea.

This eccentric, glamorous company even produce wax busts of Napoleon and Marie Antoinette. The latter commissioned candles from them.

Cire Trudon
78 Rue de Seine
METRO: Mabillon

We love the nightlife

Holiday Goddess editors agree that the best nightlife in Paris lies in the bars, cafes and restaurants. It's not necessarily the place for live music, unless a big name happens to be touring – or you get lucky and tickets for Air are on sale. Check *Time Out* online, months in advance, to snap them up at *timeout.com/paris*.

Yes, we know there's an opera in Paris. And what an opera! But although we love the Marc Chagall ceiling we're not sure we want to sit through *La Traviata*.

There are nightclubs in Paris (like the famous Rex) if you like clubbing – but we also can't help remembering what one Holiday Goddess editor said about French DJs: a lot of the songs they play seem to be like some weird kind of English lesson for locals.

The answer? Learn to love and cherish a French wine list and French liquors. Even the longest relationship or marriage can be revived over a half-bottle. Or, a grand affair, begun. The best nightlife in Paris lies in the clinking of glasses (make ours Pol Roger).

How do you work your way around the wine list in Paris? Comedienne and writer **Helen Lederer**, a familiar face on *Absolutely Fabulous*, is also an admired wine reviewer. We asked her to be our tour guide.

Absolutely Fabulous wine

The cheap date: For a cheap date, I suggest Blanc de Blancs! It's a great sparkling cheapo one-grape wonder – at least you can enjoy yourself and get high on the bubbles. If you go for a medium dry Blanc de Blancs they've only crushed the one grape – a Chardonnay (less fuss and hoo ha all round) and the price of F Dulac's demi-sec, for example, are just crazy – we're talking a mere few pounds. Admittedly, demi-sec is quite sweet but then if it's a cheap date you might as well cut out the middle man and go straight for the pudding and get pissed alongside an economy pavlova. If it's made in France you can be sure it has passed their exacting excess of standards and labelling. The large bubbles may give you a headache, but who cares – it's only a cheap date!

The date with a multi-millionaire: Go for a Romanée-Conti. From Côte de Nuits, Burgundy, made from Pinot Noir grapes by a small but exclusive winery that makes only a few bottles at a time. We're talking possibly £2500 a poke. And the least you deserve! Plus, the multi-millionaire will most likely will be married so he owes you big time.

Lunch with the girls: You simply have to settle on Sauvignon Blanc. Every woman always sighs 'oh yes!' with sheer relief whenever this is suggested.

The grape gets its name from '*sauvage*' – meaning 'wild' and frankly that's what girlie lunches are FOR. Choose a classy Pouilly-fumé for that aftertaste of girlish laughter tinged with bittersweet thoughts of peer group pressure and camaraderie.

After dinner liqueur: Why not try something tangy, like Mandarin Napoleon? Napoleon was partial to this as it's macerated and blended with cognac – and it's a bit of an aphrodisiac – even after a five-course French meal which leaves you belching.

The best champagne: The best champagne has to be a full flavoured Louis Roederer – the best vintage champagnes really do taste superior and can age for ten years. It's blooming gorgeous and you can taste the blend of almonds and toasted brioche – it's a general orgy. Delicate heaven.

Don't forget that when you visit Duty-Free on the way home there is always a multi-purpose, pretty bottle of Grand Marnier to consider. It has a nice free red ribbon on the front and it also slips easily into your trouser pocket. It's orangey, aromatic and luminous – great with cocktails, ice-cream and truffles.

Helen Lederer

Finding passion in Paris

After she left *Rolling Stone* magazine, author and columnist **Sue Ostler**, the UK's Flirt Diva, began writing books about dating, mating and relating. So where does she find passion in Paris?

'Predictably, each time I've been to Paris with a boyfriend in tow, it's ticked all the romantic boxes. But deep down I would curse its glamour, resenting the fact that tapping into the real Paris seemed impossible. All that changed one weekend when I visited with a girlfriend.

We'd been the perfect tourists and, come nightfall, we were ready to be rewarded. Our tour driver dropped us off at Rue Mouffetard in the 5th arrondissement, a cool and quirky foodie's paradise crammed with restaurants and party spots.

The bars were spilling over with locals. Hoping to blend in, we settled on the lively Roadhouse le Vieux Chene for a cheeky Kir Royale. Feeling cheerful, we strolled around the area soaking up the vibe. All of a sudden, and seemingly from out of nowhere, there was a wave, a wink and a smile and we were lured into a tiny, dark venue. An acoustic guitarist serenaded the room, bringing to mind a youthful French version of Thom Yorke.

Minutes later, the house lights went down, the disco lights went up, a DJ appeared and then, much to our astonishment, two hot guys approached. "Hey, there's a party and free drinks. Will you stay?" We looked at each other. Jackpot!

They handed us a glass of vino as the party swung into action. And for one night only, I was in the right place at the right time, evidence perhaps, that in order to infiltrate the cool side of Paris you might consider leaving your partner at home.

It's not as cheap some of the tourist pubs, but it has the distinction of being in a location that has been selling wine since the late 1500s – hence the choice is mind-boggling. It also features good happy hour deals ranging from €3.50 beers to €6 cocktails.'

Sue Ostler

Mouff'tot mouff'tard
71 Rue Mouffetard

Roadhouse le Vieux Chene
69 Rue Mouffetard

TOP TEN

Romantic Places

1. Montmartre
2. Palais de Chaillot
3. Luxembourg Garden
4. Arc de Triomphe
5. Pont Neuf
6. Île de la Cité
7. Jardin du Palais-Royal
8. Pont des Arts
9. Canal Saint-Martin
10. Pont Alexandre III

A night in Boho Bellevilloise

Holiday Goddess editor **Donna Wheeler** has spent some of her best Paris nights in the northern neighborhood of Belleville, home to the city's bourgeois bohemians – known to locals as bobos.

The kids are drinking rosé from carafes, beneath olive trees that spout fantastically out of timber tables, and the talk is of love, death, Maghreb politics and what became of Justice (the electropop act, not the ideal). The Bellevilloise is, as it is most nights, cheek-by-jowl, and the crowd trips across three floors, and out onto the terrace, with Paris glowing below. Next door, it's BB Brunes or arbouretum or Florence sound checking at La Maroquinerie. Welcome to the XXème, the 20th, current playground of the bobos – bourgeois bohemians.

The frantically fashionable Bellevilloise's lovingly crafted surrounds, however, hark back to another time: 1877, to be precise, when the neighbourhood had been subsumed into the city, becoming its final arrondissement, out on the tip of the snail's tail. The Communards had, by then, been exiled or executed, but their heady spring wasn't forgotten up here. It was then a cooperative, home to the neighbourhood's radical worker-artisans, and hummed round the clock with organising, performances, poetry and barter. Its leaflet-printing days are long gone, but the music, bonhomie and just a glimmer of that dissenting spirit remains. Not to mention a nice line in bucolic stage-set whimsy.

I was first lured up to the 20th to visit a friend whose sprawling apartment sits on the crest of Rue Ménilmontant. Used to the tight corners (and frequently uptight atmosphere) of Marais and St Germain-des-Prés hotels, it was a revelation.

Not only was there breathing space, rustling treetops and a stunning view of the city, but my friend's local corner bistro was Michelin-starred, most of the city's hippest bars were just down the hill, and the Bellevilloise in stumbling distance. And so, with ensuing visits, Mama Shelter, on rue de Bagnolet and across from idiosyncratic live venue Le Flèche d'Or, became my hotel. The poetic, melancholy paths of Père Lachaise my morning walking track, Piston Pélican my bar and Alexandre Dumas or Gambetta my metro stops.

Paris's northeast has, of course, been partying hard since the late 18th century. Not then part of Paris proper, but in striking distance of the city's workshops and factories, hilly and green Belleville and the neighbouring village of Ménilmontant, were flush with rough-and-ready bars, restaurants and guinguettes – open air dancehalls. These offered the city's workers tax-free alcohol come Sunday or holy days, with fresh air thrown in as a bonus. With fantasy rural settings begetting 'country' pleasures, sybarites from all classes were soon arriving in droves; noble women were known to frequent summer's particularly debauched all-nighters disguised as sailors or cobblers or blacksmiths.

The 20th isn't the Paris of big-ticket sights or name galleries or famous shops. Instead I discovered a neighbourhood unusually at peace with its past, where gentrification continues apace but is also gently resisted, diversity flourishes and its brand of cool is one that isn't yet entirely for sale. The neighbourhood's 19th century worker–poets – who saw sleep as a distraction, literally burning the candle at both ends – would, I hope, have approved.

Donna Wheeler

Our seven wonders of Paris

Catching sight of the Eiffel Tower in Paris around the corner of a building is a little like glimpsing Jane Birkin in the street: it makes us want to say 'sacré bleu!' and 'erk alors!' but we don't really want to get any closer. We don't need Jane Birkin's autograph. Nor do we want to get up close and personal with the Eiffel Tower. Or indeed, *up* it. Is this sacrilege? Not really, when Paris offers so many other wonders ...

Coco Chanel's oracle cards

When my friend Justine Picardie was researching her book on Chanel, she introduced me to her oracle cards – the famous Lenormand deck. The appropriately numbered cards for Chanel's fragrances – 5, 19 and 22 – can still be seen lying on her desk, inside her private apartment, above the Chanel flagship store. One of the seven wonders of Paris for me – and perhaps for you – is this deck.

Even if you're unused to tarot or oracle cards (and even if you can't read French) these make beautiful decorations for a pin board, or a small frame on your dressing table. I occasionally use my deck to give complimentary readings to Holiday Goddess readers about their travel plans (see *holidaygoddess.com* to find out how you can request a free Lenormand consultation too).

The deck was created by the mysterious Madame Lenormand, who used to read for Napoleon and Josephine. It is printed with beautiful old-world watercolour illustrations of odd symbols: a book, a family of foxes, a skipping child, a haystack.

Rumour has it that Lenormand's deck helped save Josephine – and made Chanel a business superstar.

Trust the Parisiennes to be different. This isn't a tarot deck – it's a far more gentle collection of images which trigger natural intuition. Unless you can read the French verses you'll have to draw on your gut feelings, but do write down what you see about your future. You may be pleasantly surprised at your fortune-telling skills. The term *clairvoyance* is French after all.

Jessica Adams

Your best chance of finding Lenormand Oracle cards is here: Librairie de l'inconnu, at **84 Rue du Cherche-Midi**.

Also try Librairie du Graal, **15 Rue Jean-Jacques Rousseau**. The deck often turns up on market stalls too.

Marc Chagall's ceiling: The Paris Opera

The Paris Opera is perfect heaven, open during the day (without the shrieking, sorry, we mean the singing) and free. Walk around the empty red velvet seats and gaze up at the ceiling: there lies one of the seven wonders of Paris – painter Marc Chagall's vision of heaven. Children love the way he sees animals. Grown-ups can't believe the hours of work. This is a place to stare, and stare.

Afterwards, make sure you are photographed descending the famous marble Opera staircase. And don't miss the stone angels blowing bugles outside.

The Paris Opera
Place de l'Opéra

METRO: **Opéra**

WEBSITE: **operadeparis.fr**

Shakespeare & Co

This famous bookshop is the last remaining place in Paris to keep the spirit of the old Left Bank alive. The Left Bank (*Rive Gauche*) was the home of young, creative and the cash-strapped Parisiennes last century – the place for jazz, beat poetry, radical left-wing views and modern art. Now it's all down to Shakespeare & Co, which still stages events for, and by, alternative types.

Our favourite book at Shakespeare & Co is *Love on the Left Bank* by Ed van der Elsken.

It's a 1954 photo essay which captures *Rive Gauche* style perfectly – Gitane cigarettes, thick black Bourjois eyeliner, cognac, bare feet, bedroom hair, rollneck sweaters, espresso, Cinzano ashtrays, hash, chess and serious paperbacks. Shakespeare & Co is a magnet for Parisiennes who still believe in the good old days. It rocks when it rains.

Shakespeare & Co
37 Rue de la Bûcherie

METRO: **Saint-Michel**

WEBSITE: **shakespeareand company.com**

Musée Carnavalet

Everything we ever wanted to know about the French Revolution, we learned here. As you walk into the courtyard of the Musée Caravalet you will see a statue of Louis XIV, the Sun King, who symbolises all the self-indulgence and arrogance of the old French monarchy. He looks rather silly, with his podgy stomach and pretentious hand gestures. An Australian Holiday Goddess editor took one look and pronounced him 'totally poncey' before walking away. She completely understood why the old kings and queens revolted the peasants. And indeed, why the peasants revolted. The whole story is inside this fantastic museum.

Off-season, the Musée Carnavalet is happily uncrowded, one of our American editors reports. Thus, you can fully absorb the atmosphere of stunning rooms that look like film sets from *Dangerous Liaisons*. They are actually carefully reconstructed salons and boudoirs, taking you from the era of one King Louis to another.

After you've started reeling from the beauty and extravagance, you'll appreciate why starving, over-taxed peasants wanted to guillotine Louis XVI and his wife Marie Antoinette.

Everyone knows that Marie Antoinette never *actually* said 'Let them eat cake'. But even without that quotable quote, one look at the shameless extravagance inside the Musée Carnavalet and you'll understand why the peasants wanted her head in a basket.

There is a small model of a guillotine in here – an original, working version. Nearby, there are old execution orders in glass cases which still have the power to terrify. By 1795 it was all over for the French monarchy, and the wigs and beautiful clothes vanished from Parisian life. French babies were named Egalite, not Louis.

Still the popularity of the guillotine continued – 20,000 people lost their heads that way. Then came Napoleon. His picnic hamper is in the Musée Carnavalet too. It's our favourite Parisian museum for so many reasons.

Musée Carnavalet
23 Rue de Sévigné
METRO: Saint Paul – Chemin Vert

Notre Dame

When people think of Notre Dame, they think of hunchbacks and gargoyles. It is a sacred site that goes back to the time of the Romans, though. There was a shrine to Jupiter here once – the God of Good Fortune. The old cathedral must have been protected by Jupiter because even the revolutionaries couldn't destroy or steal everything. Even though it was a wreck by the time Victor Hugo made the place famous with his 1831 bestseller, *The Hunchback of Notre-Dame*, its new popularity with readers saved it.

Notre Dame is a peculiar place, full of mysterious esoteric, occult and alchemical symbols, alongside traditional Christian images. There's also a wishing spot – the brass stud which marks the centre of Paris. We've heard one writer who wished on this spot met his wife that way!

Place du Parvis Notre Dame
METRO: **Cite**
WEBSITE: **cathedraleparis.com**

Joan of Arc

Joan of Arc is the patron saint of France. Ingrid Bergman and Milla Jovovich have both played her in films. She lives on in Paris, thanks to a fabulous golden statue by Fremiet, in the Place des Pyramides. The statue reveals her as more Milla than Ingrid, but the attitude is all Joan – defiant, courageous and not quite of this world. She was the peasant girl who heard the Archangel Michael telling her to lead the fight to make Dauphin Charles VII King of France.

She prayed all night in a famous vigil at Saint-Denys de la Chapelle, at 16 Rue de la Chapelle. It's still there. Despite her prayers, she was betrayed and sold to the English, then convicted of witchcraft and burned at the stake. In the absence of royalty, she's Queen.

Place des Pyramides
METRO: **Pyramides**
Saint-Denys de la Chapelle
METRO: **Marx Dormoy**

French Resistance memorial plaques

I once met a heroine of the French Resistance, although she was actually from New Zealand. Her name was Nancy Wake and she was nicknamed The White Mouse.

She loved freedom and France, in no particular order. Every time I look up in Paris, and see a blue plaque commemorating a Resistance fighter, I think of Nancy.

She risked torture and death to cycle across France, dressed as a peasant girl, carrying vital information for the allies. She braved every checkpoint, fooling the Nazis along the way. There is history in those houses which bear a plaque. Nancy's friends were in there, plotting the path to D-Day. It bothers me that very few visitors to Paris ever look up and photograph them: they should!

Jessica Adams

The eighth wonder of Paris: Le French bulldog

Nicknamed 'frog dogs' by the British, French bulldogs are only walked by the smartest Parisiennes (though you may see one tucked under an arm on the Champs Élysée).

Spot a genuine French bulldog by looking for a sweet, grumpy face, along with an adorable snub nose and big, bat ears. They are top-heavy and have trouble swimming in the Seine without a flotation device. They also overheat, which is why you will often see Frenchies (as some call them) lying under shady trees, panting.

They are as much a part of Paris life as the poodle, but there is something about a frog dog which makes us drool. Just like them.

Spas, sanctuaries, sacred spaces

It's all about the Seine in Paris, which is a spa, sanctuary and
sacred space all at the same time. And yes, you can work out
there too. Mia Freedman, editor and publisher of the cult website
mamamia.com.au says, 'I adored running along the Seine in the
mornings in Paris. It made me feel like a proper Parisienne'.
In summer, women spread out their towels on the banks and
organise their manicures – and their boyfriends' massages.

Paris Luxe
hotel spas

You don't necessarily have to
stay at these hotels to book
their luxurious spas:

1. Hôtel Fouquet
2. Hilton Arc de Triomphe
3. Le Meurice
4. Ritz Paris
5. Hôtel Plaza Athénée
6. Hôtel le Bristol
7. George V

The Nuxe spa

I'm not a spa person. But I love Nuxe. In fact, I seem to have a relationship with them. Unfortunately it has to exist online, as Nuxe is a body and beauty brand hardly exported outside France. But I do get a bit desperate if I don't have a small glass pot of their lip balm. It's the only one that's ever worked. The secret ingredient is honey, apparently. I was pleased to find so many other Holiday Goddesses who were also addicted, once the hushed topic was raised. It did feel a bit like a secret Nuxe club.

Their other famous Nuxe product (which you may request at their Paris spa) is the *Huile Prodigieuse*. It's a big, golden bottle of precious oil, with borage, St John's Wort, sweet almond, camellia, hazelnut, macadamia and vitamin E. It's a dry oil, so it's not moist and gluggy – it 'dries' on the skin and hair at the moment that it moisturises. There is also a glittery version, full of soft, powdered gold flecks, which Parisiennes slather on for summer evening parties. The great thing about the Nuxe spa is that you can try, then buy. And it's not expensive. They will use the oil you request during your massage.

If you are used to the somewhat ho-hum scent of budget aromatherapy oil from other massages, you might go a bit silly when you breathe in the warm, sexy, nutty fragrance of *Huile Prodigieuse*. Choose from a Kashmir or California massage. We hear super cool DJ Josephine de la Baume (whose romantic links to Mark Ronson have guaranteed instant coolness) is a Nuxe fan too.

The Nuxe Spa is so relaxing that women tell us they can barely fill in the questionnaire afterwards. I'll vouch for that. Try not to be so relaxed that you forget to take home the lip balm though.

Jessica Adams

The Nuxe spa
32 Rue Montorgueil
WEBSITE: nuxe.com

The Seine

We know some like the idea of haunting Cimetiere du Père Lachaise, where Jim Morrison, Oscar Wilde and Édith Piaf are buried. And yes, Père Lachaise is a sacred space. But we think the banks of the Seine are even more precious.

Morrison, Wilde and Piaf live on every time you walk the length of the river. That's where you'll see today's 18-year-old Doors fans, wired into their iPods, in second-hand leather jackets. And it's also where today's batch of Oscars and Édiths strut their stuff. The Seine is so much more than a river. Because of its endless curve (like a classic Dior hat) it unites the whole city. It's designer water, but not in a bottle.

On the left side, *Rive Gauche*, you will still find the intellectuals and modern bohemians drinking coffee, even though corporate coffee chains have moved in.

Across the river, there is the wealth and splendour of the Grand Palais, the Place de la Concorde, the Jardin des Tuileries, and in the middle of it all, Notre Dame, one of our seven wonders of Paris.

It is possible to walk along the Seine for miles, at sunrise, uninterrupted. Mystical types tell us the Seine crosses several ley lines, or powerful, sacred energy lines. Perhaps that's why Notre Dame, which centres it, also holds the centre of Paris – on every traditional map.

Even the least mystical Holiday Goddess readers and editors swear by a walk along the Seine. 'It connects you with poets and painters, and princesses,' said one. 'And it's free. You can just sit in Square Jean XXIII behind Notre Dame and watch it flow past you.'

Christian Dior's sacred space

Christian Dior's sacred space (and one of ours) is at 30 Avenue Montaigne. It's a great place to make a pilgrimage. It is where Dior started work, after the war, creating the biggest revolution in fashion for a decade – The New Look.

Dior was an art lover long before he became a famous designer. Twenty years earlier he was exhibiting work by his friend Picasso. Then he had the worst years of his life. The Great Depression forced him to close his gallery. His brother was sent to an institution. His mother died. Then he was so ill with tuberculosis his friends paid for him to be sent away to the country, to save him.

When he came back, it really was a comeback. And when he moved into 30 Avenue Montaigne, it was immediately painted pearl white and grey – Dior's favourite colours. White and grey was also the palette of choice for Picasso.

And here at 30 Avenue Montaigne is where women were reinvented, with small waists and big hips. It's also where Dior dreamed up the idea (borrowed from the art world) of giving each of his collections a theme and name. A young Pierre Cardin (aged 25) also worked here.

This is what Dior said about his very first collection: 'After so many years of wandering, weary with consorting with only painters and poets, couture wished to return to the fold and rediscover its original function which is to adorn women and to beautify them.'

That's not written in stone at 30 Avenue Montaigne, but it might be. When Dior died, Yves St Laurent took over, so this place became sacred to him too. And to all women.

We heart Parisian art

Holiday Goddess editor **Emma Killick** has spent enough time in Paris over the years to know that she is a committed fan of art for the people – but without the people. These are her favourite places.

Rodin Museum

The **Rodin Museum** is a beautiful, simple building where Rodin once lived, set within a gorgeously laid out garden, and small enough that you can stroll through it all in a couple of hours. Plus, it seems surreal that some famous sculptures balance on precarious plinths that wobble slightly as you approach them on the squeaky old parquet floor. You can lean over *The Kiss* and be face to face with the individual casts for *The Burghers of Calais* before you head outside to see the finished sculpture in the garden. *The Thinker* is there too, as is *Balzac* (with and without his robe). After the tranquility of Musée Rodin, you can then go and join all the people you just avoided at Les Deux Magots or its rival, Café de Flore, about a 15 minute walk away, or keep going and hang a left just after St Germain des Prés into the smaller streets filled with bars and restaurants (start on Rue de Buci).

Rodin Museum
79 Rue de Varenne
WEBSITE: musee-rodin.fr

Atelier Brancusi

Atelier Brancusi is another great place to see art for the people, without the people.

Romanian-born Brancusi bequeathed his studio and contents to the French government on the condition that his studio be recreated, making for a special and highly personal museum. The spaces are packed with Brancusi's streamlined forms in wood, marble, limestone and bronze in a unique arrangement that was the artist's – not a curator's – imaginings. Because of the way the works are arranged, as you move through the space some pieces come into view as others recede and there seems to always be something more to admire. My favourites are the Sleeping Muses (I must have about 200 photos of them).

The museum at the Pompidou centre is worthy, but doesn't fit the crowd-beating criteria (although the entrance fee to Brancusi gives you access to the Pompidou, so head in if you are feeling tolerant). Otherwise, go to the large terrace at the top of this iconic building for a café au lait and a jaw-dropping view.

Emma Killick

Atelier Brancusi
Place Georges Pompidou
WEBSITE: centrepompidou.fr

There's something about Picasso

Picasso arouses a surprising amount of passion in Holiday Goddess editors and readers. Some like the Picasso they can understand – the man who created simple line drawings of his mistresses. Others prefer the cubist. He captured his lover Irene Lagut both ways, in 1916, the year that broke his heart. The self-portrait photographs he took at that time show him looking ridiculously sexy in a pair of shorts – no wonder Irene submitted, as all Picasso's women did.

Pablo Picasso possessed a yellow kimono (with flowers) and kept a monkey. He appears to have cut his own hair, or had his lovers cut it for him. Yet he is still the biggest art-throb of the twentieth century. Maybe we adore him because he was so in touch with his female side: his famous paper cut-outs were made with borrowed dressmakers' pins from his lover Eva Gouel (another kimono fan). Whatever the reason, Paris is Picasso and Picasso is Paris.

The **Picasso Museum** has more than 3000 of his own works, plus some well-known pieces by other artists from his personal collection. Like the Rodin Museum, there's a serenity here that I think comes from a clever combination of the building's size and the well-planned arrangement of the pieces. The museum's layout takes you on a chronological journey of Picasso's work from the beginning of the twentieth century to the early 1970s. It's a great way to see how versatile, brilliant and prolific he was. The museum was recently closed for renovation, but get ready to bang on its doors as soon as it reopens – it's worth it.

Picasso Museum
5 Rue Thorigny
WEBSITE: musee-picasso.fr

Freya North, a Romantic Novelist of the Year, also loves the Rodin Museum. In a previous life she collected a Masters Degree in History of Art from the Courtald Institute.

Amongst the posters of pop stars and ponies, which adorned my teenage bedroom wall, was a framed print of Rodin's *The Kiss*. A daydreamer, I spent much time gazing at my wall – but it wasn't the brooding bass guitarists nor pretty palominos which captivated me – it was the woman in *The Kiss*.

One day, I used to muse, *perhaps one day I'll be kissed like that*.

So began a lasting passion for the great sculptor, Auguste Rodin. I spent hours in the Tate Gallery, awestruck by this lip-locked couple and made regular pilgrimages to Paris, giving Monet and Manet a mere moment, before heading to the Musée Rodin – my favourite art gallery to this day.

It was quite a shock to discover that far from being some iconic apotheosis of romantic love, *The Kiss* isn't a chaste embrace at all. This is the furtive moment between sinners that precedes their murder. *He* is *her* husband's brother. They are Paolo and Francesca, characters from Dante's *Inferno*, which itself was the inspiration for Rodin's *Gates of Hell*.

The Kiss encapsulates what fascinates me most about Rodin – there's an edgy contradiction in his work where surface details often contort the deeper truth. Look at *Balzac* – that arrogantly hasty sweep of seemingly unstructured bronze topped by a near-monstrous head. Rodin's preparation, however, was obsessive. A multitude of sketches on paper, in plaster, of Balzac naked, Balzac clothed, Balzac from every conceivable angle, enabled the final pared-down version to have such force – there's a very real body beneath all that bronze.

My favourite work? A relatively small plaster of 1889, *The Eternal Idol*. These two figures, entwined in intimacy, are so lost in each other that the viewer almost feels a voyeur. It's beautiful and erotic and I wish I was her and I wish I knew *him*!

Freya North

Vintage and markets

Paris is vintage, retro and second-hand heaven. Designers send their assistants out to trawl the markets and return with inspiration for the season ahead. Holiday Goddesses make a point of starting with their favourite designer labels on market trestle tables first, before they even enter the hallowed halls of Printemps, next door to Galeries Lafayette. Our best bet though? Shop like a local and discover the astonishing 'empty attics' markets in Paris and surrounds.

You'll look in vain for St Vincent de Paul, Red Cross, Oxfam or other good-cause shops in Paris. Apart from the fabulous Merci in Le Marais, which is in a different class altogether, Parisiennes tend not to op-shop, as Australians call it (or go thrift shopping, as they say in New York). However, they do have *les vide greniers*, where the contents of French attics, garages and junk rooms hit the streets.

Holiday Goddess reader **Liz Challis** spends part of each year in France, painting, but has a long history as a retro and vintage fashion dealer specialising in the kind of finds which make us squeak with excitement. She thinks the trick to discovering Parisian treasure is the *vide greniers* – the 'empty attics' markets.

Vide greniers

Every week I go to the *vide greniers* website, which gives a comprehensive list of the *vide greniers* in France – and you can look at any specific area, including in and around Paris.

Vide greniers literally means 'empty attics' and it's when almost the whole district participates by setting up a table in front of their house (or in the main streets). It is such fun because you never know what will turn up and sometimes there are over 400 stalls in one place.

Generally, the French don't have charity shops, so this is what they do with unwanted items. This is their opportunity to buy second-hand clothing, and children's toys, along with lots of old collectables and antiques. Most are open to bartering and there are many bargains.

Amongst the many treasures I have bought are retro sunglasses, bisque dolls from the 1920s, vintage clothing, German vases from the 1950s and French fashion magazines from the 1930s.

I always arrive early: 6–7 am for the first one, but have still found bargains later in the day when I have gone to two or three on the same day. My tip for travellers is to use the international prepaid postage box at any French post office which holds up to 6kg – you can post around the world for just 41 euros. Visit *vide-greniers.org*.

Liz Challis

Holiday Goddess editor **Janine Brown** is the author of several beautifully illustrated books carried by fashion chains and bookstores around the world. She also designs and creates her own clothes and accessories. We asked her to recommend the most user-friendly, easy to find Paris vintage shops.

Didier Ludot

Find vintage haute couture heaven at the Palais Royale. Avid collector, historian and designer Didier Ludot presents an immaculate collection with vintage *prêt-à-porter* next door, including Chanel, Dior, Lanvin, Courreges, Balenciaga, YSL.

Didier Ludot,
20–24 Galerie de Montpensier,

METRO: Palais Royal – Musee du Louvre

WEBSITE: didierludot.fr

Mam'zelle Swing

The swing music playing here puts you in the mood, with a carefully selected range of clothing from 1900 to 1960. Well stocked with good condition and reasonably priced pieces, you could find that rare jacket with matching shoes or anything from a 1900s shirt to a Courrèges suit.

Mam'zelle Swing
35 Rue du roi De Sicile
METRO: Hôtel-de-Ville
WEBSITE: mamzelleswing.fr

Ultramod

Step back in time when you enter this *mercerie* that has been selling dress, hat making and sewing supplies since 1890. The unique merchandise is all vintage. Beautiful loomed silk ribbons, felts for hats more than 50 years old. Precious silks and French netting. Buttons, threads and notions from a bygone era. Directly across the street is a spectacular boutique dedicated to hats and hat accessories.

Ultramod
2–3 Rue de Choiseul
METRO: Quatre Septembre

La Jolie Garde-Robe

Great presentation of a trendy selection of vintage, this shop has the intimate feel of a lovely antique wardrobe, and sells clothing and accessories from all eras. Flirty and romantic vintage to outrageous designer garments from the '80s. Colourful, wearable pieces, a little whimsical and out of the ordinary. All French designers are represented here.

La Jolie Garde-Robe
15 Rue Commines
METRO: Filles du Calvaire

Thanx God I'm a VIP

Well selected collection of vintage designer pieces from quality to luxury, immaculately set out in colour co-ordinated racks. Find gems from Yves St Laurent, Balenciaga, Chanel, Hermès, Lacroix, Rochas, Prada as well as no-label pieces from the '60s by local couturieres, sailor striped shirts and timeless wool peacoats.

Thanx God I'm a VIP
12 Rue de Lancry
METRO: Jacques Bonsergent
WEBSITE: thanxgod.com

Come on Eileen

A favourite amongst celebrities, this three level vintage emporium is stacked with Lanvin, Chanel, Courreges, Cardin, Hermès, Dior, Mugler, Givenchy, mixed with quality but less impressive labels at good prices. Bohemian but well organised and accessible. Loads of unusual and authentic accessories plus a denim haven with jeans of every age and variety. Other treasures to be found here include:

- Princess Diana memorabilia
- John Galliano at Dior
- Jean-Paul Gaultier 1990s scent bottles
- 1990s Prada rucksacks
- Gianni Versace 1990s scarves

Come on Eileen
16/18 Rue des Taillandiers

METRO: Bastille

Our favourite daycations

There are two places outside Paris where you will find both Joan of Arc and Marie Antoinette. Allow a day for each.

Reims

Reims might be under an hour from Paris on the fast TGV, but its serene pale-stone streets feel as if from a long-off, storybook version of France. While one could quite happily just wander, peering at Gallo-Roman ruins, Art Deco gems and Saint-Remi's 11th century basilica, it's no use pretending you're not here for the bubbles.

With a roll call of Champagne's *grandes marques* – Mumm, Veuve Clicquot, Piper-Heidsieck, Taittinger and Pommery et al – in walking distance, it's hard not to feel kid-in-a-sweet-shop giddy. Thirty metres below ground, sipping Blanc de Blancs (a graceful though never uncomplicated drop) in the *crayeres* of the house of Ruinart, one wonders at the serendipity. Lime mining was big business here, from the Roman era on, and left the city riddled with subterranean chalk chambers. Quite a few centuries later, thanks to Madame Clicquot's savvy spotting, they continue to be the perfect place to bottle age Champagne.

As most houses offer tastings with their tours, plan for a substantial lunch in between visits (L'Assiette Champenoise boasts one of France's best young chefs, Arnaud Lallement), or pace yourself with non-liquid diversions. I can't resist Maison Fossier for their so-pretty *biscuits roses de Reims*, and am always moved by the wholly preserved war room – 1940s tat and all – at the Musée de la Reddition.

Most stunning of all is the High Gothic Notre Dame de Reims: all French coronations were held here for over a thousand years, with Jeanne d'Arc herself heading up the procession for Charles VII. Significantly rebuilt after shells rained down upon the city in 1914, the cathedral features Chagall's stained-glass designs. Jesus on the cross is reassuringly jolly, doughy round the middle; it's in the background one glimpses the sublime. When the Champagne glow fades, I like to drink in Chagall's deepest, luminescent blue.

Donna Wheeler

Versailles

Here's the thing about the palace and gardens of Versailles. It's a commitment. Versailles is only a short train ride from Paris, but because of the queues, and the crowds, and the sheer size of the place, it needs a little homework first. Otherwise it may all seem staggering and glorious, but be a rather empty experience, like going to the collections without knowing the back story.

Tourist walkie-talkie devices for the general public are so bland and chatty they always leave me cold. I can't think of a worse way to ruin the peculiar, glittering atmosphere at Versailles than jamming a listening device against my ear.

Signs will not do and pamphlets are no good. It's all too glib, like fast-food information. And Versailles is so much more. If you're going to take the day out of Paris that Versailles requires, then you need a good reading list.

I do think you have to make it *your* Versailles. In this respect it's like the Louvre. You have to understand it, then edit it, then turn it into a private experience rather than a big blur.

Everyone has her own way into Versailles. For some Holiday Goddess editors it's via the wonderful Sofia Coppola film about Marie Antoinette. For others, it's the Glenn Close and John Malkovich classic, *Dangerous Liaisons*.

For me, Versailles is best seen and appreciated after reading the definitive biography, *Marie Antoinette* by Antonia Fraser. Lie on the hotel bed and indulge.

From Antonia Fraser, I learned that Marie Antoinette had a little pug called Mops. And also that she had girlie crushes, which the gossips thought made her a lesbian.

She lived a public life, rather like the late Princess Diana. There were no cameras, but the people were allowed to watch her eat in the palace, and she was often forced to dress in front of a crowd. Her fan may have been encrusted in diamonds but she couldn't hide herself from the masses, or the courtiers.

In 1770 Marie Antoinette wrote, 'I put on my rouge and wash my hands in front of the whole world'. Think of the gawping, as you see the mirrors at Versailles: in the absence of paparazzi and social pages, people had reflections to gawk at.

If you want to know more about the origins of Versailles, turn to Nancy Mitford's book, *The Sun King*. She is best known for her classic romantic comedies, *The Pursuit of Love* and *Love in a Cold Climate*. She was also a British aristocrat who was fascinated by France and French life. Her version of the life of Louis XIV is wonderful. (Nancy heartily disliked Marie Antoinette, though.)

The spectacular spaces at Versailles will come alive for you once you know just how mad palace life was. Guards with spaniels used to roam the grounds to weed out all the people hiding in the nooks and crannies. And nobody ever knocked – according to palace etiquette, they had to scratch on the door, like cats.

The place reeked of wig powder, apparently. Is there still a whiff of it, hidden in the palatial walls? At times it must have been like a circus, given the public's access to the place. Ironically, Marie Antoinette wore her rouge like a clown, as was the fashion. The ladies of Versailles had scarlet circles below each eye.

Close your eyes inside the palace and hear the harp music, and the whispers. Court life could be bitchy. Later on, Marie Antoinette had worse to deal with. There is a famous engraving of the march of the market-women on Versailles from 1789 that says it all: they have the cart, the axes and the pitchforks, and they want her blood. When she was eventually guillotined, her head was held aloft and shown to another mob.

Versailles can be an emotional experience, and it probably *should* be. It was, for poor Marie Antoinette. There is so much more to say about this place, but let Fraser's *Marie Antoinette* and Mitford's *The Sun King* be your guides. They are also available as audiobooks on *itunes.com*.

Jessica Adams

Getting to Versailles

Catch the train to Versailles from any Metro (train station) in central Paris, using the yellow line (the C line), in the direction of your final destination, Versailles-Rive Gauche.

From there it is an easy five-minute walk to the palace, which is well-signposted.

Playlists and downloads

Any Paris playlist for your iPod just has to include the following:

Plastic Bertrand, *Ça plane pour moi*

A New Wave classic from a Belgian, not a Frenchman (but it still helped every schoolgirl to learn a bizarre kind of French, when first released). For us, Bertrand will always be the king of the divan, no wonder if he did seem to be as high as a kite, on a trampoline, in the original film clip. Full marks to you, if you can sing this word for word, when it turns up in your taxi on Paris radio. Although you may be asked to get out of the car.

Serge Gainsbourg and Jane Birkin, *Je t'aime moi non plus*

The ongoing war between the British and the French has nothing to do with Joan of Arc. It is all about beautiful Jane Birkin. British men resent the fact that 'sleazy' Serge Gainsbourg wooed her with this heavy-breathing song, which they believe typifies Gallic male behaviour. Holiday Goddess editors completely understand why Jane Birkin was seduced by this song. It has been described as pre-orgasmic and also post-coital by music critics.

Édith Piaf, *Moi, Je N' Regrette Rien*

Holiday Goddess editor and illustrator Anna Johnson keeps Édith Piaf (the DVD and the CD) on permanent standby in her kitchen. This is Piaf's most famous song. The Little Sparrow could roar like a lion when she wanted to, and despite her upsy-downsy life, she remained defiant to the end. This loosely translates as 'I regret nothing' and thus it is the Parisienne's version of *My Way* by Frank Sinatra. Or Sid Vicious.

Jean Michel Jarre, Oxygène

Okay, we love the dreamy, soporific electro-pop of Air too.
In fact Air might just be our favourite Frenchy musicians of all time.
But nobody can deny that Jean Michel Jarre is the king of late-night
keyboard swoon. In cunning Gallic fashion, he created an instrumental
which would cross all known global barriers, and ended up with a huge,
classic hit. It's timelessly cool, and Jarre is still the sexiest thing to come
out of the 1970s.

Asterix and Tintin: Painless French Lessons
This is a guilty secret that some Holiday Goddess editors were
embarrassed to share: however, their secret is now out. The painless
way to learn French is to download Tintin and Asterix cartoons.
In French.

   The DVDs can never capture the charm of the original books, but
there is nothing like a short program designed for nine-year-olds to
break through any fear and loathing we might have about learning the
French language. Note the fact that the boy detective Tintin (why does
he hardly ever take off his raincoat?) has a dog which actually barks in
French too. If you don't believe it, just hear what happens when Snowy
sees a baddie: 'Whoa! Whoa!' he cries – as opposed to woof, woof.

You can download the perfect Paris playlist, free, at *holidaygoddess.com*.
The eight-track album, *Is This Not Paris*, from Foghorn Records and
Sounds Like Cafe, provides wonderful, chilled music for your Eurostar
trip from London to France. It's *almost* as sexy as Serge Gainsbourg

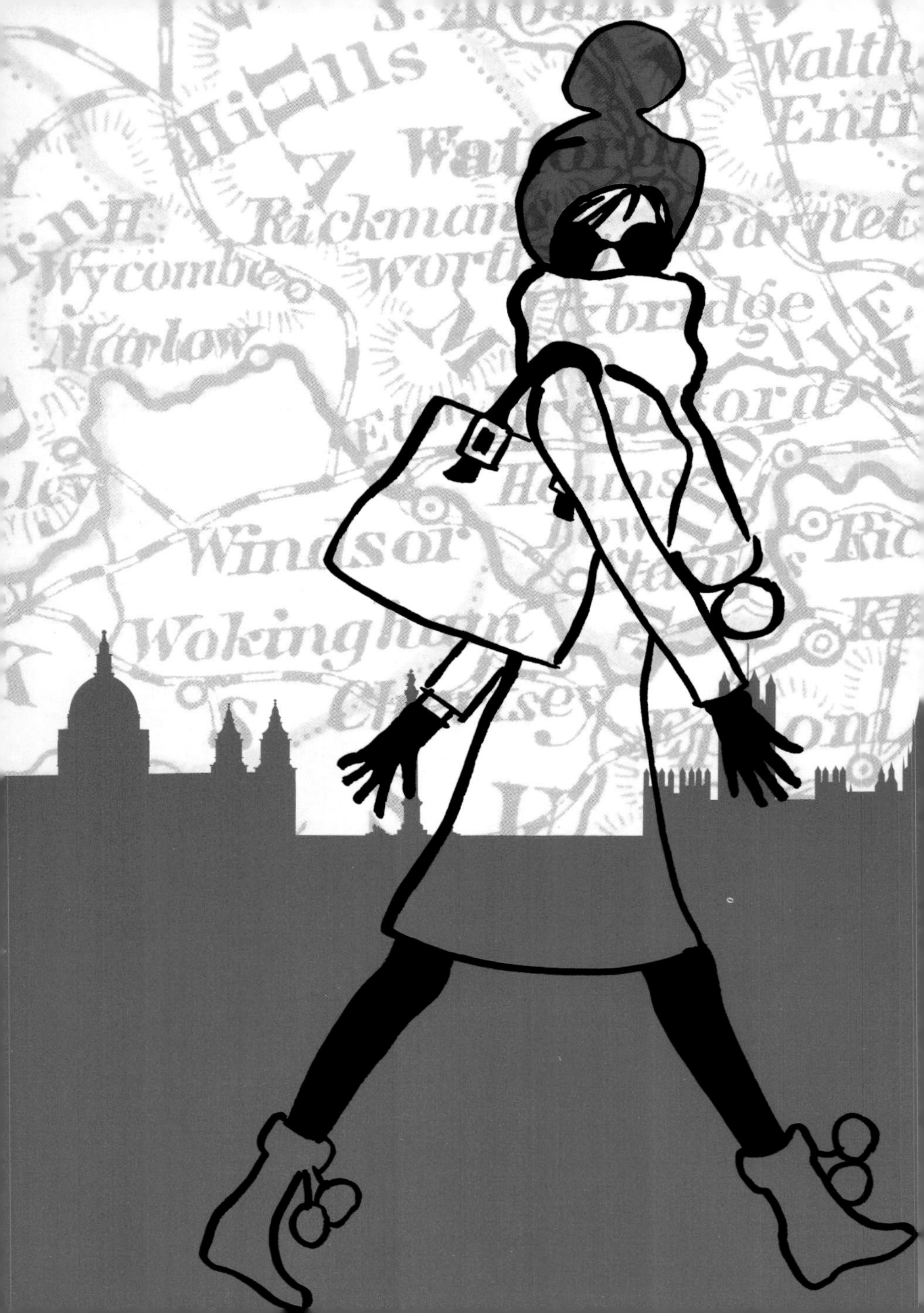
Wycombe
Marlow
Windsor

London

It's a real life Monopoly board.
Pass Go and collect!

Why go to London, or go again? The pubs. Walk inside and you will find dogs, Monopoly games, jokes shouted across the bar, antiques, French wine, British cheese, copies of Dickens on the shelves and smirting in the garden. What's smirting? It's a cross between smoking and flirting. Before the pub, visit the world's best museums. After the pub, see the world's best plays and gigs. Just don't forget your tube map.

Before you go

It's all about the trains

Even if you've been to London many times, you can never re-acquaint yourself with the importance of her trains too often (or buy your tickets to Bath or Brighton too far in advance). The train – not the car, nor the bicycle, nor even the double-decker bus – is the London way.

The London Underground map, created by the fiendishly clever Harry Beck, is both a work of poetry and modern art. The lyrical names (Swiss Cottage, Elephant and Castle, Upminster) have been celebrated by everyone from travel writer Bill Bryson to musician Ian Dury, who wrote an album called *Lord Upminster*. There are several cult alternative maps of the tube, including an anagram version. *The Great Bear* is the most famous 'other' tube map and you can find Simon Patterson's masterpiece in the Tate Gallery.

The London Underground is also the magical pathway to the rest of the United Kingdom and Europe, connecting you from the most romantic stations to the most romantic destinations: Kings Cross, St Pancras to Paris, Paddington to Bath, Victoria to Brighton.

If you are rich, famous or have a country pile you'll go first class. (One Holiday Goddess editor once shared a first class compartment with Nick Cave en route to Victoria Station. She informs us he was the only man she has ever seen catch the train in a pale blue velvet suit. Her quote? 'Sexy Peter Rabbit'. She has paid extra for first-class tickets ever since, but sadly never seen him since.) Even if you don't go first-class you can still shake out *The Guardian* or *The Daily Telegraph*, block the view of your neighbour and order a glass of wine and some peanuts from the drinks trolley. Brit bliss!

London knowledge

The Knowledge

No matter where you are going in central London, you need only instruct your driver once. Then you can lean back with a magazine and relax. London black cab drivers are the best in the world because they have to pass a test known as The Knowledge, which grills them on their knowledge of every street (and some obscure alleyways) within six miles of Charing Cross. It takes them between two and four years to pass The Knowledge. You can hail a cab anywhere – if the orange light is on, it's yours. There are ranks outside every major hotel, department store and train station in the city.

On the Buses

Still prefer the bus? Writer and Holiday Goddess reader **Bethea Jenner** is a long-time London resident who knows her double-deckers. These are her survival tips:

- Some buses have air conditioning, but not all, and they can get very hot in summer, so always have bottled water with you. A dinky little fan might come in handy as well. The best seats for sightseeing (the front of the top deck) are also the hottest unfortunately as the windows don't open!
- Drivers are unlikely to remember where you want to get off so there is no point in asking. Luckily you won't miss your stop as buses are now equipped with recorded messages and LCD destination boards on both decks. And finally ...
- Get hold of a night bus schedule from the Transport for London website (*tfl.gov.uk*) as this will save you a fortune in cab fares after the Tube shuts at night. Do bear in mind that everyone using them will be drunk though!

Boris Bikes

Boris Bikes are the blue bicycles, sponsored by Barclays Bank, which were introduced to London by Mayor Boris Johnson. (His sister, bestselling novelist and editor Rachel Johnson, contributes to our Notting Hill guide on page 172.) For hiring details visit *tfl.gov.uk*.

Walking the tube

The London Underground (the tube) distorts the true geography of the city, so it's easy to assume you can't walk the distances between some stations. You can! Visit *holidaygoddess.com* for our links to London's best tube-walking maps. On those agonising Sundays when three tube lines are shut at once, these maps can save your day.

Andreina Cordani commuted to her rather high-powered job at *Cosmopolitan* magazine, in the heart of London, for years (nearest tube station: Oxford Circus). This is her advice for absolute beginners, and for anyone who has forgotten The Rules of Tube.

The tube for absolute beginners

It all starts with The Map. *Don't* hulk a guidebook around. Ticket offices have free tube maps. You can also download one at *tfl.gov.uk* (which has a handy journey planner). The network is divided into zones 1–6. I think most of the good stuff is in Zone 1–2.

The Fare. Buy a one-day or one-week Travelcard, or ask for an Oyster pre-pay card – load money onto it, then swipe it on the yellow readers at stations or on buses to deduct the fare.

Stand on the right, climb on the left. If you're lazy or wearing crazy heels, stand on the right side of the escalator and ride it to the top. If you're feeling energetic (the longest escalator is 60m long!) then scramble up on the left, and feel the burn in those calf muscles.

Keep cool. The tube is *old*. The first one opened in 1863, and this means two things: air-con is hard to find, and trains sometimes get held in tunnels. Carriages can be humid, so I carry water in summer, and in winter I peel off my coat before I get on to avoid wilting.

Follow the signs. If something looks like a short cut, stick to your route or you can end up wandering through miles of identical tunnels!

Holiday Goddess editors and readers also advise
- Don't scream if you see the Tube Mice. They are small, black, covered in soot and part of London life. They forage for food on the tracks, then dart away when a train rumbles in.
- To really appreciate the tube while you are on holiday in London, make sure you catch the train from Oxford Circus to Victoria at either 8am or 6pm on a weekday. It will be such hell that every other trip you take while you are here will seem like paradise.

Where to stay

London is the home of the £600-per-night luxury hotel. If you want to indulge yourself completely at the grand old duchesses – The Dorchester, Claridge's or The Ritz – then prepare yourself for carpets you can roll around on, hand-sewn mattresses you'll never want to leave and baths you can accommodate two people in. When London does grand, she really does grand. For hotels at sensible prices, though, you will need to book months ahead as demand is fierce.

Bargainista London hotels (£75 and under) typically involve sharing bathrooms, or dealing with England's wimpy power showers. Sometimes they work, sometimes the Victorian plumbing ensures that they don't. So what to do? The best way to get a good, cheap hotel room in London is to wait until the day before, then trawl the late-booking hotel websites. For the ultimate list, visit *holidaygoddess.com*.

The best foodie hotel: Alain Ducasse at The Dorchester

The Dorchester is on Park Lane, one of the top Monopoly spots. It is also within tottering distance of Selfridges so if you really are in London to fulfil a fantasy, you can bring armfuls of shopping bags back to your room, just like a character in a book. Expect the sleep of dreams. Heavy, luxurious curtains and absolute peace, even minutes from the heart of London. Shower heads like dinner plates. Marble bathrooms. The fluffiest robes. And room service that reminds you why the Beatles and Winston Churchill stayed here. The reason most people stay at The Dorchester, though, is Alain Ducasse.

This is the Frenchiest French chef in the world, who once pronounced, 'A turbot without genius is better than a genius without turbot'. His restaurant here holds three Michelin stars. You can book The Dorchester from *holidaygoddess.com*, often at a deep discount (because we are bargainistas).

The Dorchester Hotel
Park Lane, Mayfair, London.
WEBSITE: thedorchester.com
and holidaygoddess.com

The Goring: Kate Middleton stayed here!

Good luck getting a room at The Goring, now that it's become world-famous as Kate Middleton's hotel of choice for *that* wedding. It's an old-fashioned home away from home in Belgravia, much loved by politicians, who walk up from the Houses of Parliament nearby. The last time the goddesses dropped in for a glass of champagne at wine o'clock, former Australian prime minister John Howard was here, parked with a silver teapot. The veranda terrace, which overlooks the small private garden, is lovely for spring or summer drinks.

Try not to think about the fact that Prince Harry is supposed to have scaled the roof at 3am (according to some newspapers). There are lots of reasons we love The Goring. It's not just the glittering chandeliers, over-stuffed sofas or the fact that the staff wear yellow silk to match the curtains. It's the fact that we feel so beautifully taken care of.

The Goring Hotel
15 Beeston Place, Belgravia
WEBSITE: thegoring.com

Your first day

Londoners run on tea, and it's not herbal. Strong, reviving, brown tea. Brits call it Builders' Tea because (a) builders drink it and (b) it's the colour of bricks. Tea is served at breakfast, 11am (Elevenses), 3 to 5pm (Afternoon Tea) and at various points in between, depending on stress levels. Putting the kettle on is a time-honoured way for London women to deal with problems, no matter if it's World War Two or their husband's mistress. So join the cult. Devote your first day to the pursuit of good tea. Our two dream choices are also in wonderful parts of London. The Wolseley is near the shops of Piccadilly and The Orangery flanks Kensington Palace.

Breakfast at The Wolseley

The Wolseley serves the best breakfast in London. Glamorous, luxurious and, best of all, not remotely crowded. Try the haggis with fried duck eggs. Or if you've won the lottery and lost your mind, the caviar omelette (£60). Children may order boiled eggs and toast soldiers too – but don't be surprised if you see elderly gentlemen asking for them.

More modestly, try The Wolseley's own muesli and its super-strong tea. No matter how jetlagged you are, this is a fantastic way to start the holiday.

The Wolseley
160 Piccadilly

NEAREST TUBE: **Green Park**

WEBSITE: **thewolseley.com**

Afternoon tea at Kensington Palace

The Orangery, Kensington Palace, serves tea from 12 noon until 5pm. The Orangery is behind Kensington Palace, where Princess Diana lived. Prices are around half those charged by smart London hotels and we think the food is better. Choose from finger sandwiches, éclairs, orange tea and even chocolate tea. Queen Anne used to heal commoners in The Orangery, believe it or not. We find the scones and champagne very healing too.

Many princesses walked within a scone's-throw of your table. As you pour the tea and gaze at the exquisite gardens and glorious muffin-shaped hedges, clink a glass to Diana and feisty Princess Margaret, sister to the queen.

The Orangery
Kensington Palace

NEAREST TUBE: **High Street Kensington**

WEBSITE: **hrp.org.uk/ kensingtonpalace**

Wine o'clock in London

At around 6pm the streets of London fill with women on an urgent mission. It's wine o'clock! So where do they all go? There are thousands of choices, as this is the city that pubs built. But if this is your first night, try the Cellar Door. We can't think of a better way to end your first day in the city.

Just north of the Thames, on the corner of Aldwych and the Strand, is a doorway sticking up out of the pavement. A flight of stairs leads down to what was once a public toilet, but which is now a plush, be-mirrored and elegant bar, Cellar Door.

In this tiny, tiny bar every square inch counts. You might just about, if you were cruel enough, be able to swing a cat in there but still somehow they manage to cram a good selection of drinks and cocktails and a range of snuff (less antisocial than smoking, the owners say).

Perch on one of their strange lips-shaped bar stools or cram into a booth and play with the SMS Jukebox – text your requests in from the bar and eventually it pops up on the playlist. Then marvel at the fact that they've somehow managed to cram a cabaret act in there with you!

Some singers can be a bit overpowering in such close quarters – especially if it's a Tuesday night and you've just popped in for a quick glass of wine with friends – but it adds to that strange combination of decadence and cosiness which makes this tiny bar one of my favourite London places.

For more information and listings, go to *cellardoor.biz*.

Andreina Cordani

London pub life

Only Dublin can rival London when it comes to pub life. And we're not kidding. It's a way of life – several working days a week (for lunch or 6pm drinks) and then again on Saturday night for dating, and Sunday afternoon for roast beef, gravy, brussel sprouts and Yorkshire pudding.

Even if you're the biggest detox queen Los Angeles ever produced, you have to give in to pub life eventually if you're ever going to really know and love London.

After a suitably boozy lunch with pickled onions and Red Leicester cheese, this is what London Holiday Goddess editors and their informants agreed.

The perfect London pub has:

- A name on the sign which is poetic, witty or historically profound. We think 'The Slug and Lettuce' is clever, but we sadden at the sight of another chain (corporate) pub with a boring name. Our favourite joke London pub name is 'The Kebab and Calculator', for accountants.
- A wealth of games. Monopoly, Scrabble, Trivial Pursuit, backgammon and anything that has the potential for pieces going missing. Add two bottles of wine and let the fun begin.
- A pile of dogs, randomly arranged in front of the fire, or in summer – in the beer garden. Extra points if the dogs are ancient Brit breeds like greyhounds, spaniels or bulldogs.
- A proper pack of true locals. Not mere visitors, like us. Locals walk in, are greeted by their nicknames ('Hello, Porky!') and then join in conversations stretching the length of the bar.

The Great British bath

To make sure your second day in London is wonderful, end your *first* day with a long bath. The Brits acquired the habit from the Romans, and in the absence of decent plumbing (at least until the 1980s) became a Bathing Nation rather than a showering one. Here are two quintessentially British stores which cater for bathtime – and the wonderful Liberty even has rubber ducks. Look carefully at the front of the building as you go in – Liberty is built partly from two ships, the HMS *Impregnable* and the HMS *Hindustan*. Say 'Ahoy!' as you walk in.

D. R. Harris, the smart chemist and perfumer, produces blissful bath oils and candles. D. R. Harris is also the appointed chemist to Prince Charles. The lotions and potions are all encased in lovely retro packaging. Actually, it's not retro at all – it's just *never changed*. The Mayfair Silky Bath Essence is divine, and named for Mayfair – everyone's favourite Monopoly stop. Or try almond soap-on-a-rope.

Liberty has the best handpicked bath and beauty range in London. It also has everything else, and as it is England's most beautiful department store, you may have to be dragged away, weeping. Once you reach the bath shop, try Liberty's own-brand Samphire and Seaweed Bath Oil. Samphire is an old British plant first mentioned by Shakespeare in *King Lear*. The soap makes a lovely present.

Liberty
Great Marlborough Street
NEAREST TUBE: Oxford Circus
WEBSITE: liberty.co.uk

D. R. Harris
29 St James's Street
NEAREST TUBE: Green Park
WEBSITE: drharris.co.uk

Get the fast flat habit

London is the home of fast flats. Racks of flat pumps and ballet shoes in every kind of leather, fabric and colour, sold on racks and carousels, like paperbacks. You can see them all over the world now, but Londoners started the trend. Because I can't drive, I always seem to be running to appointments, or pelting down stairs. Thus, I had to develop a split shoe personality. Towering Terry de Havilland platforms for special occasions, and Fast Flats in my bag.

The best Fast Flats (FFs) in the world are sold in London fashion chains and department stores. I love the fact that you don't have to wait to be served, or wait while someone disappears into a time-and-space vortex, to look for your size.

If you think Fast Flats are boring, it's because you've never been inside Top Shop's sublime Oxford Street shoe department. Look down, whenever you walk London streets, and you'll quickly realise that every second fashionista is wearing them. I'm convinced part of the boom in It Bags began because party shoes became more vertiginous, and greater bag space was needed for the life-saving FFs.

Not in a rush? London's biggest and most stunning shoe range is at Selfridges (see page 119). The ballet shoes and pumps here are handpicked from the world's biggest and best designers. Everyone do the Fast Flat Fandango!

Jessica Adams

Chiconomical secrets

Oyster Card
Buy an Oyster Card the moment you land at Heathrow or Gatwick. Swipe it at train stations and on buses to save money and time. The cheapest way to get from Heathrow Airport to central London is by normal tube on the dark blue Piccadilly line. Ignore the Piccadilly Express, which costs £18 for a one-way ticket.

Marks and Sparks
London restaurants are expensive. Thus, if you're here in warm weather, throwing Marks & Spencer sandwiches in your handbag for lunch in the park is the only way to go. (They do mozzarella and tomato salad too, and prawns with dipping sauce.) See *marksandspencer.com* for locations. And pick up a free copy of the *Evening Standard* – London's most fabulous newspaper – outside the store, to read over lunch.

The Magic Number 11 bus
Despite the high cost of hotels and restaurants, London's most spectacular museums and art galleries are also free. And as goddesses know, it costs nothing to take the number 11 bus. Holiday Goddess editors and their friends agree that apart from the Sandwich Secret, catching this magical double-decker is the best visitor's trick of all.

If you sit on the top deck, you'll have the best cheap London tour in the world. The number 11 runs from Fulham, home of the famous football team, past Sloane Square, where Sloane Rangers originally came from. The bus will take you through to Westminster, so you can wave at Big Ben, Westminster Abbey and the Houses of Parliament. Then to Trafalgar Square (more waving, this time at Lord Nelson), then past Fleet Street and onto St Paul's Cathedral. Magic!

British glampacking

Holiday Goddess editors and friends rely on glampacking to wander the country for under £50 a day (much less if you are with a partner or friend who will split the cost of your YMCA room). And make no mistake, the YMCA rules, despite its connotations with the Village People and malodorous backpacking males. There have been pretenders to the British bargainista throne for twenty years, but in London and her daycation destinations (Bath, Brighton, York, Oxford, Cambridge) there really is no other choice – mainly because the YMCA has a knack for snapping up prime locations. Their rooms are frequently near smart hotels (the Bath branch is opposite The Hilton) and always uber-cheap. A room with two single beds and a shared bathroom can be snapped up for £30 or less, overnight. Endless breakfast (toast, cereal, tea or coffee) is included, along with free wi-fi. Simple dinner is £4 or under – be amazed. Beyond that, there are certain considerations if you are trying to fake glamour on a budget in London and beyond. Our Holiday Goddess tips are:

- Pack a magic shrinking towel (the kind that folds away to nothing in a plastic pouch). Otherwise you'll be hiring them.
- Pack earplugs too – the best are from Muji at *muji.com*. You can never account for your neighbours in a YMCA, and the Bavarian drinking team may check in.
- Packing a sarong and wearing it into the share bathroom, but throwing it over the (usually garish) bedlinen the rest of the time.
- Throwing lavender oil into the room sink, with hot water, to vaporise the room on arrival, then dropping more oil into the mist in the showers.
- If staying more than two days, buying fresh flowers and fruit, and a travel candle. Add mini-speakers for your iPod with your favourite music and you'll feel completely at home, no matter how many church or school groups check onto your floor.

The fine art of Swishing

Swishing is swapping, but more interesting. It has also taken over London – the home of Swishing – and spread as far as the United Arab Emirates, home to our Dubai Holiday Goddess editor Tamara Pitelen.

For travellers, it's great news – and it's also ecofabulous. Decant your suitcase of the clothes you wish you'd never packed, and the stuff you deeply regret impulse-purchasing.

The organisers we know (and boy are they well-organised) have invented clever rules to stop kicking, scratching, biting and screaming. Lindsay Lohan helped kick it all off three years ago, and Londoners haven't stopped swishing since. Pay a fee, get a colour-coded ticket (reflecting the value of what you wish to swish) and then watch all your fashion swishes come true. To find your nearest next event go to *swishing.com*.

Charity shop tricks 101

The smartest parts of London offer the best charity shopping – but at realistic eBay prices, so be warned. The good old days of the bargainista Paul Smith tweed jacket have long gone, and now you will pay a hefty amount for designer labels, should they be in your size. Serious competition for good clothes (see Swishing, above, along with eBay) has diminished the charity shops, but if you're nearby anyway, see if you can't resist a quick visit. Holiday Goddess editors say, trawl the charity shops near these tube stops: Sloane Square, South Kensington and Gloucester Road.

TOP TEN

The best of free London

1. The National Portrait Gallery
2. The British Museum
3. The Victoria & Albert Museum
4. The Wellcome Collection
5. Geffrye Museum
6. Horniman Museum
7. Imperial War Museum
8. Museum of Childhood
9. Natural History Museum
10. John Soane's Museum

London in children's books – free

The London you know and love from children's books is absolutely free.

Paddington Bear

Paddington Bear (in bronze) lies near YO! Sushi at Paddington Station – the big overground branch, above the tube – on Praed Street. He was born in 1956, when his creator first saw him in a shop near the station. Fame followed, perhaps because of Paddington's wellington boots, which actually help to keep him stable.

Harry Potter's Platform 9 ¾

J. K. Rowling was living in Manchester when she created her fictional platform. Kings Cross station management now have a sign announcing 'Platform 9¾' along with half a luggage trolley, stuck in a wall.

Coram Fields Children's Park

Holiday Goddess reader Helen Basini was a team editor on the bestselling *Kids' Night In* series in aid of War Child, for which J. K. Rowling chose a favourite poem by Walt Whitman. Helen's favourite place for children is Coram Fields Children's Park. 'Adults may only enter with a child under 16, but there's a literary connection. Jamila Gavin's novel *Coram Boy* is set here. It also appears in a novel by Jacqueline Wilson.'

Peter Pan

The Peter Pan statue in Kensington Gardens was put up secretly on the night of April 30 1912 so that on May 1, children seeing it would think Peter Pan had arrived by magic. He is still there.

The secret diaries of several shopaholics

More than any other city in the world, London is divided into fashion tribes. And each part of London caters for those tribes. Whether you're vintage or vamp, prefer second-hand markets or haute couture, there should be a London fashion district with your name on it.

If you thought Mayfair was expensive on the Monopoly board then you'd better bring more than Monopoly cash. Mayfair is filled to the upper-crust brim with globalites who call royal providores **Fortnum and Mason** their corner store and **Savile Row** their tailors. The area is home to **Balenciaga**, **Louboutin**, **Vivienne Westwood**, **Marc Jacobs** and their friends on Bond Street.

But if you only have time for one store make it **Selfridges** department store, the one-stop shop for fashion-forward trends and celebrity watching. Comme des Garçon's uber-schmick **Dover Street Market** is a den of cutting edge design that must be seen, and do not miss London fashion institution **Browns** on South Molton Street or the hidden enclave of St Christopher's Place for one of a kind boutiques alongside **Marimekko** and **Mulberry** classics.

Rachael Oakes-Ash

Soho and Covent Garden

The saucy Brit streets of Soho are part red light, part Italian, part French and part modern media. Add in the cobbled laneways of Covent Garden and expect some fashion finds.

Our top tips? **Coco de Mer** serves up luxurious erotica from girlie toys to corsets, **Twenty8twelve** is Sienna Miller's sister's shop (we're sure she has her own name), **Jelly Pong Pong** is a British take on retro-style make-up glamour as found in the **Vintage Magazine Shop**.

Foot fetish? Do not pass **Poste Mistress**, a divine den of tootsie fashion from shoe gods around the world. You can't go wrong at the **Seven Dials** hidden village in Covent Garden especially at the highly coveted **Fifi Wilson** – expect racks of hand-picked designer fashion.

Grab something for mister on Floral Street, the shrine to male design. Choose from **Paul Smith** for men, **Nigel Hall**, **Jack Wills** and **Ted Baker** but not before you've got yourself a present from cult brand **Maharishi**.

Clerkenwell, Shoreditch, Hoxton

The East End of London offers an eclectic mix of cockney locals and plum-in-the-mouth media and financial types.

You'll find haggling in Petticoat Lane market here, and curry houses in Brick Lane, but you'll also find uber-cool brands like **CA4LA** for Japanese designed hats, **Bernstock Speirs** for British-designed eye turning headware, the burlesque inspired **Bordello** boutique for lingerie and **Tatty Devine** where art, music and jewellery combine.

Shoreditch and Hoxton are also the creative Mecca for vintage wear in London. Try **Absolute Vintage** for shoes and bags and their sister store, **Blondie**, for seriously stylish dress-up-box fashion. Then get lost in a culinary journey at the **Spitalfields Market** and indulge in some nose to tail dining at **St John** restaurant where nothing is wasted (don't ask, just eat).

Knightsbridge to Kensington

Double-barrelled last names, family crests and trust funds define the inner south-west of London from Knightsbridge to Chelsea and South Kensington.

Name-droppers wander Sloane Street for **Hermès**, **Dolce & Gabbana**, **Dior**, **Jimmy Choo**, **Chloé**, **Cartier** and **Tiffany** before hitting **Harvey Nichols**, the doyenne of department store fashion in London for three floors of female fashion and the Fifth Floor dining emporium.

Down the road is the famous **Harrods** – over a million square feet dedicated to retail therapy complete with twenty-two dining outlets and a private bank (as you do).

Rachel Trevor-Morgan is the milliner of choice for Ascot-loving pony types, royal lingerie boutique **Rigby & Peller** to indulge the princess within and **Cosmetics à la Carte** for bespoke make-up.

Sure, peruse Chelsea's Kings Road but be warned, it's not the fashion central it used to be, though it does have the odd gem thrown in, like **R.Soles** for classic cowboy boots from around the world.

Notting Hill & Westbourne Grove

Westbourne Grove is the new fashion heartbeat of once-bohemian Notting Hill. Let your feet lead you to **Fiorentini + Baker** for shoe heaven as favoured by Sarah Jessica Parker, **Question Air** for one-off fashion finds and **Brissi** for chalky white and neutral toned homeware and gifts.

You'll find antique shops filled with everything from furniture to books to clocks and lampshades, and **The Travel Bookshop**, which is not dissimilar to its cameo in the *Notting Hill* film (just don't expect to meet Hugh Grant). Then there are the **Portobello Markets** and vintage galore with our faves **Virginia Vintage** and **Mensah**.

Stop off at the **Electric Brasserie** for sidewalk people-watching or inhale a vanilla cupcake or three at **Hummingbird Cafe**.

TOP TEN
Our favourite shops

1. Liberty
2. Selfridges
3. Top Shop
4. Harvey Nichols
5. Primark
6. Fortnum & Mason
7. Marks & Spencer
8. Rigby and Peller
9. Lulu Guinness
10. Office

Top Shop

There is only one reason we will put up with the heaving crowds on Oxford Street and that is Top Shop. It's on every British high street, of course, but the enormous flagship is on Oxford Street, across the road from Oxford Circus tube station.

If French designers have always been chic and tailored, then British designers have long been eccentric and creative. Top Shop is a huge, heaving homage to those witty Brits. You'll see Mary Quant's 1960s Pop Art shift dresses and mini skirts recreated here. And a nod to Paul Smith's reinvented tweed jackets. Even the Royal Family's designer-by-appointment Hardy Amies is remembered in the wonderful Top Shop evening frocks.

Top Shop designers and buyers are afraid of nothing. Enormous diamanté earrings that fall from earlobe to shoulder? No problem. Leopardskin jeggings? They had them five years ago. It's the most rock'n'roll emporium I know. We can still remember Kate Moss' Rolling-Stonesy waistcoats, designed by her, on racks above her special leopardskin floor when she launched her range.

Yes, the queues for the change rooms and the till will drive you mad. But you won't find a bigger range of delicious fashion, bags and shoes anywhere else in the country. American supermodels bring their wheelie suitcases here, and leap around the store like beautiful gazelles, before dashing out for a taxi, and the plane. Top Shop is on our no-map guide to Oxford Street shopping. See *holidaygoddess.com*.

Top Shop
216 Oxford Street

NEAREST TUBE: Oxford Circus

WEBSITE: topshop.co.uk

Selfridges' stationery department

Okay, so there's a lot more going on in Selfridges than birthday cards and notebooks. It can be overwhelming. Come out alive (and under budget) say Holiday Goddess editors, by focusing on their sensational stationery department. It stocks the hippest and the best for handbag and desk. It's where we found an *On the Road* key ring (an homage to Jack Kerouac). And also a jokey Elton John–David Furnish card to celebrate gay nuptials.

Here's another reason to go: it's adjacent to the magnificent chocolate and confectionery floor, where they sell Prestat (see page 134). And scorpion lollipops.

Selfridges
400 Oxford Street

NEAREST TUBE: Bond Street

WEBSITE: selfridges.com

Vivienne Westwood's London

There are two Vivienne Westwoods. One is the outrageous punk rocker from 1977. The other is the fabulous (but still rather outrageous) Dame, who is part of the global glitterati. Sadly, many of London's punk haunts from the 1970s have gone.

To see the famous bright blue, mock-croc platforms (captured by our artist Anna Johnson on the opposite page) pay a visit to the fashion collection at the Victoria and Albert Museum (see page 153). They are 30 centimetres high, and Naomi Campbell fell off them. Dame Vivienne donated them.

   Her favourite places are The Courtauld Institute of Art, the Wallace Collection, Whitechapel, Hampton Court, Brixton Market, Electric Avenue and the National Gallery. (Visit *holidaygoddess.com* for a link to a short clip about these magic places.)

The Wallace Collection

Stunned visitors who see a noble, flame-haired woman (like a cross between Elizabeth I and Boadicea) pedalling on a bicycle in the direction of The Wallace Collection should probably hail a taxi and follow. It is very likely to be Dame Vivienne Westwood, en route to one of her favourite places. Admission is free, and it's an easy walk from Bond Street tube station. Find the Wallace Collection at Hertford House, Manchester Square. The website is *wallacecollection.org*.

   Leonie Edwards-Jones worked for Dame Vivienne: 'I know that she really loved the Wallace Collection,' she says, 'and particularly the Fragonard and Poussin paintings there – from the Rococo period.'

There is one painting showing a woman on a swing, and her lover is lying at her feet looking up her skirts – I think the story was that she didn't have any knickers on. Vivienne loved that painting – I seem to remember that she even put it on the front panel of one of her corsets.'

Want to buy a bit of Britain from a place where it was actually created? To find the famous Westwood label boutique with the backwards-spinning clock, head to Sloane Square train station and take the long (but lovely) walk down Kings Road, until you reach the very end.

Just near two of the best charity shops known to womankind, you will find World's End. This is where the Westwood legend began. The crazy clock-hands on the front of the shop are part Alice in Wonderland, part witty Brit. It's a reminder that for Vivienne Westwood, fashion is nothing without the past. If you're serious about the homage, then you'll take a copy of Proust under your arm.

'I remember my job interview with Vivienne well – she saw on my CV that I'd studied French at university and was very keen to discuss Proust with me. However, we never did – probably a good thing as I had managed to study French for four years without ever touching one of Proust's books!'

London in books and film

Shut your eyes and think of London. Are you running down Carnaby Street in 1967 wearing a mini-skirt or lining up for soup in 1837 wearing rags? Either way, you've been seduced by British writers, who have had longer to work with the English language than anyone else. We asked bestselling novelist **Sara Foster** to walk us through the literary and cinematic landmarks.

The London of book and film is a contrasting landscape – coupling the historical and the zeitgeist, the suburban and the iconographic, home to British high society and thriving multiculturalism. One thing is clear, however: it has long reigned supreme in nurturing imagination and invention, playing home and host to everyone from Harry Potter to Sherlock Holmes, Mary Poppins to Bridget Jones.

Many literary pioneers lived in and wrote about the capital – including Chaucer, Shakespeare, Pepys, William Blake, W B Yeats, Oscar Wilde, Henry James, H G Wells and Sylvia Plath. Jane Austen gave her readers glimpses of class-obsessed London in the early nineteenth century, while Dickens wrote voraciously about the city in the Victorian era. His house is now open to the public at 48 Doughty St, not far from where the infamous Bloomsbury set of Virginia Woolf, Lytton Strachey, E M Forster and T S Eliot, among others, met for intellectual discussion and edification between the world wars.

The upheaval and turmoil of the capital in conflict is the backdrop to Woolf's classic *Mrs Dalloway* (1925), which chronicles a day in post-WWI London, and other greats have been similarly inspired. Graham Greene's *The End of the Affair* (1951) moved through the city post-WWII, while Ian McEwan's *Saturday* looks at a day in the life of Henry Perowne, who lives in Fitzrovia post-9/11.

In other literary classics, London is cast as a merciless, threatening place. In George Orwell's chilling study of the future, *1984*, the city has become a metropolis of surveillance and oppression, while one of its most lauded writers, Martin Amis, writes of degradation and decay in the black-humoured murder–mystery *London Fields* (1989).

The more tender, romantic aspects of England's heart can be found in Sophie Kinsella's *Confessions of a Shopaholic*, Jane Green's *Mr Maybe*, Marian Keyes' *The Other Side of the Story*, and books by Lisa Jewell and Harriet Evans.

Hanif Kureishi's *The Buddha of Suburbia* (1990) is a masterful exploration of suburban cultural diversity, and has been joined in recent years by Monica Ali's *Brick Lane*, Andrea Levy's *Small Island* and Zadie Smith's *White Teeth*.

Over the same period, Nick Hornby set many of his sharply observed novels in North London, including *High Fidelity*, *About a Boy* and *A Long Way Down*. And in 2009, Audrey Niffenegger chose Highgate Cemetery as the location for her surreal tale of twin sisters in *Her Fearful Symmetry*.

London's film credits are as prolific and varied as its literary heritage. Hitchcock used the place as a setting numerous times, and the seamlessly shifting kaleidoscope of London life repeatedly blossoms in the endless permutations of filmmakers' imaginations, attracting the biggest box-office stars.

Colin Firth and Renée Zellweger played London residents Mark Darcy and the unforgettable Bridget Jones, alongside Hugh Grant, who seems almost synonymous with the city and the genre (*Notting Hill*; *Four Weddings and a Funeral*; *Love, Actually*).

The award-winning drama *Closer* features Clive Owen, Jude Law, Julia Roberts and Natalie Portman in an interwoven tale of complicated relationships; while Owen also plays Theo Faron, a man confronting the chaotic, barren world of London in 2027 in the adaptation of P D James' *Children of Men*.

Tom Hanks races around the city in *The Da Vinci Code;* while Judy Dench metamorphosises from the eccentric promoter of nude female performers in *Mrs Henderson Presents* (the true story of the Windmill theatre), to starring alongside Cate Blanchett as the obsessive, bitter teacher in the psychological thriller *Notes on a Scandal* (based on Zoë Heller's novel).

London has also played its part in some cult classics. Who could forget *Withnail & I*, where two out-of-work actors living in a squalid flat in Camden take a disastrous holiday; or Ray Winston's orange, pot-bellied, Speedo-clad body and Ben Kingsley's chilling arrival into his life in *Sexy Beast*.

The mercenary and often merciless underbelly of London's East End is also depicted in the Guy Ritchie-produced films *Snatch* and *Lock, Stock and Two Smoking Barrels*, while *Eastern Promises*, starring Naomi Watts, and *Dirty Pretty Things*, featuring Audrey Tautou, each submerge viewers within disturbing subcultures of the metropolis.

Landmarks of London are well-represented in a variety of films. One of the most striking depictions begins the zombie flick *28 Days Later*, where Cillian Murphy walks across a deserted Westminster Bridge towards a silent Piccadilly Circus.

Historical dramas such as *Elizabeth* and *The Other Boleyn Girl* (adapted from one of Philippa Gregory's bestsellers) use the world-renowned palaces, grand houses, and the River Thames to portray historical London at its cruel yet graceful, glittering best. And in *Sliding Doors*, Gwyneth Paltrow's character Helen leads a double life, dependent on whether she catches or misses the tube. *An American Werewolf in London* also features the underground, but beware: one or two scenes might put you off travelling through it at night!

London's innocence is recaptured through some well-loved children's characters – from Michael Bond's Paddington Bear, to Mole, Mr Toad, Ratty and Mr Badger in Kenneth Grahame's *The Wind in the Willows*. *Finding Neverland*, featuring Johnny Depp and Kate Winslet, is set around Kensington Gardens, and tells the story of how J M Barrie came to write *Peter Pan*. And young heroes Harry Potter and Alex Rider each know the city well.

But when you are in the capital, don't waste time indoors! Venture out to hunt down the best book and film experiences the city can offer. Breathe in the atmosphere of the writing greats by visiting the Reading Room in the British Museum, beloved by everyone from Mark Twain to Arthur Conan Doyle. Find Poets' Corner in Westminster Abbey or the Poetry Cafe in Covent Garden. Download one of the movie maps from Film London and go on a locations tour. Or look out for Secret Cinema, which shows classic films as part of a unique, interactive theatre experience. And when you come away, you can bring this city of contrasts to life again and again, by immersing yourself in the imagination and inspiration of others.

Sara Foster

Follow the white rabbit to Oxford

Oxford, England is the best place to find Alice in Wonderland and other wonders. I first stayed at Jesus College, Oxford, ten years ago. I was attending a summer school, and booked a room next to a large bell on the Turl. Big mistake. It clanged on the hour, every hour, and my jetlag was indescribable. Still, there were wonders to compensate – chiefly of the Alice variety.

The best place to follow the white rabbit is online. Visit the (appropriately) wonderful Alice in Wonderland site on the web at *aliceinoxford.info*.

Alice's Shop in Oxford is the original Old Sheep Shop from *Through the Looking Glass*. The shopkeeper bleated like a sheep, so Lewis Carroll turned her into a character, and the shop into a location.

It has been a gift shop for all things Alice since the 1960s. The fascination with Carroll's trippy, deeply dippy stories was revived in the era of psychedelia, and students loved it. Today it's the only place to go, if you have young girls to buy presents for at home. The calico bags, with beautiful illustrations of the Mad Hatter, Alice and the famous dodo are easy to pack, and exclusive to the shop.

There are fabulous Lewis Carroll artefacts at the Oxford Museum. Most interesting of all is his watch, given his strange perception of time and space. You may also find the original 'Drink Me' bottle there.

The dreamy river and ancient trees help set the scene – though get up at 6am to wander around, as I did, if you want to have the atmosphere and the space, rather than the coach-loads of people with backpacks and cameras. The museum won't open for ages, but go wandering, across the cobblestones and down to Oxford's famous bridges and playing fields.

It's hard to imagine Oxford as she was in Carroll's time, or even in Waugh's time, when he was absorbing it all for *Brideshead Revisited*. The shops selling university scarves tend to take away from the magic. As do the fast-food containers in the gutters – *tch!*

Wake up early enough, though, and you'll find a little of what transported past students and academics – and what inspired their work. Time only stands still on Lewis Carroll's watch, but you can catch glimpses of the past if you try.

Jessica Adams

Eat, love, eat more

Along with tea and wine, London runs on carbohydrates. Thus, the famous fat injection at Heathrow. The legend runs, that when you arrive in the capital, you will be secretly injected with a huge quantity of liquid fat. Within a week, you will be several kilos heavier, with a Bridget Jones bottom, and have absolutely no idea why.

At this point, we should probably let you know about Tube Escalator Maths. You divide the number of kilojoules you've just consumed by the number of escalator steps you've taken on the tube that day. Then you can scoff down that delicious pork pie.

If Paris is the home of the pâtisserie and the boulangerie, then London is the home of the proud pudding. And also the great British cake. It is also the capital of toast, and Londoners eat it with anchovy paste, known as Gentlemen's Relish. They are also obsessed with marmalade – particularly Cooper's Oxford. An awful lot of tutting goes on if all the marmalade has been taken at breakfast.

Are you salivating yet? Because the truth is, while London is hell on your skinny jeans, it is heaven for anyone who likes comfort eating. Almost *everything* about food in London is comfort. The porridge reminds you of Goldilocks and the Three Bears. The toad-in-the-hole reminds you of eccentric British children's books. A great deal of what Londoners like to eat is actually nursery food – the cuisine of childhood.

This is not a yeast-free, gluten-free city, so if you have to watch what you eat, do your web homework before you visit. Our tip? Start with the YO! Sushi chain at *yosushi.co.uk*.

St Martin-in-the-Fields' Cafe in the Crypt

Holiday Goddess editors and readers all recommend the Cafe in the Crypt. You will be dining on top of ancient gravestones, inside a church – but sometimes that's the only way to avoid coach-loads of tourists. The Cafe in the Crypt lies in the gloomy basement of St-Martin-in-the-Fields, which is the pretty church across from the National Portrait Gallery and Trafalgar Square.

There are lots of reasons we like this place. The candles on the tables. The spooky atmosphere. The smartly-dressed women in velvet jackets and sensible shoes. Their hungry husbands in Barbour coats, who load their trays until they are ticked off by their wives.

It's cafeteria-style eating, so just grab a tray and slide it along the stainless-steel bars to heaven. The Cafe in the Crypt has the best auntie food in town. Afternoon tea with vast scones, clotted cream and strawberry jam is under £5 too – so these are old-school, auntie prices.

Come for breakfast, lunch, afternoon tea or dinner. The Crypt has everything. It's close to Nelson's Column, so you can stroke Nelson's famous lions afterwards. And the National Portrait Gallery is over the road. It's easy to reach, because of the tube. And it's a licence to eat a lot of custard.

The Crypt is vaguely secret, although all our mothers' friends seem to know about it. Jilly Cooper even launched one of her books here. It's beautifully lit, so if you come here on a date, you'll look gorgeous.

The church above you, St-Martin-in-the-Fields, dates to 1222. Kings used to worship here. Below your feet, as you pop your bag under the table, you will see the names on the graves have been rubbed away by time. Still, the atmosphere remains.

A large bowl of home-made soup and a bread roll is just fine for lunch. Or consider the apple crumble or bread-and-butter pudding.

Old-fashioned British cooking has slowly made a comeback over the last ten years, thanks to Jamie Oliver, Delia Smith, Nigel Slater and Nigella Lawson. This is one of the very best places to find it, without the crowds, and without the usual London price tag. Just don't take a king's ghost home with you.

Cafe in the Crypt
St Martin-in-the-Fields

NEAREST TUBE: **Charing Cross or Leicester Square**

WEBSITE: **www2.stmartin-in-the-fields.org**

Perfect London picnics

All those royal parks. All that impromptu cricket. All that strange behaviour when the barometer hits 20° celsius and the secretaries sunbathe in their bras. London is a big summer picnic town, and Holiday Goddess readers can't resist foodie superstores like the Wholefoods Market at 63 Kensington High Street. It's a short trot from High Street Kensington tube station, and next door to Hyde Park. Just bring a tartan rug and bottle opener.

We asked our most trusted advisors for their best inside knowledge on where to gather the ingredients.

Justin North was just 22 when he became Raymond Blanc's youngest 2nd Sous Chef. Last year, he was named *GQ Magazine*'s Chef of the Year: 'At Borough Market, you can opt for oysters or pick up paella. You can surrender to sausage or ogle olives. You can buy hot baked bread or become a fruit-fancier. There are French pâtés and Melton Mowbray pork pies, as well as deli delights from Sardinia, Poland and Germany.

I find fantastic barbequed chorizo and rocket buns there, that scent the air and make the mouth water. Or try something quintessentially English like a ginger pig banger sarnie while you're shopping.

A stall at Borough Market at 8 Southwark St produces the most palatable and portable Parma ham, smoked mozzarella and rocket wrap.'

Alison Carmichael-Rulten has had several media career adventures including *delicious* magazine and *Vogue Living + Entertainment*: 'I agree that if you're going to shop for the best weekend picnic ingredients in London, then you *have* to visit Borough Market. It's set beneath the railway viaducts between the River Thames and Borough High Street in South East London and it's open on Thursdays, Fridays and Saturdays. It's the best place to find the basics. After that, find your favourite park!'

Andreina Cordani likes visiting Borough Market then strolling the Thames afterwards, or popping into The Globe pub on Bedales Street, the fictional site of Bridget Jones' flat. 'At the market, the scent of fresh organic steak sandwiches sizzles in the air and there are veggie treats too. Try the free samples of cheese, cold meats, dips, chutneys and breads. Do get cash out before you come to Borough Market though – there's always long queues for local ATMs and many of the vendors don't take cards.'

Luxe picnics for less

How do you enjoy a luxe picnic in spring or summer, for less? Holiday Goddess editors have a sneaky trick. They make sure they are in Selfridges' Food Hall at closing time. That's when all the delicious takeaway sushi is marked down to half price. From there, they nip over the road to Marks & Spencer's Food Hall, where the sandwiches are also marked down. Add a bottle of the excellent M&S Beaujolais, and then wander down to Hyde Park. For around £10 per person, you'll dine in style.

Marks & Spencer
458 Oxford Street

Selfridges
400 Oxford Street

NEAREST TUBE: Bond Street

Perfect Picnic Parks

1. Green Park
2. Hyde Park
3. Bushy Park
4. Kensington Gardens
5. Regent's Park
6. Richmond Park
7. St James Park
8. Greenwich Park
9. Alexandra Park
10. Holland Park

The non-Starbucks guide to London coffee

London is dominated by the big three coffee chains – Starbucks, Nero and Costa. **Emma Killick** prefers the cappuccinos, biscuits and atmosphere at these three Soho alternatives:

Milk Bar at **3 Bateman Street, Soho** is one of the many Antipodean-owned coffee houses taking over London. I've always found a great range of coffee caringly presented (patterns drawn into frothy milk seem to tug at my heart strings). It's a tiny space with bench seating and comfy stools, groovy music and a buzzy atmosphere.

Bar Italia at **22 Frith Street, Soho** is voted by Holiday Goddess editors as the most intriguing coffee bar in London. 'A mere walk from Leicester Square tube,' says one, 'and I have escaped corporate coffee chain hell.' Television was invented in the flat above Bar Italia, and Will Self name-checked it in a novel. The interior is totally 'Ciao!' and it's like time-travelling back to 1960s Rome in 21st century London. Bar Italia has been a family run business for more than 60 years and the brusque service is as authentic as the full-bodied Italian coffee. Check out the good people-watching tables out the front (heat lamps mean you'll see people sitting outside even in January).

LJ Coffee House at **3 Winnett Street, Soho** has very friendly, personal service and rich, creamy lattes. The last time I visited for Holiday Goddess I was greeted with an accented 'Yes, I am listening' and a smile. Comfy sofas encourage you to stay and lounge, a rarity in hustle-bustle Soho.

Two good options before the theatre in Covent Garden or on the South Bank:

Notes Music and Coffee at **31 St Martin's Lane, Covent Garden,** sells music in the back and coffee in the front – they do both well, unlike most establishments that try to multitask. Great staff and a light and airy space make this an inviting spot.

Concrete on the South Bank has as industrial an interior as you would expect from a place named Concrete, but manages to feel warm and appealing. Its location begets an arty, laidback crowd. The smooth and strong coffee always leaves me wanting more and the proper kitchen in the back means there are real food options, too. **Hayward Gallery, The South Bank Centre. Nearest Tube: Leicester Square**

Eat like an English eccentric

Mad dogs and Englishmen go out in the midday sun, and then eat truly peculiar food. Join in and sample these goodies.

Jellied Eels
The original London jellied eels come from the Thames and they are a traditional Cockney delicacy, eaten cold.

Cockles
Miniscule clams, served on tiny plastic plates from dollies' tea sets, with a toothpick, salt and vinegar.

Toad-in-the-Hole
No actual toads, as children dread – just a lot of sausages (bangers) encased in Yorkshire Pudding.

Yorkshire Pudding
Not a pudding – actually a puffball of light golden dough. Tasteless without gravy. Best eaten with a roast.

Gobstoppers
Everlasting Gobstoppers were made famous by Roald Dahl in Willy Wonka's Chocolate Factory. See your dentist first.

Scotch Eggs
Hard-boiled eggs wrapped in a ball of sausage-meat, then deep-fried in breadcrumbs. Invented at Fortnum & Mason.

Best Eccentric Restaurants

St John, in Smithfield, is wonderful. Sausages are served with snails and pigeon pie is also available. For a brilliant British breakfast under £10 drop into the St John Hotel restaurant, near Leicester Square tube in Soho. We rate the home-made toast and marmalade.
St John Bar and Restaurant, 26 St John Street
Website: *stjohnrestaurant.com*
St John Hotel, 1 Leicester St
Website: *stjohnhotellondon.com*

Dinner, Heston Blumenthal's latest restaurant, uses British recipes from as far back as 1390. We'd walk a million miles for the Brown Bread Ice-Cream, though we're not sure about the beetroot porridge, Heston. Dinner lies inside the **Mandarin Oriental Hyde Park Hotel, 66 Knightsbridge**.
Website: *dinnerbyheston.com*

Made in London: Cult local brands

Let everyone else drag home the Burberry perfume or the Harrods' teddies. You're here for True Brit brands, which are only selectively exported and (even in New York City) devilishly hard to find.

Several of our favourite cult local brands have royal warrants, which means they have are favourites of the Royal Family too. And yes, they *do* pay for them. *Ahem.*

Prestat

The Queen Mother apparently used to keep a box of Prestat chocolates in her desk drawer. Princess Diana liked them too – and Prestat also delivers to Her Majesty the Queen, by appointment. You can even find Prestat chocolates in Roald Dahl's novel, *My Uncle Oswald* (where they are fictitiously injected with love potion). We can't throw the famous hot pink and turquoise boxes away, because they're so good to keep ribbons and buttons in. Try the Earl Grey tea flavoured chocolate wafers, or the old-fashioned rose and violet cremes. Just as importantly, Prestat also has a fair-trading partnership with farmers in Ghana as joint Managing Director Bill Keeling was once West Africa correspondent for the *Financial Times*.

The woman who has re-imagined Prestat's beautiful packaging for the 21st century is artist and designer Kitty Arden. She also designs pet coffins for fish, pigs, tortoises and snakes. Until that sad day arrives for your pet, just keep eating the chocolate.

Prestat
14 Princes Arcade, Piccadilly
NEAREST TUBE: Piccadilly Circus
WEBSITE: prestat.co.uk

Smythson

Smythson is where the best stiffies in the land are created. And a stiffie from Smythson (a stiff, white, card invitation – engraved, not printed) is always worth keeping. You may have your own personal writing paper and visiting cards created here, at huge expense, but they will keep your design in their files forever. The tiny leather-bound notebooks in hot pink and emerald green are future heirlooms. Some are engraved with the legend 'Blondes, Brunettes, Redheads'. To pick up a chap at Claridges, lick your pencil seductively and point the pencil at him in a meaningful way.

Smythson
40 New Bond Street, Mayfair
NEAREST TUBE: Bond Street
WEBSITE: smythson.com

Emma Hope

The aristocracy would court each other barefoot (and marry barefoot) if it wasn't for Emma Hope. Her most beautiful store lies off Sloane Square, near Sloane Square tube station, in the old eighties heartland of Sloane Rangerdom. Holiday Goddess editors go nuts at sale time, and do a lot of window-licking for the rest of the year. Emma Hope, who is gratifyingly real, pioneered old-school sneakers in velvet, the colour of 19th century drapes. She also creates beautiful boots, in the Georgian style. The evening slippers glitter under the light of the chandeliers in London ballrooms.

Emma Hope
513 Sloane Square
NEAREST TUBE: Sloane Square
WEBSITE: emmahope.co.uk

Neal's Yard

Neal's Yard – one of our all-time favourite bathroom shelf shops – looks Victorian with its beautiful dark blue glass bottles and herbal ingredients. It dates from the big organic and alternative health push of the 1980s, though, when a visionary woman named Romy Fraser created the chain. The travel-friendly kits will waft you from hotel to plane in a cloud of frankincense, rose or orange. The bottles are made from Scottish sand and Yorkshire limestone, so recycle before you fly. Another reason to visit Neal's Yard? It lies in Covent Garden, where more Best of British brands also dwell.

Neal's Yard
15 Neal's Yard
NEAREST TUBE: Covent Garden
WEBSITE: nealsyard.co.uk

Covent Garden

Catch the tube to Covent Garden and you will find the Best of British. However – we guarantee you'll get lost unless you walk with your eyes glued to a map. One way to do it? Exit in the direction of Marks & Spencer, the big store right in front of your eyes beyond the turnstiles. If you walk past it, you're on your way to **Neal's Yard**, for the eponymous potions (see previous page). And minutes away, in the same direction, you'll also find **Cath Kidston** at Shelton Street. There are other goodies up there too, beyond Neal's Yard and Cath Kidston. It's cosmetics and shoe heaven. And you'll also be able to wander into **The Astrology Shop**, where both Britney Spears and Robert Downey Jr ordered charts.

To discover the most elegantly retro shoe shop in the land, double back on yourself, walking past Marks & Spencer again, towards the old-fashioned collection of buildings known as Covent Garden proper. There is an entire street of **Paul Smith** boutiques here. And also a mad ice-cream parlour called **Icecreamists**, which sold a human breast-milk flavour, until it was told not to. For our no-map guide to Covent Garden see *holidaygoddess.com*.

TOP TEN

Cult Local Brands

1. Prestat
2. Dr Harris
3. Smythson
4. Cath Kidston
5. Emma Hope
6. Neal's Yard
7. Anya Hindmarch
8. Lulu Guinness
9. Lush
10. L.K. Bennett

Cath Kidston

Cath Kidston (she is delightfully real) has single-handedly made unfashionable parts of female life from the 1950s–1970s desirable again. That's why women salivate at buying pretty peg-bags (to hang up the laundry) or charming ironing-board covers (to do the bloody ironing). She also sells wellies, beautifully reproduced tea-frocks from the 1950s, polka-dot luggage and tiny children's suitcases with images of cowboys and Indians.

Once seen, never forgotten. Often imitated, never bettered. You may even enjoy doing the washing-up with her tea-towels and washing-up liquid.

Cath Kidston
28 Shelton Street,
Covent Garden
NEAREST TUBE: Covent Garden
WEBSITE: cathkidston.co.uk

L.K. Bennett

L.K. Bennett is where London ladies shop for their Good Shoes for weddings and balls. It's also where beautiful 1950s and 1960s influenced suits, frocks and separates lie in wait for unwitting shopaholics. Just when you think you've spent enough money in London, you walk past the front windows of L.K. Bennett and lose the plot. Like Emma Hope, L.K. Bennett gives good sale. We also like their shoes sizes, which range from Imelda Marcos through to Elle Macpherson.

L.K. Bennett
43 King Street, Covent Garden
NEAREST TUBE: Covent Garden
WEBSITE: lkbennett.co.uk

**Lulu Guinness
3 Ellis Street**
NEAREST TUBE: Sloane Square
WEBSITE: luluguinness.com

Lulu Guinness

Six tube stops from Covent Garden, on the chic blue Piccadilly Line, you will find the chic British handbag queen, Lulu Guinness. If your personal style is somewhere between Helena Bonham-Carter and Dita von Teese, then Lulu is your woman. She creates bags that museums love, as they are tomorrow's collectables. Holiday Goddess illustrator Anna Johnson, creator of the iconic book *Handbags: The Power of the Purse*, is a confirmed fan.

We love the nightlife

London after dark is all about live music. And music is wired into Londoners. You will hear more impromptu singing on the streets than anywhere else in the world. Even more impressive – Londoners actually *know all the lyrics*. It is a city where grown men sing 'Wuthering Heights' complete with Kate Bush's flapping hand movements. London is also the place to discover tomorrow's stars. Everyone from David Bowie to Lily Allen started out here.

We asked global clubbing star **Victoria Aitken** and former *Rolling Stone* staffer **Sue Ostler** to open up their address books, to give you *our* inside advantage.

Victoria Aitken's London nightlife address book

Victoria Aitken has been in the Top Ten of the UK dance charts four times. She's performed everywhere from her native London to Berlin, Istanbul and Paris. She is also a Holiday Goddess editor.

If you're going to start anywhere after dark in London, you must begin with **The Troubadour** at **263–265 Old Brompton Road**. This is a classic old-timer nightlife venue. The legendary Bob Dylan played his first London gig here. Other troubadours have included Jimi Hendrix, Joni Mitchell and Elvis Costello. The basement is very dark, with a single rose on each table.

The Cobden Club at **170 Kensal Road** is Notting Hill's grandest live music venue. Outside it looks like a stately home. Inside you'll find a vast, sweeping staircase, leading to a majestic hall the size of a football pitch. The vibe is cool eighties disco, with a huge glittering disco ball above the floor. I like the long bar, which serves both drinks and dinner – and the sofas!

Freedom Bar at **66 Wardour Street, Soho** is an electro-music classic. The promoter Sam Samuels finds the best acts and puts them on in this seriously sexy basement, in the heart of Soho. The interior is furnished with plush purple cushions, mirrors, and poles in the centre of the room (one act I saw here pole-danced his way across the audience and DJ booth).

The Half Moon at **93 Lower Richmond Road**. This is one of the most elegant pubs in London, located in Putney. Getting there is half the pleasure, as you stroll down the Thames. From the outside, The Half Moon almost looks like a Swiss chalet. Inside, it's known for promoting amazing new talent.

The Pigalle Club at **215 Piccadilly**. This is London's most chic and elegant live music venue. The first time I went, I heard jazz genius John Altman. The second time I went, I heard Puff Daddy play to a small audience of 100. Beware – Pigalle's has scary bouncers and they are immune to sweet-talking. Once inside, if you'd rather admire the show from afar, you can take a seat on the balcony and sip a (wildly expensive) champagne. This is where Prince came after his Wembley concert for a secret jamming session.

XOYO at **32–37 Cowper Street**. I stumbled on this by accident. When I arrived there was a line round the block, and only 20 tickets left on the door for none other than DJ Starsmith. Downstairs, Monarchy were on the stage. This is the place to see acts before they go absolutely insane!

Proud Camden at **The Stables Market**. The last time I came to Proud Camden (in Camden) to see Jessica 6, the queue was so long that I heard someone screaming, 'I came all the way from New York! You HAVE to let me in!'

Unfortunately, only half the queue did. Is it worth it? Yes. This venue is actually a series of warehouses joined together. If you don't like the act you came to see, you can always jump over to another stage to see what's going on.

The Blagclub at **11 Russell Gardens** has a speakeasy vibe. It's very hard to find, as there is no sign – just a nondescript door with a number. Even if you ring the bell, the music inside is so loud that they may not hear you, so be warned. The club is the size of a studio apartment. It's really for singer-songwriters, rather than bands, and to lounge around on an armchair seeing the coolest new talent.

London legends after dark

Sue Ostler saw hundreds of bands during her time at *Rolling Stone* magazine – and she loves London so much she moved there. This is her handpicked selection of the best places to go out, and stay out:

Alexandra Palace at **Alexandra Palace Way, Wood Green**, or Ally Pally as it's better known, is a massive, sprawling palace that's played host to all the big names from The Stones and Led Zep to Morrissey and Stone Roses. I saw Franz Ferdinand here recently. The best way to experience it? Arrive early, and have a drink on the roof terrace. The first time I came, nothing had prepared me for the panoramic views across London and the surrounding parkland. Whoa! They even have a skating rink in winter.

The Forum at **9–17 Highgate Road, Kentish Town**, was an Art Deco cinema. Now it's a rock 'n' roll magnet. Oh look, there's Kate Moss making eyes at Carl Barât! Courtney Love and Julian Casablancas falling about out on a jolly! It's a big venue, perfect for big, dirty gigs. Upstairs on the balcony it's too restricted – you need to be down on the floor, to really soak the music up. The Forum's heritage includes the wildest gigs ever from the Velvet Underground, the Pixies and Happy Mondays.

Hope & Anchor at **207 Upper Street, Islington**, (known affectionately as the Hopeless Wanker) attracts a mix of skuzzy rockers and tourists but is mainly a favourite of local boys, if you're man-hunting. The Hope & Anchor also attracts loads of bands with its cheap booze and unsigned newbies every night. Its new wave/punk pedigree is amazing. Ian Dury, The Specials, Madness and Joy Division all played here. It's a great three-level space with a hard-rocking jukebox and comfy booths at ground level, and a pool room upstairs. A makeover has taken some of its punk character but the live music remains.

Boogaloo at **312 Archway Rd, Highgate** is the scene of many a debauched night. You'll find secret gigs and showcases from the latest indie darlings to Libertines reunions here. It's a real insiders' place, and *very* industry – you'll see plenty of important-looking dudes in dark glasses skulking about. This is where famous musos party. But be cool, otherwise you'll be out the door.

Jazz After Dark at **9 Greek St, Soho** lies in the middle of Soho. It's a tiny and somewhat dingy room, adorned with rock portraits painted by owner/artist Sam Shaker who, if you ask nicely, may lead you into to a tiny back room where behind a black curtain are more portraits of rock royalty. It's not all a rock fiesta, however; they also lay on a mean jazz night. There's food here as well – it's all very civilised. Come for the food, atmosphere and surprise bands and stay for the mayhem.

Sue Ostler

London's Karma Kabs

To begin or finish your night out in London in rock-star style, book a Karma Kab. The bumpers are decorated with flowers. The interiors sparkle and gleam with sequins and beads. Sadie Frost, Kate Moss and Lily Allen have been all been chauffeured in a Karma Kab. Fares can be expensive, so ring for a quote first. The website is *karmakabs.com*.

Lady Mini Cabs are another excellent option. They take children and pets unaccompanied and pride themselves on being a more caring, woman-driver service. They charge as much as a black cab. The only catch – they are not 24-hours. Book at *ladyminicabs.co.uk*.

London's best night out: The Hawley Arms, Camden

Holiday Goddess editors nearly fought a duel (handbags at dawn) over their choice for London's best night out. In the end, though, they realised it had to be about the city's two great charms – pubs and music. All of which makes The Hawley Arms a wonderful place to be.

So why does London's best night out begin in Camden? Because, as Jane Owen (author of *Camden Girls*) tells us, it's where the best live music can be found. And why go to The Hawley Arms? Because, as our other informants tell us, this is where you may find Amy Winehouse cheerfully serving behind the bar on some nights. Also, its huge Victorian mirrors; its turquoise loo tiles; its Gaggia coffee machine; its signed album covers on the walls; its nooks and crannies – and its fantastic music.

Author **Harriet Griffey** is a Camden local, and loves The Hawley Arms: 'Camden, home to some of the hippest shops, venues and eateries, is like Covent Garden's younger sister in Doc Marten shoes. At weekends it's so busy that the Northern Line tube station is exit-only, but with music venues **Koko** at one end of Camden High Street (at Mornington Crescent) and the world-famous **Roundhouse** at the other end (at Chalk Farm) you'll find Camden's most famous pub, slap in the middle. If you see paparazzi outside you'll know Jude Law may be inside.

Or Liam Gallagher, Peaches Geldof or other famous visitors.

In many ways it's an old-fashioned boozer with attitude, serving Greene King beer and a decent wine list, food that ranges from traditional meat pies to Caesar salads, vegetarian lasagne, steak sandwiches (delicious) and a traditional roast lunch on Sundays, with English apple pie or sticky toffee pudding to follow, and a really good cappuccino. Food is served from noon until 7pm, after which it gets too busy and the focus is on music, including new bands hosted by Apocalypstick every first Thursday of the month, with free entry but donations to a charity.

The Hawley Arms is great all year round. In the summer you can spill out onto the small back patio, the roof deck, or the pavement, and in the winter a fire and old Chesterfield sofas create a warm welcome. What I love about it is that it's not so agonisingly hip you feel out of place if you're over 30, but relaxed enough to drop in for a coffee and read the paper, or a full-on celebration drink.' *thehawleyarms.co.uk*

London's amazing pub jukeboxes

Some London pubs still have old-fashioned jukeboxes with vinyl singles. Others are computerised. All of them have the best playlists we have ever seen, anywhere in the world. Holiday Goddess reader and guest contributor Professor **Jane Pirkis** is a big Elvis Costello fan, and couldn't believe her luck when she walked into a Paddington pub and found no less than 20 of his greatest hits on one machine. (The whole pub was soon singing along to 'Oliver's Army'.) Whatever your taste in music, though, there is bound to be a pub with a playlist that suits you. Put in a pound and start a conversation. Or a singalong.

The Social: London's best pub jukebox?

The Social is the pub dreamed up by the chaps from Heavenly Records, the label that gave the world Saint Etienne, Manic Street Preachers, Doves and Magic Numbers. This is the place for seriously good jukebox options, especially late at night. There is a mailing list and membership base, so if you want to adopt a pub before you land in London (or be adopted by one) it's easy. The Social boasts that it has launched a million hangovers – but we just go there for the music!

The Social
5 Little Portland Street
NEAREST TUBE: **Oxford Circus**
WEBSITE: thesocial.com

Private members' clubs

If you're planning to visit London often (and drink long and late) then membership of a private club is the only way to go. An existing member will have to introduce you, though, and there may be a waiting list (The Groucho Club list is so long that you may have grown a lady-beard by the time they admit you). There are sneaky ways into London's exclusive club land, though. Try Associate Membership at Frontline, the journalists' club. You only need an interest in current affairs to apply, and for £50 a year you can attend screenings, discussions and nice-to-meet-you events. Visit *frontlineclub.com* for more information. It's a short walk from Paddington tube station.

Pub quiz nights

The British are obsessed with television quiz games, from *University Challenge* with Jeremy Paxman (we can never answer a single question) to *QI* with Stephen Fry. No wonder pub quiz nights are every Londoner's guilty pleasure. Some are hi-tech and involve iPods and TV footage. Some are low-tech and involve very poor photocopies of celebrity teeth ('Question Five, for three points: Whose tooth is this?').

At least two people counts as a team, and the occasional lone genius will even play by himself/herself. Pay a small fee to join in, and think of a suitably silly name for your team.

At one celebrity pub quiz, David Tennant (*Doctor Who*) was auctioned to the highest bidder. Seems to us like a pretty good reason to find out more. For the best quizzes visit *timeout.com/London*.

Perfect London pubs

The best London pubs are a few tube stops from the centre of the city, but worth the pilgrimage:

The Dove at **19 Upper Mall, Hammersmith** is a lovely, peaceful 17th century pub right on the River Thames so you can sit outside in warm weather. You can walk from Hammersmith tube station. Graham Greene drank here.

The Hawley Arms at **2 Castlehaven Road, Camden** (see page 144) is decorated with album covers and signed messages from Brit music legends, and Amy Winehouse sometimes serves the beer. **Nearest tube: Camden**

The Queens at **49 Regents Park Road** in Primrose Hill is light and airy, in the heart of chic Primrose Hill bookshops, vintage stores, parfumeries and restaurants. Fantastic food.

The Hootananny at **95 Effra Road** in Brixton is famous for its reggae and Mexican kitchen. It's loud, hot and happening and it stages live band karaoke. It's a nationwide award-winner.

The Falcon at **33 Bedford Road, Clapham** is another award-winner. It has a huge beer garden for warm weather, and has dogs, board games and home-made Sunday roasts. **Nearest tube: Clapham North**

The Gilbert Scott Bar

The St Pancras Renaissance Hotel is a short walk from Kings Cross Station. It looks like it should be in the next Harry Potter film. Step inside and turn sharp left – towards The Gilbert Scott Restaurant. Next door to this, you'll find the bar, and dozens of women in an advanced state of happiness. Beautiful painted ceilings, huge chandeliers, carved owls above the windows – we could go on. But how about the wine list? Try cocktails called Herbalist and English Garden, or from Somerset, real English Apple Brandy. Better still, the Sussex version of champagne is sold by the (exquisite) glass. We think it's equal to Bollinger, Moët and Pol Roger.

The bar is named for George Gilbert Scott who designed the hotel, which opened in 1863. It was bombed three times in one month during the Second World War, but survived with all its original Victorian grandeur intact.

Holiday Goddess editors Faith Bleasdale, Julian Venables and Jessica Adams love it. So does **Gillian Anderson-Price**, who runs the celebrity cult interiors boutique, Judith Michael & Daughter, in Primrose Hill: 'The Gilbert Scott bar at the St Pancras Hotel is a gem. The service is faultless and effortless.

The wine list is compact perfection, and includes the wonderful British 'champagne' Nyetimber. For me, though, it's the architecture and sympathetic contemporary interior design that enthralls. Master designer David Collins has surpassed himself with this intimate, cosy, imposing bar. The original gothic gilt illumination is complemented by sleek modern styling, attention to detail – and a hint of railway utility.'

Our seven wonders of London

What are the seven wonders of London? Could one possibly be a pickled bishop's rectum? Holiday Goddess editors and their friends came up with all kinds of weird and wonderful ideas when asked to ponder life in London. For some of us, though, London's wonders are exactly the same – the fashion collection inside the Victoria and Albert Museum, and the women's pond on Hampstead Heath were all high on the list. And oh yes. The bookshop with a bar …

The bookshop with a bar

Waterstone's Piccadilly is the only bookshop in London with a well-stocked bar – and sweeping views across the city. I have launched two books here, and I often tell friends to meet me in the bar because, if either of us is late, there is plenty to read on every floor. Waterstone's used to be Simpson's, the grand old department store where my grandmother bought her clothes. The original Art Deco staircases are still there. It's always amusing to see young Harry Potter fans being told by their parents not to slide down them. Waterstone's Piccadilly is the place to meet your favourite (famous) author and have a first-edition signed and dedicated to you.

Many visitors to London never realise there is a bar on the top floor, but it's a great place for a champagne at sunset.

Jessica Adams

Waterstones
203–206 Piccadilly

NEAREST TUBE: Piccadilly Circus

WEBSITE: waterstones.com

The Hampstead Heath bathing ponds

When I lived with my boyfriend in his Tufnell Park council flat in London in the 1980s, we never felt poor, because Hampstead Heath was just a short walk up Highgate Road.

There, in the winter, I'd go for a run up Parliament Hill and then down the paths, passing others, bundled up against the gloom and the damp, while their dogs happily chased the scent of a squirrel.

From there, I would find my way to the Hampstead Heath bathing ponds, where a brave (or certifiable) person or two would be splashing around in the 5 degree water. They were in on the delicious secret that these ponds are the only open-water swimming areas, complete with lifeguards, open to the public every day of the year.

There are more than 25 ponds on Hampstead Heath. The Mixed Pond (opened in the 1860s), is open to men and women. But the best places are the Highgate Ponds, originally dug as reservoirs.

You'll also find a model boating pond, a wildlife reserve pond and even a fishing lake there, separating the Kenwood Ladies' Pond from the Highgate Men's Pond.

Because the water is so cold and the thought of pond slime is so off-putting, these treasures are rarely crowded even on the hottest days. A day's swim costs only £2 for entrance and £1 for concessions.

Goddesses will revel in the privacy of a female-only pond, hidden deep in the middle of thick vegetation. It's one of the loveliest ways to spend a sultry summer's evening.

Karen Moline

Hampstead Heath, Hampstead
NEAREST TUBE: Hampstead
WEBSITE: cityoflondon.gov.uk/hampstead

The English language

There were several nominations for the seven wonders of London that all dovetailed towards one conclusion: The English Language. This is logical, given that Londoners helped to invent it. If you are a first-time visitor to the city, though, nothing can prepare you for the wholesale worship of words.

Find all versions of the English language at Shakespeare's Globe Theatre, in the hilarious columns by Charlie Brooker in *The Guardian*, or in the signed first editions in Hatchard's on Piccadilly. The best English language repository of all, though, is BBC Radio. Download free from *bbc.co.uk*.

London's Egyptian mummies

To really enjoy London's biggest and best collection of Egyptian mummies, try to visit the British Museum *without* the mummies. And the nannies. For an uninterrupted view, always avoid weekends and school holidays, and go at opening time. The Egyptian floor is the museum's most famous (partly because of its perfectly wrapped cat) but don't skip the ground floor either.

That's where you'll find a room dedicated to the Enlightenment. Not many people know there are mummies here too. And the crystal ball once owned by Queen Elizabeth I's soothsayer, Dr John Dee.

British Museum
Great Russell Street,
Bloomsbury

NEAREST TUBE: Russell Square
WEBSITE: britishmuseum.org

West End Wednesday matinees

On my first trip to London, as a student, I didn't realise that West End theatre tickets required months of planning. Thus I was heartbroken when I realised I would never get to see my favourite playwright, Alan Bennett, starring in his own play, *Talking Heads*, with Patricia Routledge.

Then someone told me about Wednesday matinees. These post-lunch performances are a warm-up for the cast, but a great way for you to score an otherwise unavailable ticket.

So I eventually saw *Talking Heads*. I laughed and cried, and I never forgot it. I now book months ahead, of course, but I've acquired the matinee habit.

Don't leave London without slinking into a theatre for the afternoon.

Imagine seeing Danny Boyle directing Benedict Cumberbatch and Jonny Lee Miller in Mary Shelley's *Frankenstein*. Well, you don't have to imagine it. And tickets start from just £12.

Jessica Adams

Victorian Gothic London

For me, London's sixth wonder has to be its Victorian Gothic buildings.

The Victorians were fascinating people. They ruled the waves, they had strange notions about the afterlife, they were fascinated with horrible crimes and scandals – in fact they were rather like us, except they did it with more style and less plumbing. The Victorians have also left a trail of macabre relics and pure eccentricity behind them, which is fascinating to follow.

For a glimpse of the vast, crumbling, ivy-clad grandeur of the Victorian afterlife, take a tour around Highgate Cemetery on Swain's Lane where a guide will spin tales of tragedy, murder and midnight exhumations amidst the gravestones and mausoleums.

To see the sharp end of medical science visit the Old Operating Theatre Museum on St Thomas Street. Or walk among the specimen jars at the Hunterian Museum on Lincoln's Inn Fields where grisly artefacts include a pickled bishop's rectum. Yes, really.

After his death, 19th century collector John Soane's home became a museum where you can wander through rooms crammed with sarcophagi and sculptures, and get up-close to some amazing Hogarth paintings.

Or to step directly into the past, go to Dennis Severs' House. It's an eerily effective three-dimensional work of art, recreating the sights and sounds of the centuries past, as though the family living there has just left the room.

Still not strange or macabre enough for you? London Walks arrange ghost tours around Westminster and Jack the Ripper walks in Whitechapel where you can retrace the steps of London's most notorious murderer.

Andreina Cordani

GOTHIC ADDRESS BOOK

Highgate Cemetery, Swain's Lane
Nearest Tube: **Archway**

The Old Operating Theatre Museum, St Thomas Steet
Nearest Tube: **London Bridge**

The Hunterian Museum, Lincoln's Inn Fields
Nearest Tube: **Holborn**

John Soane's Museum
Nearest Tube: **Holborn**

Dennis Severs' House, 18 Folgate Street
Nearest Tube: **Liverpool Street**

The Victoria and Albert Museum

The Victoria and Albert Museum, known to Londoners as the V&A, is every woman's favourite museum. Some of us love the Buddhas, enormous and serene. They are a comfort in London, when life can be maddening. The fashionistas among us head for the dimly-lit Dior, Chanel and Yves St Laurent, in glass cases, downstairs.

Faith Bleasdale is the author of several bestselling novels, including *Rubber Gloves or Jimmy Choos?* As you might guess, she has a thing about shoes. And she loves the V&A:

'I love the fashion at the V&A. They regularly hold special exhibitions (the Versace exhibition was amazing – and they also had Kylie's costumes on display). It is a place that makes you feel beautiful – because, it is astoundingly beautiful.

The V&A cafe is in the Morris, Gamble and Poynter Rooms, and serves hot and cold dishes, along with great wine. But if you want to take a packed lunch that's absolutely fine – if it's a sunny day then you might want to venture outside into the impressive courtyard. The John Madejski Garden is incredibly elegant and the perfect place to rest after a busy day where fashion and culture live in perfect harmony.'

V&A Museum
Cromwell Road

NEAREST TUBE:
South Kensington

WEBSITE: vam.ac.uk

The big, big, Big Ben climb

If you have a British passport, and have a London trip planned, then you're one of the lucky ones who can climb all the way up and inside Big Ben – if you're prepared to wait for your application for a tour to be approved. (Unfortunately access to overseas visitors is not available.) To get your (flat) shoes on the very first step inside, though, you'll first need to contact your local Member of Parliament, some months ahead, and obtain permission. Only 16 visitors are allowed up at a time and there is a long waiting list in peak seasons, so plan well ahead if you want to see the famous clock faces from the inside.

The clock is famously reliable, though the weather may not be: if it rains (it did when Holiday Goddess editors visited) the steps behind the large clock face can be quite wet – wear sensible shoes, as your grandmother would have said: this is not Manolo-friendly.

Climbing up the winding stone staircases is hard work. You're allowed to rest part of the way up, to explore a small museum, but otherwise you will have to be fit to take on Big Ben. Anyone with the slightest degree of vertigo may have to think twice about going. The view is spectacular but if you are terrified of heights, we think Big Ben is probably one of the most intimidating places to stand in the world! Once inside, though, you'll find out all kinds of odd facts about the world's most famous clock. Believe it or not, the time of the clock is adjusted with a small stack of old penny coins. They sit on top of the pendulum, and adding or removing just one penny is said to change the clock's speed by a fraction of a second.

During wartime, Big Ben's bells have been silenced, and the clock faces darkened (during the Blitz, there was a fear that the illuminated faces would be used as a guide by German pilots).

Londoners rely on Big Ben to chime in the New Year, although in the 1960s snow and ice delayed the chimes by ten minutes. Extremely hot weather a few years ago also stopped the clock.

The bell is nicknamed Big Ben in honour of a heavyweight boxer of the day, Benjamin Caunt. At least, that's one theory. It was transported to the tower on a trolley drawn by a vast team of horses, whereupon it cracked and had to be replaced. Peering inside the tower, it's hard to believe that men actually pulled this 13-tonne monstrosity up nearly 200 feet. Some other trivia – if you happen to live in Westminster, then on New Year's Eve you will hear Big Ben strike thirteen if you have the radio on as your ears detect the chimes from the real Ben, and the radio Ben. It's something to do with the speed of sound, apparently.

So how does it feel to be up there? It's a little bit like being in your own spy movie. It's impossible not to think of Richard Hannay hanging from the clock face in *The Thirty-Nine Steps*. (Hannay was trying to stop a bomb by delaying the minute hand.) This great British icon has also been in a James Bond film (*Thunderball*) and of course, *Doctor Who* and *The Avengers* – and *Captain Scarlet*. It's a heart-thudding experience, partly because climbing the 334 limestone stairs is like the biggest workout you will ever experience. Realising that you could trip and fall through the clock face at any point also made Holiday Goddesses' hearts race! The guide kindly checks on everyone's progress all the way up though; if you want to return to terra firma, just say the word and you will be helped by an escort.

There are three tours a day. Small children are not permitted. Don't be late either – you'll need to be smartly on time in the foyer of Portcullis House, nearby, to meet your guide. For more details and a free Big Ben download striking the hour, see *visitbigben.com*. Try a Big Ben hourly alert on Twitter too: *@big_ben_clock*.

Spas, sanctuaries, sacred spaces

The Romans exported the spa habit to London when they invaded England, and it was revived in the Regency period. Thus, some spas in the city are living museum pieces – two of London's best spas are Grade II listed. If you don't want to succumb to the delights of a fluffy white robe, though, the capital also offers other kinds of sanctuaries. We even know where the druids go, on the solstice.

The Sanctuary

Holiday Goddess editors know some women who have been going to The Sanctuary for decades, since it first opened. **Sue Ostler** is a confirmed fan:

'The Sanctuary in Covent Garden is so exquisite that if you don't look your best, you'll simply feel shabby. I don lashings of waterproof mascara and my best swimming costume so I can languish regally in the manner of Aphrodite, lying alongside European nobility. It's a mere pirouette from the Royal Opera House, and when it opened, offered the most precious commodities to be found in Covent Garden – space and tranquillity for local dancers. As a spa, it still lies firmly in the OMG stratosphere. Is it the dramatic backdrop, where streams of water gush and gurgle from jacuzzis and plunge pools over five sprawling levels?

Or the stunning Koi Carp Lounge where the fish glide idly by? Or the famous trapeze-like swing set high upon the blue mosaic pool, where you can glide around like a Bond girl?

Afterwards you can curl up in your robe for a snooze. All of which gives me that 'I must be dreaming' feeling whenever I visit. Expect a sublime massage too, followed by dainty finger sandwiches and fragrant chai tea.

After six hours you will emerge revitalised, revamped and ready to face the world again – reinvented as a goddess.' Look on the website for regular deals and discounts.

The Sanctuary
12 Floral Street, Covent Garden
NEAREST TUBE: Covent Garden
WEBSITE: thesanctuary.co.uk

The College of Psychic Studies

Sherlock Holmes creator Arthur Conan Doyle was a spiritualist. He believed in the afterlife, and the fact that the spirit world can communicate with us. Thus, his portrait hangs on the wall as you enter The College of Psychic Studies – a short walk from The Victoria and Albert Museum. This is the real Hogwarts. You may drop into classes for crystal therapy, aura reading, tarot for beginners and more. There is a healing sanctuary in the basement, and a small bookshop and library on the ground floor. Upstairs, the best mediums and psychics in England offer private readings or Monday-night demonstrations. Some even involve transfigurations, when spirit people show themselves. Curious? The College of Psychic Studies has been intriguing (and occasionally spooking) Londoners for decades. Visitors welcome. For a program, and more details, visit *collegeofpsychicstudies.com*.

TOP TEN

London's Best Spas

1. The Sanctuary
2. Ironmonger Row Turkish Baths
3. Porchester Spa
4. Spa London
5. Berkeley Spa
6. Bliss
7. Spa at Brown's
8. Spa InterContinental
9. Spa at Mandarin Oriental
10. Groom

The Yogini's guide to London

Yoga is *huge* in London. And we can't think of a better way to unwind than a drop-in class. Holiday Goddess editor **Kris McIntyre** is well-known for her syndicated program, *Yoga TV*. When we asked her about drop-in yoga classes in London, she suggested visiting *localyogaclasses.co.uk* before you go. Kris asked the beautiful and talented opera singer and Kundalini yoga teacher, **Kathryn McCusker** (*kmyoga. com*), for her inside tips on the best drop-in classes in London. Every yoga centre on this list lies in a hip shopping area too. So once you've shopped and dropped, you can always unroll a mat and breathe again.

Triyoga (*triyoga.co.uk*) has studios in Primose Hill, Soho and Covent Garden, with a range of different yoga styles including Ashtanga, Vinyasa, Kundalini and Iyengar, as well as Pilates, with an array of teachers including renowned Ashtanga teacher Ryan Spielman, at the Primrose Hill studio.

Alchemy (*alchemythecentre.co.uk*), located in a heritage-listed building above the Camden markets, puts the focus on Kundalini yoga and meditation.

For something different, Simon Andriesz's Meditation and Gong class is popular, and there's a host of other activities including dance and music evenings, book launches and guest speakers.

The Life Centre (*thelifecentre.com*) is a complementary health centre in a converted church in Notting Hill (they also have another studio in Islington). There's a packed timetable of different yoga styles and Pilates classes with respected teachers and more than 30 kinds of natural therapies on offer.

Kathryn's favourite 'sacred space' is **Primrose Hill Park**. 'It has a beautiful view over the city, a wonderful sense of history and especially during the summer months when there's people out and about drumming and doing all sorts of rituals, there's a real sense of community,' she says. The nearest tube stop to Primrose Hill is Chalk Farm.

Note: Primrose Hill is where modern druids gather on sacred occasions, like the solstice, following a tradition that has taken place in London for centuries. Tiptoe respectfully away if you see them.

St James's Church, Piccadilly

This lovely little church is between Fortnum & Mason and Piccadilly Circus tube station. It's also where William Blake was baptised and, funnily enough, where Nick Hornby once read from his novel about single mums, *About a Boy*. St James's was built by Sir Christopher Wren and survived the Blitz, despite being heavily bombed. It survives today, welcoming all forms of spirituality, from those who believe in crop circles, to those who believe in God. It also welcomes outright agnostics (also known as The Unsure). The author and poet Robert Graves (*I, Claudius*) married here. St James's is truly unusual, in that it welcomes all souls, of all beliefs. St James's Church also backed the ordination of women in the Anglican church, years ago. William Blake has a memorial here.

It's a very special, quiet place, but some Holiday Goddess readers and friends tell us their lives have been changed here – just a little bit.

**St James's Church
197 Piccadilly
NEAREST TUBE: Piccadilly
WEBSITE: st-james-piccadilly.org**

We heart London art

London art today is primarily about Damien Hirst and Tracey Emin.
He pickled a shark, she put her bed in a gallery. But the antics of Hirst
and Emin make us wonder, what is art anyway? For Holiday Goddess
Karen Moline, it's about the living art of the Romans, which you can
still find in secret parts of London.

When in London

Anyone interested in seeing more of Roman London (Londinium)
should plan a day in the Museum of London, to see their collection of
Roman objects – particularly the glorious marble sculptures from the
Temple of Mithras.

Ancient Rome is all around you in London, though. And this is how
I discovered the Roman Bath of Strand Lane. One uncharacteristically
sultry Saturday, I went out for a long run in the city, heading down
along the Thames. Walking back, sweaty and nearly dizzy from the
heat, I decided to meander through the crooked streets up to the flat
when I suddenly saw a sign that said 'To the Baths'. The sight of it was
so bizarre that I felt for an instant that I had somehow become lost in
time. I caught my breath, followed the signs until I came to Strand
Lane and, there it was: a rectangular Roman bath made of well-worn
stone, illuminated and sitting silently a few feet below street level,
protected by window glass and a sturdy grille. I looked around, but
there was not another soul to be seen. And I saw no one else as I stood
there for a long time, sweat trickling down my neck, wondering who
had bathed there and when and why, and marvelling that such a thing
still existed.

Karen Moline

Hopeless romantics: The Pre-Raphaelites

London's Tate Britain Gallery is the best place in the world to see paintings by the hopelessly romantic Pre-Raphaelite Brotherhood. They were more like a rock band than a group of artists. When they started working together, William Holman Hunt was 21. Sexy Dante Gabriel Rossetti was 20. And John Everett Millais was just 19.

Charles Dickens hated the Pre-Raphaelite Brotherhood, but women love them. How do you spot a Pre-Raphaelite? If you own a postcard or birthday card with a lush redhead on the front, or a swooning beauty in a velvet gown, then chances are it's a print of a Hunt, Rossetti or Millais.

Their sensual paintings will instantly want to make you grow your hair down to your waist and book a spiral perm. Best of all, every painting has a story behind it. As you gaze at the painting, remember that John Millais originally put a water vole (what friends called a 'rat') in the scene. After they objected, he got rid of the animal but a sketch of it remains, on the edge of the canvas. It can be seen whenever the frame is removed for cleaning. His gorgeous red-haired model, Elizabeth Siddal, posed in a bath for this painting, then caught a cold. Her furious father threatened to sue Millais, unless he paid her doctor's bills. Millais famously drank from the river he painted, filling up a child's mug with water as he worked. The beautiful dress you see Elizabeth wearing in the finished work was actually a dirty second-hand frock that Millais paid £4 for (this would be around £250 today). If only the Pre-Raphaelite Brotherhood had known about Top Shop.

Jessica Adams

The Tate Modern

Tyne O'Connell's travel adventures on the Holiday Goddess website are among our most widely-read. She is the author of 13 books including the Royal Match series. Hailing from an artworld background, courtesy of two previous marriages, she is now travelling the world – 'drinking tea with the people that matter,' she tells us, on an 'amortality gap year.' She is also the only person we know who owns a Damien Hirst.

Damien Hirst

Damien Hirst is a classic English mummy's boy. He hangs on to ideas, people and dead stuff. To understand this is to understand *The Physical Impossibility Of Death In The Mind of Someone Living* – otherwise known as a shark floating in formaldehyde. I first met him at A Fête Worse Than Death in Hoxton. We shared a bottle of whiskey, did splatter paintings on a potter's wheel and chucked sponges at Gilbert & George – all for the price of a pound. My Hirst splatter painting still hangs in the loo. He said, 'I wanted to be stopped but no one will stop me.' It's a combination of this anarchic energy, soundbite brilliancy and grit that made Hirst the King of Brit Art and the world's richest living artist. In his own words: 'It's amazing what you can do with an E in O-level art, a vivid imagination and a chainsaw.'

The Tate Modern
5 Atterbury Street
NEAREST TUBE: Southwark
WEBSITE: tate.org.uk

Tracey Emin

Tracey Emin is the mistress of show and tell. I met her in the early '90s in a shop she ran with Sarah Lucas in Shoreditch where I wisely bought a T-shirt announcing 'I'm so fucky'. Drinking tea laced with gin, Emin emerged as every girl who has gone to bed with a guy while on the wrong side of tipsy, and shared the story with her girlfriends. Later she shared with the rest of the world, via a tent embroidered with the names of *Everyone I've Ever Slept With 1963-1995*.

They say never cross an author – they'll end up writing about you. Emin's proved the same is true for artists. It's a girl thing; drinking, talking, hoping to make sense (or not) of the mystery of life, boys, and fashion.

Her first solo show in 1993 at White Cube featured her old passport and bits of fabric from her sofa when she was three years old. She rocketed to fame with *The Bed*; essentially *Bridget Jones's Diary* – the art installation.

Now sponsored by Bombay Gin, a muse to Vivienne Westwood and a bag designer for Longchamp, Emin has emerged as the cultural taliswoman of reality culture.

Tyne O'Connell

Taking London home

How do you steal a Londoner's style? Begin with her secret weapon – body-shaping underwear. Perhaps inevitably in a city dedicated to Guinness and Cornish pasties, there is a huge (too huge) demand for magic knickers. And who can refuse a magic padded, uplifting bra? When you leave London, one local habit that's worth taking home is an addiction to miracle undies. And how do the Brits do it? They shop at Marks & Spencer, where first they buy the Cornish pasties, then they buy the pants.

Marks & Spencer underwear

Jenny Valentish is a journalist who has edited *triple j magazine* for the cult Australian radio station, as well as the raucous anthology *Your Mother Would Be Proud*. She was raised just outside London and rectified this, aged 18, by moving inside. She thinks it's about time Marks & Sparks knickers were immortalised in a book: 'Marks & Spencer's underwear is as firmly entrenched in the modern Englishwoman's psyche as black leather boots and Earl Grey tea. Hell, I've worn sturdy black lacy pairs all through my teenage cider-punk phase, my roaring (drunk) twenties (during which time

they adorned the radiator of many a share house), and now they're girding my loins in the land girt by sea, Australia. And it's not just me. "On a sunny June day Trinny Woodall answered the door of her Kensington flat wearing nothing but a white Marks & Spencer bra and matching knickers," began an *Observer* profile on the great British fashion orthros that is Trinny and Susannah, while national treasure Joanna Lumley has voiced an ad campaign for the company, and there's a Facebook page calling for the quintessentially English Nigella Lawson to follow suit.

The 127-year-old retailer, also beloved for its food range (Bridget Jones would drop in for white wine and extravagant girly snacks, hence her need for shapewear undies) has forged a reputation for good quality, feminine underwear that caters to a woman's every need – even offering a pretty post-breast surgery range of bras.

Mothers and daughters will happily shop at Marks together (I was alarmed on a recent visit home to notice that Mum and I had identical M&S satin smalls in the airing cupboard without having consulted each other), and with bargains like three pairs of knickers for a tenner, Marks & Sparks (as it's affectionately known) doesn't discriminate against any class of bottom. Now delivering internationally!'

Marks & Spencer
380 Oxford Street
NEAREST TUBE: **Bond Street**
WEBSITE: **marksandspencer.com**

Great heroines who ought to have been wearing Marks & Spencer knickers

Emma Woodhouse Jane Austen's meddling minx understood fully the need to be both flirtatious and tactical.

Mary Elizabeth Ponsonby Earl Grey tea is the perfect complement to Marks & Spencer knickers, and Mary was the woman behind the toff who gave his name to it.

Emma Bovary Like Bridget Jones, Flaubert's creation dreamed of escaping the dullness of provincial life and bought way too much on credit. She would have made excellent use of Marks & Sparks shapewear briefs.

Boadicea Some heat-generating thermals would have stood Boadicea and her feisty daughters in good stead on their murderous rampage towards Londinium.

Taking the London look home

Londoners love rock'n'roll make-up and retro beauty. This is a city where nobody is frightened of pillar-box red lipstick. Or theatrical Cleopatra eye make-up. There are two reasons for this. One is the light, which is soft, pale and watery, and lets women get away with anything. The other is the huge influence of The Body Shop's Anita Roddick, who was the first person to break away from the big US corporation style of cosmetics, to pioneer fun, creative products which she invented with Princess Diana's make-up artist, Barbara Daly. What's special about London? Indie cosmetics and beauty salons. You'll find them everywhere. And a more daring approach to beauty is a great habit to take home.

The very indie, very beautiful **Tamara Pitelen** has covered many stories for Holiday Goddess, from scaling Dubai's highest tower, to running from life-threatening hippos. When in London, she always visits **The Powder Room**.

'For a touch of '50s glamour and an adorable 'up do' for a special night, check out The Powder Room in the East End. It's a darling little beauty boutique on Columbia Road in Shoreditch, and I love it. Drop in for a quick beauty fix or more industrial-sized primping and preening. This is affordable, fun and chic. I especially liked the champagne cocktails in bone china tea cups.

If you need some eyebrow-tidying then go to **Browhaus** in Covent Garden because every girl knows the importance of a well-shaped eyebrow for transforming a face. Browhaus – inspired by the German art movement of all things – is a one-stop brow and lash grooming shop, the place for unruly brows to be tweezed, threaded or tinted back into shape ... even resurrected. For me, the discovery of threading has been a life changing revelation. No, I am not being dramatic. Give threading a try and if you don't get the sharpest brow arch you've ever had in your life, I shall eat my bikini wax.'

The Powder Room
136 Columbia Road

WEBSITE:
thepowderpuffgirls.com

Browhaus
19a Floral Street
Covent Garden

WEBSITE: browhaus.com

Vintage and markets

Vintage in London really does mean vintage – as in, 18th century, if you know the right place. For most of us, though, the fun lies in trawling for classics from the 1940s–1980s.

Vintage clothing is a big part of London fashion. Whether you're wearing an '80s romper with Converse and tangled hair to London Fields for a boozy picnic, or slipping into a '60s cocktail dress with red lips and an alligator clutch bag, heading to The Wolseley for tea, this city has garment to fuel your unique looks.

Vintage shopping is fast becoming essential shopping, with more choice by the second. My favourites are two London staples that have been around for over twenty years.

Blackout II is my top choice for reasonably-priced vintage. Conveniently located in Covent Garden, the shop boasts two floors displaying handpicked and flawless vintage dating from the '20s to the '80s. With all the accessories to match, diamante necklaces and plastic fruit earrings spill from the counter.

The fashion forward staff are both friendly and efficient. On my last visit they knew to give me enough space to feel comfortable trying to squeeze my ugly stepsister sized feet into ten pairs of Cinderella-sized shoes before finding a cute navy pair of sandals that fit. For £40.

You're sure to find the shoe to match your outfit, no matter your size, in the back room stocked with hundreds of pairs of heels, dubbed by the frequent shoppers as the 'Aladdin's Cave of Shoes'.

Blackout II is about finding a quality piece. That pristine ruby red silk dress may be £80, but it'll make you look a billion dollars.

It's the kind of vintage fairground that you could spend hours in, so it's a good thing they have a menswear section to busy your boyfriend.

My other favourite is **Virginia Antiques**, 98 Portland Road in Holland Park. This gem is the most lustworthy vintage shop I have ever known. Entering the store you are surrounded by sequins, chiffon and garments hanging at every angle, more fantastic than any display at the V&A Museum. Long darting feathers, hand-sewn embroidery, dazzling beaded dresses and the finest and most fragile lace pieces are all draped over and around antique lampshades the colour of cupcakes.

The prices may be high for some, as dresses run into the hundreds, but they are truly exquisite. Customers include original supermodels Helena Christensen and Naomi Campbell.

The owner is the wonderful Virginia Bates, former model and actress, now *Vogue* blogger and socialite. With her signature white bob and heavy eyeliner, she has so many fantastic stories to tell. She has hand picked every exquisite garment herself from film sets and far away vintage fairs.

The shop is more like a den, a cosy world of vintage wonderment, with a range of garments from 1900s to '40s. When I asked Virginia what it is she loves about these clothes, she spun off into an enthusiastic speech, but there was one word that trailed in my head: romance.

Lily Evans

Portobello Market

Never go to Portobello Market on the weekend unless you want someone to run over your foot with a wheelie suitcase, or inhale a lot of other people's cigarette smoke. The old advice remains: always go for breakfast, on a Friday. The best cafe in the area is Tom's, where they have builders-strength tea.

The best bit is under the railway bridge, down the very end. The last time we looked here, I found a rack of Pringle cashmere twin-sets in almost every colour, dating from the 1960s and 1970s. And lovely costume jewellery for under £10.

This is also where you will find old riding boots (much sexier than Hunter wellies) and even a stall selling beautiful 1940s vintage wallpaper. I bought two sheets, lined my suitcase with it, and felt instantly happy every time I packed. If you have spent your entire life hoping for a fabulous faux leopardskin maxi-coat with a big collar and a fur hem, this is probably where it will appear. And it will cost you. But you will keep it for ever.

The other great thing about Portobello Road Market is its proximity to chic shops and restaurants.

Our favourite lunch spot is E&O. Its fans include *Hotel Babylon* series creator Imogen Edwards-Jones (see page 172 for her favourite Notting Hill places). The last time a Holiday Goddess visited E&O Kate Moss was dining with Jamie Hince, designer Henry Holland was outside having a fag and Ruby Wax was table-hopping. There's a reason the windows at E&O are so dark.

Portobello Market is all about vintage, but it's also about the lovely sidestreets heaving with artful bookshops, chic boutiques and gift stores. Head straight for Westbourne Grove and Blenheim Crescent, just off the market stalls, and start drooling.

The best Portobello lunch: The Ledbury A finalist in the UK Sommelier of the Year competition and Holiday Goddess reader, Wiremu Andrews loves **The Ledbury**, at **127 Ledbury Road**. It's also an excellent place to dine after the market. Don't be surprised if you duck homesick Australians as you take your seat.

Head Chef Brett Graham began his career at Banc in Sydney. We like the two Michelin stars, but also the three course £25 lunch.

Notting Hill

Notting Hill *is* London to millions of people, as the Julia Roberts DVD remains on permanent hire from Milan to Minsk, thanks to Richard Curtis' impossibly romantic screenplay and Hugh Grant's sexy perfomance. It's a classic film we reckon we'll still be watching fifty years from now. But is the real Notting Hill still worth the pilgrimage?

Novelist and editor of *The Lady*, **Rachel Johnson**, knows Notting Hill so well that she wrote a book about it called *Notting Hell*. She was the first writer to spot the phenomenon NHM (Notting Hill Mummies). To qualify as an NHM, Rachel notes you must:

1. Be invited to join a private, celebrity-studded, yoga group/book club/Pilates class
2. Have at least one gifted child
3. Have at least one special needs child
4. Weigh less and, even spookier, look younger than you did at puberty
5. Employ a family nutritionist, a personal PA, plastic surgeon, a weekend nanny as well as a live-out nanny, a homework nanny, a housekeeper and team of alternative therapists ...

If you're prepared to duck the NHM brigade, though (scarier than Egyptian mummies), you can have a wonderful Friday morning, as you wander from Notting Hill Gate tube station along Portobello Road, exploring the side streets.

Imogen Edwards-Jones, the bestselling creator of the outrageous Babylon series, which began with the hit book and TV drama, *Hotel Babylon*, has lived in the area for nearly 20 years.

Imogen loves Notting Hill, but also says that two decades of living on the edge of the famous markets had a price: 'Every morning in Notting Hill, no matter how bad my hangover was, I would always be woken up at 4.30am by people saying "Oi, Trevor!"'

We asked Imogen for some of her recommendations for your visit:

The Pub: 'The Cow is one of the the best pubs in London where you can buy oysters and Guinness. On summer nights it's chock-a-block with the young groovies. Upstairs there's usually a lot of Ralph Fiennes action.' **The Cow, 89 Westbourne Park Road**

The Cafe: 'Tom's is an institution and it's been here for years.' **Tom's, 226 Westbourne Grove**

The Lingerie: 'In Portobello Green, next to the market under the bridge (down the end of Portobello Road) there is a wonderful underwear shop in the arcade called What Katie Did Next – with brilliant '50s bras. These are proper Mad Men outfits. And they do really brilliant bikinis.' **What Katie Did Next, 26 Portobello Green**

The Bookshop: 'Lutyens and Rubinstein is a gorgeous little bookshop. The kids' section is great – it's the kind of place where you can always find a copy of *Milly-Molly-Mandy*.' **Lutyens and Rubinstein, 21 Kensington Park Road**

The Spa: 'The Cowshed is a little bit further away, but it's great for a mani-pedi-fanny!' **The Cowshed, 119 Portland Road**

The Cinema: 'The Electric Cinema is brilliant. You can have a vodka and tonic while watching a film, and order chips. The seats are like big airline double-beds – absolutely huge!' **Electric Cinema, 191 Portobello Road**

Our favourite daycation

London is blessed by trains to *everywhere*. So think beyond the tube and take yourself away to the real England. We call it time-travelling. It's your chance to revisit the 1960s (Brighton) or the 1700s (Bath). Book your ticket online, months ahead, and you'll have one of the most unforgettable days of your life, for the price of a Marks & Spencer bra.

Our only real problem was deciding on the best daycation destination, from what is an embarrassment of riches.

Several Holiday Goddesses have lived in Brighton over the years and some still do. All of them immediately declared it the best London daycation of all because of the magic one-hour train ride through the English countryside from Victoria Station. (And also the on-board trolley, with its miniature bottles of wine, Cadbury's chocolate and piping hot tea.) Thus, the quest for London's best daycation seemed to be finished. Settled.

But then Holiday Goddess editors and their friends had another handbags-at-dawn duel over Bath.

'If you don't put Bath into your book I may have to take serious action,' one said, hyperventilating.

So that settled it. Almost. Our favourite London daycation is a tie. But we know one thing. You're crazy if you visit London and don't take a day out to catch the train to beautiful Bath or brilliant Brighton.

Skip the London Eye, Buckingham Palace and the Tower of London and just *go!*

Brighton

Trains to Brighton take just under an hour from Victoria Station. Catch the tube to Victoria and walk upstairs to the big overground station. Book your ticket online at *thetrainline.com* months in advance and you may travel from under £15 return.

If you want to see the Royal Pavilion, the most eccentric and glittering palace in England, then come on a weekday to avoid the crowds. Be there at opening time and you may be lucky enough to have entire rooms to yourself, just as Prince George once did.

If you want to visit one of the cheapest and best markets in England, catch a train at what the British call Stupid O'Clock (6am–7am) on Sunday morning. Long-time vintage dealers say you won't regret it. If you're serious, take a wheelie suitcase with you. One retro store owner we know pinched a supermarket trolley from the carpark. And when she'd filled that, she made her husband find another one!

One way to 'do' Brighton, as the locals say, is to find a gig, play or comedy act and enjoy Saturday night here, with an overnight stay at a beachfront bed-and-breakfast (or the luxurious Hotel du Vin) then spend all day Sunday wandering around the market, the beach, the shops, the museum and the Royal Pavilion.

Brighton
Devonshire
Tea
£8.50
Served Here

Brighton Marina Markets

At around 6am on Sunday, often in the dark, the big removal vans arrive at Brighton Marina Market with the contents of house clearances from all over Sussex. Boxes of ephemera are tipped onto trestle tables without prices, which often means incredible finds for £2.

Old-fashioned vans with coffee, bacon-and-egg rolls and tea open their doors early for stallholders, so you can eat breakfast here too. Don't expect glamour or charm. This is a very windy market, on top of a multi-storey carpark at Brighton Marina, which is a short taxi or bus ride from Brighton Station. There are, however, amazing views over the English Channel. This is a seaside market.

It's all over by 12 noon and the best stuff goes at dawn. There is no rhyme or reason to any of it and the stalls we tell you about now may have vanished by the time this book comes out.

Still, we can't think of any other market where you can devote an hour of your time, and walk away with a crocodile handbag, a French bedspread, a Victorian diary and a 1960s tea-tray for under £25.

We've heard Portobello dealers come here first, then drive their booty down to London, where the prices go up. And up.

Along with the house clearance stalls, there are Brightonians clearing out their wardrobes for a seasonal change (always great) and old faithfuls, like the retro furniture stalls at the far end. It may be a 50p paperback for the train journey home, or an old hacking jacket, but you'll leave happy.

Catch the number 7 bus to the Marina from Brighton Station – it's the last stop. Or take a taxi, also from the station – around £10.

The Royal Pavilion

Cate Blanchett (who lived in Brighton) once described the Royal Pavilion as one of her favourite places. It's King George IV's fantasy palace. It's where he bedded his mistress, and gorged on swans for dinner (a royal privilege). The beautiful four-poster beds in the Pavilion, groaning with mattresses, must have seen a great deal of regal action. You can see the swans too (well, stuffed versions of them) in a faithful recreation of the original kitchen, with gleaming copper pans and vast fireplace. It's been restored to look just as King George's staff would have known it in his lifetime.

I always take visitors to England to Brighton Pavilion, and they always make the same noise when they walk into the banqueting hall. It's somewhere between a gasp and a squeak. It's huge, it's decadent, it's beautiful – and it's set up for a vast dinner, just as George would have requested. If the one-tonne chandelier above dropped it would be instant death, but it's hard not to stay in here for a good 15 minutes, just absorbing the beauty of the place.

You can practically imagine the roast pig with an apple in its mouth, or the terrible flatulence that must have come wafting from George's side of the table. He was notoriously greedy and also quite fat, with a gout problem. His chef used to make confectionery for his banquets that was the height of a small child – around four feet.

The blazing yellow on many of the walls looks so odd today, but it makes you want to go home and redecorate. Queen Victoria loathed this place: she thought it was extravagant. And also too Chinese, apparently. Today, of course, it just looks like some fabulously bohemian piece of Brit extravagance.

The current Queen has lent some of the furniture, so she must approve!

Jessica Adams

The Royal Pavilion
4/5 Pavilion Buildings,
Brighton

WEBSITE: brighton-hove-rpml.
org.uk

London by the Sea

Brighton is the original London-by-the-Sea. And for a lot of people, it's all about the iconic beach, which looks just as it did in the 1960s. *Brighton Rock*, by Graham Greene, is partly set on Brighton Beach. If you walk in a straight line down Queens Road, from Brighton Station, and follow the sea, you'll soon see Brighton Pier ahead of you, which is where the action is. It's the place to see a fortune-teller (if he's inside his gypsy caravan) and also the place to buy cockles, mussels and whelks.

If the Royal Pavilion sends you time-travelling back to Regency England, Brighton Beach and Pier will send you straight back to the days of The Who, mini-skirts, Minis and Lambrettas. This is where Mods and Rockers fought on the pebbles, throwing striped deckchairs over the railings. Mod still rules in Brighton (don't mention the Rockers) and you'll often see beautifully dressed Mods looking for the specialist shops here that cater to them.

And also, let's face it, looking for the alleyway where Phil Daniels had sex with Lesley Ash in *Quadrophenia*, the classic Who-inspired Mod film.

The alleyway is nicknamed Quadrophenia Alleyway and lies on East Street. Just look for shamelessly shagging Mod visitors hoping to recreate the magic.

The beach is where Fatboy Slim holds his legendary free concerts. If you walk right from the pier, along the beach, you'll find Brighton's famous clubs. They helped make Fatboy Slim famous, but they only come alive at night. Gaze in amazement at the other pier – the wrecked one – which stands like a black skeleton, further along.

Why is Brighton known as London-By-The-Sea? Because so many Londoners moved here years ago, and many still commute. Sir Paul McCartney buys his bagels here, when he's in town (he is an occasional local, at the Hove end of Brighton, where the squillionaires reside). London-by-the-Sea also has its reputation because so many fabulous shops are a short walk from the beach. Look for Cath Kidston, MAC, Kiehl's, L. K. Bennett, Top Shop, Habitat, Heals and more. The spirit of Portobello Road is here too, but without the hefty price tag. Find our no-map guide at *holidaygoddess.com*.

BRIGHTON PIER

Where to eat in Brighton

Terre à Terre, 71 East Street

This is Michelin-star vegetarian – and temporarily converts people
who think vegetarian food is boring. Terre à Terre is booked solid
on weekends, so ring weeks ahead to avoid being disappointed (or
having to head for fish and chips on the beach). Like many Brighton
restaurants it started out small, then got big. It now has its own
cookbooks. Website: *terreaterre.co.uk.*

Due South, 139 Kings Road Arches, Brighton Beach

The address for Due South is just silly, so follow our instructions –
you're never going to find a sign saying Kings Road Arches on the
beach, but walk between Brighton Pier (still intact) and the wrecked
pier, towards your right. Somewhere in between you will find lots of
Europeans licking the windows of a small place called Due South which
has won every award going (but still serves a perfectly unpretentious
Sunday roast). You can sit here with a glass of vino too and watch the
starlings do their en masse performance above the wrecked pier.

Bill's, 100 North Road

Communal tables, olive oil that is eye-wateringly expensive (and
lovely), organic vegetables and British fruit jams – it has to be Bill's,
the big London chain, transferred to Brighton. The boom in allotments
(your own garden, in a public space, on a waiting list) and the Jamie
Oliver/Nigel Slater/Hugh Fearneley-Wittingstall real food revolution
has turned Bill's into a hit. And an export on the Brilon scene
(Brighton-London). Website: *bills-website.co.uk.*

Moshi Moshi, Opticon, Bartholomew Square

Brighton's best sushi-go-round, no contest. Moshi is vast, yet also strangely quite hard to find, but worth the search for the swirling miso soup and ethically-farmed fish. Discount nights and printable discount vouchers are yours at *moshibrighton.co.uk*. Holiday Goddess editors and readers never book, because there are so many seats – try your luck. Website: *moshimoshi.co.uk*.

Cote, 115 Church Street

Cote is a huge, airy and beautiful French brasserie where you can sit with a large glass of red wine, a small bowl of olives and some Burgundian sausage – and be left in peace. There are also plenty of main dishes under £10, here, too. Cote is housed inside Brighton's old music library, and it's a ten-minute walk from Brighton Station.

Jane Austen's Bath

It's Jane Austen's Bath – we just think we visit it. This is the pristine landscape we dream about when we read *Persuasion* or *Northanger Abbey*, both of which are based partly on Austen's experiences in the town. Her parents married here, in pretty St Swithins church – and Jane Austen received her only proposal of marriage in Bath (she turned her unsuitable suitor down, which will not surprise any of her squillions of fans). Bath was big for Jane. And thanks to the BBC, she is very, *very* big in Bath.

As soon as the train pulls in from its short trip from Paddington Station, you will hear the BBC theme music for *Pride and Prejudice* trilling in your head. It's hard not to – Bath is beautifully preserved Georgian England, flanked by woods, blessed by cherry blossoms in spring and summer, and every building is a lovely biscuit colour throughout. Or, as one Holiday Goddess editor pointed out, 'a kind of designer eye shadow colour. Soft beige.'

You won't find horrible neon signs and ugly old 1970s red brick here. Even the graffiti is charming, tucked away on walls covered with ivy and hand-coloured in blue and turquoise. What's more, the Jane Austen Centre on Gay Street even has loos bearing Mr Darcy and Miss Bennett signs on the doors.

Apparently Jane Austen fainted when her parents told her the family would be moving back to Bath. The assumption is that she was horrified at the idea. Her fans, however, love the place.

Along with Bath's fabulous monuments to Georgian England (the men's calves! The Sally Lunn buns! The silly dancing! The beautiful windows!) there is also Roman England to explore in the streets around Jane Austen's old rented homes.

Rather like the TARDIS, the Roman Baths appear to be rather small and oblong on the outside, but inside you will find beautiful hot springs, and intact Roman columns and statues. It is enormous, steamy, and somehow weirdly inviting – despite the huge amount of coins thrown in by visitors, just as their ancestors did, 2000 years before.

The Roman Baths is part of the reason Bath is a UNESCO-protected world heritage site. You may also drink the water here, which the Romans believed had healing properties. After your ticketed tour, plastic cups are available for 50 pence a time. Try to move past the faint taste of salt and old boiled eggs, and you too may find a miracle, courtesy of the goddess Minerva.

Bath is too beautiful for words. And too much fun. The Fashion Museum not far from the Roman Baths has Mary Quant, Ossie Clark, Katharine Hamnett and other British legends on display – and clothes to dress up in.

There are also new baths – which Jane Austen would probably have loved to tackle, in her later novels. They are chic, luxurious and slightly pricey and le toute Bath goes there, shedding their designer lingerie as they go. There is an open-air rooftop pool and even a swirling goddess Minerva bath, which we like to think Jane would have enjoyed hugely. Minerva, after all, was the Roman goddess of wit and wisdom.

London trains to Bath run from Paddington and take almost 90 minutes. Book at Great Western on *greatwestern.com*.

Playlists and downloads

Holiday Goddess editor and writer **Julian Venables** used to share houses with some of Britain's best-known bands, and his career adventures include BBC Radio. We asked him to come up with some quinessentially London tracks to listen on the plane before you land and play it *after* you land. There is no bigger thrill than walking around Waterloo at sunset, listening to The Kinks' classic 'Waterloo Sunset'.

London music, London places

Suggs, *Camden Town*: Suggs is the lead singer of Madness, and one of their album covers features the band outside Chalk Farm tube station, on the edge of Camden.

Tracey Thorn, *By Piccadilly Station I Sat Down and Wept*: Everybody's favourite indie singer, Tracey Thorn, immortalises Piccadilly Station.

Pet Shop Boys, *West End Girls*: East End boys and West End girls. What's not to love? It's the British version of 'Downtown' by Petula Clark or 'Uptown Girl' by Billy Joel.

The Beatles, *The Fool on the Hill*: The Beatles lived and worked within walking distance of Primrose Hill, upon which this song is allegedly based.

Nick Drake, *Mayfair*: Nick Drake is an obsession with British music fans. He died young, but is one of the most downloaded cult singer-songwriters of the century.

Elvis Costello & the Attractions, *London's Brilliant Parade*: Costello left London to move to Ireland, but this is a typically wry, and strangely affectionate tribute to the city. More like a poem than a song.

Gerry Rafferty, *Baker Street*: There are two kinds of people in the world. Those who love Baker Street and those who hate it. But the street still stands, and so does this.

Eddy Grant, *Electric Avenue*: Electric Avenue, Brixton, is close to the booming reggae and Jamaican treats at Brixton Market. Eddy Grant immortalised it.

Squeeze, *Up the Junction*: Clapham Common is the setting for this small saga of love and pregnancy from two of the best songwriters of all time – Chris Difford and Glenn Tilbrook.

The Jam, *Down in the Tube Station at Midnight*: Nearly all Paul Weller's lyrics are about London life, but this is the most chilling song we've ever heard about the tube, as it used to be in the 1970s.

Fergie, *London Bridge*: Children sing 'London Bridge is falling down'. Fergie has a different take on it.

Lily Allen, *LDN*: London acquired its street name, LDN, from baggage tags at Heathrow. Lily Allen writes about London a lot: this is one of her best.

Scissor Sisters, *Do the Strand*: This Roxy Music cover immortalises The Strand and reminds everyone that London was the home of 1970s Glam Rock.

XTC, *Towers of London*: XTC are famously from Swindon, not London, but this is one of the very few songs any band has ever written about the raven-filled towers.

Sweet Tooth chanteuse Fleurtini and producer Gavin Hammond have nailed the sound of Soho. Listen carefully, though, and you'll also hear Brixton. And Mayfair. And don't miss our exclusive download of Sweet Tooth's London EP, La Vie Anglaise, at *holidaygoddess.com*.

New York

Gaze at the Hudson River.
Then shop like Holly Golightly.

New York is magical. It has the world's greatest charity shops, so you can take home Prada and Jimmy Choo shoes for under $20. Or how about ice-skating in the middle of the city under the watchful eye of a huge gold statue of Prometheus? Or building your own Muppet? This is the place for strong cocktails on top of staggering skyscrapers. It's also where professional dog-walkers take six pooches out at a time, dressed in diamante collars. The city encourages brilliance and bohemia. And also red velvet cupcakes. We heart NYC.

Before you go

It might be your first trip to New York or your tenth return journey. But the Noo Yawk Rules still apply. Packing can be a challenge. Our favourite tip is to really work your on-board packing on the plane. Take a trenchcoat with deep pockets. Fill the pockets with your iPod, phone, beauty kit and anything else that you'll need on the flight. It can double as a blanket for your knees, or be folded to go under your seat.

Cosmopolitan UK commissioning editor and 'Sex and the Single Girl' columnist **Rosie Mullender** loves New York. This is her advice:

- One of the funniest things about New York is playing 'spot the random thing that until now you've only seen in the movies'. A fire truck! An advert for Sweet'N Low! A Little League game! Really really really white teeth! Forget the Statue of Liberty, these are the things you should really be taking photos of.
- Within minutes of buying a burger/burrito/hot dog, someone, somewhere will insist you should have gone to Shake Shack/ Chipotle/F&B's instead. No need to rend your garments, shaking your fist at a cruel world: the great thing about New Yorkers is that they're black belts in making excellent junk food. A burger's a burger's a burger.
- And don't forget: New York dogs are smaller than normal dogs. New York hot dogs are bigger than normal hot dogs.

New York survival guide

- Ladies' loos are hard to find. Follow your grandmother's advice and go whenever you find one, be it on Fifth Avenue or downtown. The best standby is Starbucks. You may have to cross your legs like a yoga guru while you stand in the queue for a coffee, but once the barista hands over the key, you'll be glad you waited.

- Put a paperclip around your one-dollar bills, or zip them into a different compartment of your purse or handbag. It's all too easy to get those identical green notes mixed up – especially when it's time to tip. And tipping (20% or more in restaurants) is part of life.

- This is old advice, but never take a cab at JFK or Newark airport unless it's yellow and a lot of other people are standing in line for it. Ignore the tours.

- It helps to figure out the subway before you go. The map lacks the clean simplicity of London, Sydney and Moscow. There are many websites to assist – our favourite is the excellent Wiki at *wikihow.com/Ride-the-New-York-City-Subway*.

- Allow 45 minutes to get from your departure point to your arrival point, anywhere in Manhattan. In other cities you count half an hour, but not in New York.

- If you're determined to walk Manhattan and Brooklyn, then try our favourite map: *The New York Mapguide* by Michael Middleditch. It's a slim, silver booklet that doesn't scream 'tourist!' It is based on landmarks, so when you look at Fifth Avenue you'll see a lovely illustration of Audrey Hepburn, right where Tiffany is. And a photograph of the Grand Central Clock. Every subway is colour-coded in neon. It's the lost lady's friend.

- One of the best first-day walks in New York is across the Highline, which has views all the way to the Statue of Liberty. For the best departure point, visit *thehighline.org*.

Century 21

Before you go to New York, sign up for the VIP newsletter for advance notice on sales, offers and discounts at Century 21, the most famous designer-discount outlet in New York.

The legendary discount designer outlet store has survived everything from the 9/11 attacks (it was scarily close) to more than one recession. It's Century 21 and the best way to 'do' this store is to sign up for their VIP newsletter, free, well in advance of your holiday. Follow the store on Twitter and Facebook too, during the trip, for posting of discount vouchers, along with designer-label shipment news.

If you are a dedicated designer bargainista you'll want to compare prices on Gucci in particular at The Outnet (*theoutnet.com*) and Top Brands Cheaper (*topbrandscheaper.com*) too. Yet, everyone has a bargainista story to share from a day-trip to Century 21. The rack of Gucci shirts at 75% discount. The Donna Karan bag that was the price of a good lunch. The piles of hip, suede Hush Puppies for men. (Our secret shopaholic purchased two pairs, one for her husband and one for her never-mind.)

Alongside those big global name brands you will find floors of luggage, electronics, children's clothing, bed linen, gifts and more with labels you've never heard of but at satisfyingly low prices.

Century 21 can get seriously crowded, but its easily accessed on the subway. Find it between Church Street and Broadway at 22 Cortlandt Street, downtown, at the Wall Street end of Manhattan. Take the E Train to World Trade Center.

Century 21 has been around since the 1960s and now has other branch stores in New York. So if you don't find what you want at the Manhattan branch, look at Century 21 elsewhere in Brooklyn or Queens.

Our other tip – pay for up to six bags of merchandise (!) to be delivered to your hotel for $20. We really have seen women schlepping six bags' worth of designer shoes, coats, bags and bed linen at the infamous sales. If you pay for low-cost shipping from your hotel, you'll have fitted out a house/your wardrobe/your best friend's wardrobe in designer threads for hundreds less. Visit *c21stores.com*.

Where to stay

If you want to save a fortune, exchange your home for a New York apartment. New Yorkers were early adopters of this trend, for two reasons. Firstly, many of them have cats or dogs which require TLC when their owners are on vacation. Secondly, this is the city which made Craigslist (started by Craig Newmark) the phenomenon it is today. Before you invest in a hotel, visit *craigslist.com*.

If you happen to work in a creative field, then our resident New York fashionista Lily Evans recommends *creativecaravan.net*. It's been called the Craigslist for Creatives. It's how you get from Pretty Beach, Australia to Brooklyn – with a free listing.

Our favourite hotel – even for one sybaritic night – is The Plaza. How much does it cost? Don't ask. The Beatles stayed here on the 15th floor in 1964 and, according to the doorman, took the luxurious coat hangers back to Liverpool with them. Truman Capote threw a ball here. It's where Elizabeth Taylor held hands with Richard Burton. F Scott Fitzgerald drank here (orange blossoms spiked with bootleg gin).

Almost every part of the hotel holds a story. Everyone's favourite rich little girl, Eloise, lived here – after Hilary Knight and Kay Thompson had created her. Designer Betsey Johnson has now created a (very pink) Eloise Suite too. Holiday Goddess editors believe The Plaza is not a hotel, it's just … the best of America.

Be careful, though, or you might run into Gene Simmons from Kiss. He's stayed there more than 200 times and famously used to get room service to bring in cans of whipped cream when spending the evening with lady friends. When Catherine Zeta-Jones married Michael Douglas here, they even flew the Welsh flag for her. You can stay here, or just take tea here, but The Plaza's service is probably the best in the world. Butler? Tick. Champagne? Tick. Spa? Oh, just pass the plastic.

Your first day

- Race down to Century 21 before it opens at 7.45am, then grab a bagel and coffee from a deli, joining handsome construction workers. Then hunt for Egyptian cotton pillowcases in the Century 21 basement for the price of breakfast, or buy a designer trenchcoat by DK or sunglasses for a song.
- Risk tickets for the the new, hot comedian/band/actor that *Time Out* or *New York* magazine is recommending that week. This is how we once saw an unknown Eddie Izzard.
- Meet friends at the ticket office in the huge lobby of Grand Central Terminal. Look up and you will see brightly lit zodiac signs on the ceiling. Admire Cancer the crab, overhead, then walk downstairs to the Oyster Bar & Restaurant to eat the real thing with champagne.

Century 21
22 Cortlandt St
SUBWAY: Fulton St
WEBSITE: c21store.com

Grand Central Terminal
87 East 42nd St
SUBWAY: 42nd St Grand Central
WEBSITE: grandcentralterminal.com

Your second day: Radio City Music Hall

A wonderful way to spend your **second** day exploring Manhattan is to time your trip around a big show at Radio City Music Hall. Holiday Goddesses and our readers have seen Flight of the Conchords here, but also His Holiness the Dalai Lama.

Radio City is eclectic by nature and also has the most beautifully preserved Art Deco hall in America. The best seats are by mailing list at *radiocity.com*. If you're there from November to January, there is the Christmas Spectacular variety show, featuring The Rockettes.

The January sales

In January, **everything** is on sale in New York. Yves St Laurent shoes. Luxurious hotel rooms. Flights. Puffy jackets. It may snow, but in the bars, the hot-buttered rum is warm.

So enjoy the greatest bargains known to womankind and congratulate yourself on being here without the sticky summer queues and heaving tourist crowds.

If you are here in the second week of January, then you will be in bargainista heaven, as **Saks Fifth Avenue**, **Barneys** and **Bloomingdales** staff slash the price tags in red pen for the third consecutive time. And that's how you end up with labels you only dreamed about, for 70% off the normal price.

Expect crisp, sunny days and, if you are lucky, the romance of seeing a snowman on Fifth Avenue carrying the Stars and Stripes.

If you can ski off-piste then you can see NY off-peak. Layer the pretty new thermal vests.

The Rockefeller Rink

New Yorkers work so hard that they love to play – until they fall over. The Ice Skating Rink at Rockefeller Center is part of the fun; you will see plenty of corporate types slipping and sliding during winter. You are welcome to join them, too, for the price of a bagel. In summer, the empty space transforms into a vast bar, complete with shady table umbrellas and Cosmopolitan cocktails. Last time we checked, Happy Hour was still on. That's appropriate, as a golden status of Prometheus (whose liver was ripped out daily by an eagle) dominates the space. Paul Manship is the sculptor who created Prometheus; as an old man, he also created the John F Kennedy inauguration medal. If you are here in winter, lessons are available. On Saturday night you can skate until midnight. If it's snowing, it can be the most romantic thing on earth. The Rink (or in summer, the bar) is a strange, lovely, introduction to the city. It also happens to be the perfect excuse to get closer to your date (if you just picked up) or to rediscover sweet, old-fashioned, Victorian thrills (if you have been together forever). The flapping international flags above make the whole world feel at home here, no matter where everyone comes from.

United by embarrassment or smugness, the skaters at Rockefeller seem lost in a world of their own. Even if you don't want to participate, you can watch and enjoy. And in summer, of course, all you need are flexible wrist skills to raise those Happy-Hour Cosmopolitans.

The Rink at Rockefeller Center, on Fifth Avenue between West 49th & 50th Sts.

SUBWAY: 47th & 50th St, Rockefeller Centre

WEBSITE: rockefellercenter.com

Your new best friend in NYC: *The Village Voice*

You can pick up *The Village Voice* magazine free in New York. It's an essential part of the NYC experience. This is where we found an extra-large Yoda dog costume for $14.99 but also where we found out about downtown $30 Turkish baths (women only, robe included). *The Village Voice* is not for tourists, it's for locals.

As these are New York locals, however, the magazine is as discerning, sophisticated, hip and witty, as you'd expect. It's also the place to find hot tickets: *The Village Voice* recently presented the King Tutankhamun exhibition after dark – a special event for locals which most tourists never knew about.

If you want to feel as if you've crawled inside New York, rather than just remained outside waving a map, collect your free copy on your first day. We like it for its eminently trustworthy reviews. *The Voice* is also part of history: it was launched from a two-bedroom apartment in Greenwich Village in 1955 by Norman Mailer and friends. Henry Miller wrote for it and *Simpsons* creator Matt Groening also started out here.

We could do without the sexy lady advertisements in the back pages, but otherwise this is one of the first sources to turn to for a week in NYC.

You can also log onto the website at *villagevoice.com* before you fly.

Chiconomical secrets

A bargainista holiday in New York depends on two things – flying in unpopular months like January, February and March, and exchanging your home. Do that, and you will shrink the two biggest costs of a wonderful holiday in NYC. The rest is surprisingly chiconomical. Even cheap.

- Home exchange subscription fees cover every kind of insurance, assistance and protection. Our tip is *creativecaravan.net*. And we also love *homeexchange.com*.
- Holiday Goddess editors are constantly gathering the best chiconomical New York hotel and airline deals on the Holiday Goddess Hot List. Just visit *holidaygoddess.com*.
- The benefits of flying January to March to NYC extend beyond huge savings to far shorter queues at the airport and plenty of empty seats on the plane. (When the seatbelt sign goes off, bag 2–3 seats.)
- New York can be cheap if you organise breakfast at home, and dine in half the time. If you're cooking, Chinatown is the best source of vegetables and fruit. Trader Joe's is great too: *traderjoes.com*.
- Your best experiences in New York may well end up being free experiences. This is a generous city. The Metropolitan Museum of Art only asks for donations to view Monet, Da Vinci, Picasso, Van Gogh and Degas. You don't have to shop at Tiffany to see Tiffany altars or inside stunning St Patrick's Cathedral.

New York charity shops: Prada heaven

To find one pair of Prada shoes in a charity shop in Manhattan seems like crazy good luck. To find another pair, on the same day, reminds us just how wealthy some New Yorkers are. There are five main categories of retro fashion, across the best shops:

1. Classic separates from J Crew, Ralph Lauren and Calvin Klein that never date – around $10.
2. If the Fashion Goddess is with you, then Jimmy Choo or Prada shoes may be in your size for $20.
3. The eighties is well represented so if you want to recreate *Dallas* or *Dynasty*, shop from $5.
4. Seventies chic (tweed jackets, pussycat bow shirts, tan leather bags) can be found from $10.
5. If you can sew, raid the menswear section for Dior and Yves St Laurent clothing from $20.

TOP FIVE
New York Charity Shops

1. **Housing Works thrift shop**, 157 East 23rd Street. Subway: 23rd Street & Lexington
2. **Salvation Army thrift shop**, 220 East 23rd Street, East Village. Subway: 23rd Street & Lexington
3. **East Village thrift shop**, 186 Second Avenue. Subway: 14th Street & Union Square
4. **Salvation Army thrift shop**, 176 Bedford Ave, Williamsburg, Brooklyn. Subway: Bedford Avenue
5. **Calvary St Georges thrift shop**, 61 Gramercy Park North. Subway: 23rd Street & Lexington

Loehmann's

Vicki Arkoff recommends Loehmann's for women who have (a) no dressing room modesty and (b) an addiction to deep designer discounts.

'Communal dressing rooms equal shopping hell. But unwanted opinions from strangers in their undies are something I'm willing to bear as I bare all at Loehmann's. I'm an addict who'll sacrifice my modesty for the prospect of Prada at puny prices, as long as it's in the overcrowded, overwhelming Chelsea flagship department store.

Buy a Gold Card which knocks off another 10% and don't forget the back room for current- and past-season finds like my favourite Max Mara black dress ($89) and Donna Karan trousers ($50). My secret: call ahead for a free personal shopper who'll find gems in your size before you arrive. And don't tell, but the private dressing rooms are hidden on the second floor.'

Loehmanns, 101 7th Avenue, Chelsea (btw W 16th & 17th St)

SUBWAY: 18th St

WEBSITE: **loehmanns.com**

Bargainista books: Strand Bookstore

Want a great book for $2? It's here. But Strand Bookstore is also for millionaires. This is where Michael Jackson came with his entourage to fill his library. It's also where collectors came to view *Alice's Adventures in Wonderland* by Lewis Carroll, priced at $15,000.

If you're a bargainista, though, you'll be here for the second-hand and remaindered books.

There are 18 miles of them (they measured) on sale. Look at the wheeled stands on the street outside the entrance for the lowest prices.

Strand Bookstore, 828 Broadway, Greenwich Village

SUBWAY: Union Square, 14th St

WEBSITE: **strandbooks.com**

Brooklyn's (free) summer sanctuary: Red Hook pool

Felicity Loughrey's career adventures include *Vogue* magazine and *New York* magazine. When the weather is warm, she recommends Red Hook pool.

In summer, my favourite New York City summer swimming destination is the landmark Sol Goldman Red Hook Recreation Center. It also happens to be free.

It's possible to get to Red Hook pool by public transport but you may also book a car, from around $10, from anywhere in Brooklyn. See Arecibo Car Service at *arecibocc.com*.

Before going to Red Hook, scrutinise the New York City Department of Parks and Recreation website for opening times and pool rules. You must bring your own combination lock, and you may not bring cameras, phones or newspapers.

The Sol Goldman Red Hook Recreation Center was built to stimulate the US economy in the Great Depression. The women's change rooms are in an open gymnasium with battered metal lockers lining the walls (hence the need for your own padlock). The showers and bathrooms won't be featured in a design magazine but they're functional. Once you're out on the deck, it's wonderful.

An Olympic-sized lap area is open at certain hours (check the website). If you are travelling with children, there's a separate knee-deep kids' pool that is lined with surprisingly rough pebbledash cooled by large sprinklers painted in primary colours.

Felicity Loughrey

Sol Goldman Red Hook Recreation Center, 155 Bay St, Brooklyn
SUBWAY: Smith St & 9th St
WEBSITE: nycgovparks.org

The secret diaries of several shopaholics

Holiday Goddess editor **Rachael Oakes-Ash** is a bestselling author and travel writer, whose work also appears in LUXE Guides, along with major newspapers and magazines. These are notes from her New York shopping diary.

Nolita and Soho are great for mingling with the media and celebrities through cobbled lanes and cast-iron architecture. Pick up a toffy-styled bespoke British suit at **Lord Willy's**, bespoke perfumes from **Le Labo**, Tibetan mantra stamped jewellery at **Me&Ro**, slinky lingerie with a wink at **Kiki De Montparnasse** or vintage wallpaper from **Secondhand Rose**. Don't forget **Resurrection Vintage** for pre-loved Chanel, Dior and Yves St Laurent.

Tribeca is great for window shopping for interior design ideas. Try the **R 20th Century Design** for 20th and 21st century furniture designers worth boasting about. The cult showroom **Urban Archeology** reworks salvaged design elements from mosaics to bathtubs and **Interieurs** showcases industrial, unique and antique design for 'modern soulful living'.

Worked up an appetite with all that window shopping? **Billy's Bakery** on Franklin Street serves banana cream, coconut cream and key lime pies to raise your blood sugar levels above the Empire State Building.

In the Meatpacking, Chelsea and West Village areas, trawl the usual fashion suspects like **Stella McCartney**, **Lulu Guinness** and the late **Alexander McQueen**. Don't miss **Ludivine** which brings Parisian chic to the US with contemporary French brands or Brazilian **Carlos Miele** who shows the north how the south do red carpet glamour.

The Upper East Side is where you'll find the one-name designers: **Valentino**, **Armani** and **Lauren**. Head to the old bank turned new boutique – the Italian luxury fashion house **VBH** for lush jewels and bags.

For Art Deco jewels and classic vintage watches visit **Michael Ashton** on Madison Avenue. And remember, every NY princess needs to write thank you letters, so **Mrs John L Strong**'s contemporary twist on fine stationery will get yours noticed.

Rachael Oakes-Ash

Lord Willy's: 223 Mott Street (near Prince Street)
Le Labo: 233 Elizabeth Street (near Prince Street)
Me&Ro: 241 Elizabeth Street (near Prince Street)
Kiki De Montparnasse: 79 Greene Street (near Spring Street)
Secondhand Rose: 230 5th Avenue #510 (near W 27th Street)
Resurrection Vintage: 217 Mott Street (near Spring Street)
R 20th Century Design: 82 Franklin St (near Church Street)
Urban Archaeology: 143 Franklin Street (near Varick Street)
Interieurs: 149–151 Franklin Street (near Varick Street)
Billy's Bakery: 75 Franklin Street (near Church Street)
Stella McCartney: 429 W 14th Street (near Washington Street)
Lulu Guinness: 394 Bleecker Street (near W 11th Street)
Alexander McQueen: 430 W 14th Street (near Washington Street)
Ludivine: 172 W 4th Street (near 6th Avenue)
Valentino: 747 Madison Avenue (near E 65th Street)
Armani: 760 Madison Avenue (near E 65th Street)
Ralph Lauren: 888 Madison Avenue (near E 72nd Street)
VBH: 940 Madison Avenue (between E 74th and 75th Street)
Michael Ashton: 933 Madison Avenue (near E 74th Street)
Mrs John L Strong: 699 Madison Avenue Floor 5 (near E 63rd Street)

Fifth Avenue classics

Our idea of shopping heaven is a world without maps.
That's why Holiday Goddess editors all love Fifth Avenue.

Saks Fifth Avenue

If you only have time for one Fifth Avenue department store, make it
Saks Fifth Avenue. Every major designer in the world is here. The last
time Holiday Goddess editors road-tested Saks in a sale, they found
an entire issue of *Vogue* magazine reduced by 70%. Gorgeous Marc
Jacobs clutch bags from his previous spring collection were well under
$100. Whenever you come to Saks, you can be sure of finding
something (just one thing) to love, from a lipstick to a scarf. It is also
the place to collapse gratefully for lunch, morning tea or afternoon
tea before returning to bustling Fifth Avenue outside.

Saks Fifth Avenue, 611 Fifth Avenue between 49th & 50th Street

Bergdorf Goodman

You can never be too X-ray thin or too damn rich – apparently. That is
why the women on the escalators at Bergdorf Goodman wear skinny
designer jeans and carry vast Hermès bags. Is it really so expensive and
intimidating here, though? Not at sale time. You will be able to take
Chanel, Repetto and Manolo Blahnik shoes straight from the 50%
discount rack and try them on. No security guards. No hovering
assistants. Outside sales time in January and July, you can pick up
gorgeous candles or writing paper here. It's inexpensive luxury and
easy to take home, in the violet Bergdorf Goodman bag.

Bergdorf Goodman, 754 Fifth Avenue between 57th & 58th Street

Henri Bendel

Bergdorf Goodman is for seriously rich, sophisticated yummy mummies. Henri Bendel is younger, hipper and more relaxed. The ground floor is often as far as we go. The Henri Bendel travel candles scented with peony in square, pink tins ($15) are fabulous – or we pick up the signature brown candy-striped plastic vanity cases. It's designer fashion all the way upstairs. What interests us most are the only-in-New-York beauty and bathroom goodies, the beautiful hair accessories, and the eponymous branded gifts. There is a beautiful winding staircase, which we tend to scale at 25 kph at sales time.

Henri Bendel, 712 Fifth Avenue between 55th & 56th Street

FAO Schwarz

Over the years, we have seen everything at this children's fantasy superstore. Business cards for seven-year-olds. Talking trees. Dolls which pee in a potty. We would no more think of missing a trip to FAO Schwarz than missing the plane home. On our last trip, a man dressed as a toy soldier waved us inside, while visiting children screamed from a Hershey's sugar high (you will also find Willy Wonka bars in the same section). Attractions come and go, like the Muppet Workshop or the Harry Potter floor. The huge toy animals, though, (Grizzly Bear $1249) always delight us. **FAO Schwarz, 767 Fifth Avenue between 58th & 59th Street**

And finally ... Barneys

It *should* be on Fifth Avenue, but instead you will find the stylish, cutting-edge, fabulously pricey Barney's at 660 Madison Avenue. The window displays often feature live models. For a bigger thrill, attend their warehouse sales. Get on the mailing list at *barneys.com*.

Barneys, 660 Madison Avenue, near E 61st Street

Download our no-map guide from *holidaygoddess.com*, then take the subway to Fifth Avenue station and shop until you shop *again*.

Bargainista favourites

Anthropologie

A true bargainista walks in with $50 to spend and comes out with treasures – and change for lunch. Anthropologie is our favourite place to do just that. The tea towels make you want to wash up: they are trimmed with pom-poms and feature hand-stitched flowers and patchwork birds. The sales rack is permanent and you may find your dream retro or boho frock or shoes here. The books inspire us, the perfume is unusual, the vibe is all-American with a touch of Paris.

Anthropologie
375 West Broadway
SUBWAY: 14th St
WEBSITE: anthropologie.com

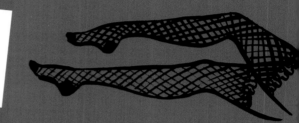

H&M and Zara

H&M and Zara are no big deal if you're from Europe, but if you don't know these wildly chiconomical clothing chains, you'll love discovering them in NY. What you see stylists showing in *Grazia* magazine at designer prices is translated in-store at H&M and Zara the same week – for $50. The sheer size of the stores means you'll probably find *something* you love. The quality and tailoring in Zara is remarkable. Only fashionista pros will guess your navy jacket wasn't YSL.

H&M
640 Fifth Ave
SUBWAY: Fifth Ave
WEBSITE: hm.com

Zara
689 Fifth Ave
SUBWAY: Fifth Ave
WEBSITE: zara.com

Sample sales

Cash only. No change rooms. But still – up the stairs we go, tramping to another sample sale. These events (when fashion samples shown to stores are sold off until they are sold out) are strictly for fashion gamblers. Still, we'd feel we'd missed out if we didn't visit New York and check out *Daily Candy* at *dailycandy.com*, *New York* magazine at *nymag.com* and *Time Out* at *timeout.com* for the sample sale listings. Our tip? If you are lucky enough to have a contact in the media in Manhattan, ask her if she can use her VIP List status to get you into the very best sales, first.

Jackie O's New York

Jacqueline Kennedy became Jackie Onassis and then Jackie O, the legend. Holiday Goddess editor **Karen Moline** once saw her on the streets of Manhattan and never forgot it: 'I remember seeing Jackie on Madison Avenue, once. I stopped, stunned, once I realised who it was, as she climbed out of a yellow cab, with her Hermès scarf wrapped around her hair and her trademark Nina Ricci sunglasses on her face'. While still in mourning for John F Kennedy, Jackie moved to New York in 1964, buying a 15th floor co-op at 1040 Fifth Avenue and 85th Street. It's still there today.

The Jackie O style list

1. Oleg Cassini created Jackie's iconic wardrobe in the 1960s, still being copied by and inspiring designers today.
2. Her silk scarves came from Hermès.
3. Her triple-strand pearls were from Kenneth Jay Lane.
4. Van Cleef & Arpels created her wedding ring from President Kennedy.
5. Gucci created the 'Jackie' bag – the slouchy shoulder-bag classic – especially for her.

Jackie O had a handful of places she cherished and visited often.

The Jacqueline Kennedy Onassis Reservoir at 90th Street and Fifth Avenue: Jackie was fanatical about keeping her trim figure, and she often ran counterclockwise on the path around the reservoir, a distance of 2.54km, so she could see who was approaching. Few runners ever recognised her. It was renamed in her honour after her death.

The Costume Institute at the Metropolitan Museum of Art at 82nd Street and Fifth Avenue: Style goddess and editor Diana Vreeland became a consultant here after she was fired from *Vogue* in 1971. When she was working as an editor at Doubleday, Jackie convinced Diana to write a book on style. The result was the magnificent *Allure*, recently republished with a Marc Jacobs foreword.

Grand Central Terminal, 42nd Street at Park Avenue: This is a great place to dine (see page 218). However it's also a monument to Jackie. When plans were announced put up a huge office block above Grand Central, she led the charge with the NYC Landmarks Preservation Commission.

Tiffany, 57th Street and Fifth Avenue: Tiffany is associated with Audrey Hepburn, thanks to the film based on Truman Capote's novel. It's also part of Jackie O's story, too. She edited six books with Tiffany design director John Loring and was so fond of the enamel and gold bracelets designed by Jean Schlumberger for Tiffany that they were nicknamed 'Jackie bracelets'.

The Grill Room at the Four Seasons, 99 E 52nd Street: Jackie O dined regularly at The Grill Room at the Four Seasons, still *the* power place to be seen at lunch. Perhaps you will feel her presence there, in spirit. There was nothing Jackie loved more during her years here than being thought of as just another New Yorker.

New York in books and film

Holiday Goddess North American editor **Vicki Arkoff** has written for *Daily Variety*, *Entertainment Weekly* ... and *MAD* magazine. She's also worked on films with Johnny Depp, Bruce Willis, Viggo Mortensen and Jeremy Irons, so we asked her for an insider tour of the cinematic and literary highlights of Hollywood East – otherwise known as NYC.

New York is one gigantic fictional set. You can't walk a block without running into a film, TV or novel location. One way to do it? Check into the **Helmsley Park Lane Hotel** and ask for a room with a view – as you gaze onto Central Park you will see locations from *Love Story*, *Hair* and *Marathon Man*. The Central Park Zoo itself appears in *The Catcher in the Rye, Mr Popper's Penguins, Madagascar* and *Summer Crossing* by Truman Capote.

You may also take a romantic horse-drawn carriage ride around **Central Park** – though hoping for a *Sex and the City* experience, rather than a *Seinfeld* one.

If you've seen *Edward Scissorhands, Beaches, The Out-of-Towners, Misery, Heartburn* or *Ghostbusters*, then you'll recognise the **Tavern on the Green** on Central Park West and West 67th Street – it's where Rick Moranis was attacked in *Ghostbusters*.

If you take the horse-drawn carriage, **The Dakota** will also feature on your journey. This is the grandiose apartment building at 1 West 72nd Street, at Central Park West. It had a starring role in *Rosemary's Baby*, and it was also the real-life home of Judy Garland, Lauren Bacall, Leonard Bernstein, Boris Karloff, and John Lennon and Yoko Ono. Strawberry Fields, nearby in Central Park, commemorates Lennon's life.

When the ride is over, you will be dropped back opposite **The Plaza Hotel** at Fifth Avenue and Central Park South. Anyone who's anyone has slept here, including The Beatles. The Plaza Hotel has also had roles in *North by Northwest, The Way We Were, The Great Gatsby, Funny Girl, Plaza Suite, Arthur, Barefoot in the Park, Home Alone 2* and *Almost Famous*.

The Plaza Hotel is the setting for the *Eloise* books and movies by Kay Thompson and Hilary Knight – about a rich girl living extravagantly in the Plaza's penthouse. You may have afternoon tea here, just like Eloise, even if you don't book a suite. (For more information visit *theplaza.com*.) And Paris Hilton also lived in the penthouse at The Plaza Hotel for 15 years. Just like Eloise. Groan. Need to escape Paris Hilton's presence at The Plaza? Head downtown to **Hotel Chelsea** at 222 West 23rd Street between 7th and 8th Avenues. This is the only hotel in New York where you might ask for the *Sid and Nancy* room, or the *9 ½ Weeks* room. Or better yet, the room where Arthur C. Clarke wrote *2001: A Space Odyssey*. Jack Kerouac also wrote some of his classic, *On The Road,* here. And Dylan Thomas succumbed to pneumonia in Room 205.

Are you a *Sopranos* fan? There's a four-hour bus tour of its New Jersey locations. I didn't take it, because the bus goes to places I wouldn't be caught dead in (bada-bing!). I skipped the *Gossip Girl* bus tour, too, as it didn't include any shopping time at Henri Bendel on Fifth Avenue.

The Seinfeld tour of New York was hard to resist though. It's a kitschy three-hour bus ride with Kenny Kramer, the real-life inspiration for the *Seinfeld* character Cosmo Kramer. When I rang, though, it was sold out. 'No tour for you,' said the guy on the phone – who turned out to be Kenny Kramer himself. (To book your seat, go online months in advance to *kennykramer.com*.)

With or without Kenny, though, it's possible to see all of *Seinfeld's* most famous locations. The 'Soup Nazi' episode was based on **Al's Soup Kitchen** at 259-A W 55th Street, between Broadway and Eighth Avenue. Jerry, George, Elaine and Kramer also frequented **Tom's Restaurant** (Monk's Cafe in the series). Find it at 2880 Broadway and 112th St in Morningside Heights. Tom's Restaurant also featured in the song *Tom's Diner* by Suzanne Vega.

More New York classics – **Katz's Deli** (205 East Houston Street at Ludlow, Lower East Side) is where Meg Ryan faked an orgasm in *When Harry Met Sally*. Prefer *Friends*? Visit their apartment building on Grove and Bedford in Greenwich Village. And don't miss the *Flight of the Conchords'* apartment at 285 Henry Street nearby – along with manager Murray's faux New Zealand Consulate at 232 East Broadway.

Over the bridge in Brooklyn, pay homage to *Dog Day Afternoon*. It was shot in an auto-repair shop, rebuilt to look like the bank where the real events took place, at 285 Prospect Park West between 17th & 18th.

Back in Manhattan, **The American Museum of Natural History** is the natural place to reflect on Holden Caulfield, from *The Catcher in the Rye*. It's on Central Park West at 79th Street, on the Upper West Side. It is also where Ross Geller worked in *Friends* and where the museum benefit was held in *The Devil Wears Prada*.

Don't miss the **Empire State Building**, central in *King Kong, An Affair to Remember, On the Town, Funny Face, Serpico, Sleepless in Seattle, Bright Lights Big City* and the Martian scene in *I Love Lucy*.

And how can you resist window-shopping at **Tiffany** on Fifth Avenue and 56th Street, holding a coffee and pastry like Audrey Hepburn in the famous opening scene in *Breakfast at Tiffany's*? Or letting the breeze from the subway grate (at 52nd Street and Lexington) blow up your skirt, like Marilyn Monroe in *The Seven-Year Itch*? Later on, strut down Fourth Avenue in Bay Ridge like John Travolta in *Saturday Night Fever* to the sound of 'Stayin' Alive'. Or would you prefer to dance on the giant piano keys at **FAO Schwarz** toy store, like Tom Hanks in *Big*, at 767 Fifth Avenue, just a hop, skip and a jump from the Plaza? Finish up on on the site of Woody Allen and Diane Keaton's famous bench under the **Queensboro Bridge**.

Vicki Arkoff

A tale of two Carries

I first met Candace Bushnell, author of *Sex and the City*, at a party in London about ten years ago. We were talking, in a random, champagne-fuelled way, about a book she had written about single women in Manhattan – which had just been picked up for TV. Candace said *Sex and the City* was about feminism. Wow. I hadn't heard that word since university.

Well, I read the book in one sitting. It was the first time I remember any single woman over 30 honestly writing about her life. And it was funny, too. Plus it wasn't hard to see that Carrie Bradshaw (CB) was loosely based on Candace Bushnell (also CB).

Do you remember the rolodex scene in *When Harry Met Sally* when Carrie Fisher helps out the newly-single Sally by going through her rolodex file of straight, unattached guys? That's not so far from the truth in Manhattan. New York City really is about a tale of two Carries.

Some years after the party with Candace, I hosted an event with her (looking dazzling in a white suit and huge cocktail ring) before hundreds of devoted fans. Afterwards, groups of them went off for cupcakes – the tiny, frosted cakes of female bonding, which *Sex and the City* made famous. Also known as Carrie Cakes.

The most famous Carrie Cake location in NY is the original **Magnolia Bakery** at **401 Bleecker Street**, in the West Village. It started the cupcake revolution here and queues still form outside.

Holiday Goddess readers are even bigger fans of **Sweet Revenge**, though. It's New York's only cupcake, beer and wine bar. The last time we checked, happy hour was still on from 4pm to 8pm, Monday to Friday. And that's when you can pull up a chair and indulge in a glass of Pinot noir and a cupcake for $10. Find Sweet Revenge at **62 Carmine Street, New York**. Find more details at *sweetrevengenyc.com*.

The men of New York have also come up with their own version of Carrie Cakes. **The Butch Bakery** is, you guessed, a testosterone-loaded cupcake delivery service. The Butch Bakery has a chocolate cupcake called Jackhammer. And believe it or not, a cupcake made with maple syrup and bacon, called a Driller. The B-52 cupcake at Butch Bakery even has army camouflage decoration on top. There is no shop, but Butch Bakery will deliver to your hotel or apartment. Order these incredible man-treats at *butchbakery.com*.

For fans of both Carries (Carrie Fisher as Marie in *When Harry Met Sally* and Carrie Bradshaw), New York's only place to dine is **The Loeb Boathouse**, in **Central Park, between 74th and 75th**.

There are no cupcakes there, but you will be sitting in a location made famous by both the first and second Carrie, as it's been a location in *Sex and the City* and *When Harry Met Sally*. For more details visit *thecentralparkboathouse.com*.

Jessica Adams

Eat, love, eat more

New York is the world capital of 24-hour food, from lunch at the fabulous La Grenouille to a plain bagel with whipped butter at 4am. It also has its own five food groups – the aforementioned Bagels, but also: Hot Dogs; Black and White Cookies; Lobster Rolls; and Pastrami on Rye. You can try any of these as part of the big new food craze taking over New York – Twitter truck cuisine. Holiday Goddess editor, author and journalist **Karen Moline** suggests you take your phone to Manhattan.

Twitter truck cuisine

Type 'Food Trucks in NYC' into the Twitter homepage and you'll instantly get listings from New York locals who are serving food, streets away from you. Then drop all inhibitions and stuff your face on the street – hey, you're turning into a local!

Not surprisingly, dessert trucks are usually at the top of many lists, but if you factor in how long it will take you to walk to one, you'll burn off so many calories you can then stuff yourself guilt-free. (A perfect New York rationale.) I have to confess I am partial to the calorific delights at The Dessert Truck (@desserttruck) and the Big Gay Ice Cream Truck (@biggayicecream) for its crazy toppings (wasabi pea dust, anyone?).

The Chelsea Market

The Chelsea Market is the old Nabisco biscuit factory (where they produced Oreos), converted into a dark and mysterious underground food mall, where you can dine in, or buy lunch to take away. You may have a perfect paper-bag bench picnic watching the boats on the Hudson River, which is a five-minute walk away, as is the Meatpacking District and the High Line.

Note Chelsea Wine Vault as you walk in: half the costly private wine collections of Manhattan are reputedly stored in its cellars. You can take wine-tasting lessons here and meet the locals, if you book ahead.

The Chelsea Market has several cafes, bakeries and restaurants inside, from hip organic, to cartoon cupcake. There is a hot pink interior waterfall, and dazzling curtains of fairy-lights to guide your way. As you enter you'll see glass cases containing old biscuit tins and packets from Nabisco's heyday. Inside, bakers in white hats and aprons throw dough around on tables, visible through picture windows: they produce the divine rolls and loaves for Amy's Bread, a fixture here.

It's all a simple five-minute walk from the subway. You'll also find a large branch of Anthropologie here – Holiday Goddess editors nickname this store Eclectic Ladyland, after the Jimi Hendrix album. It's our favourite women's fashion, fragrance and homewares store in the world. (Read more about Anthropologie on page 206).

If you dislike crowds, come to the Chelsea Market for breakfast from 7am (Though note: Anthropologie opens at 10am).

Whatever you do, don't miss The Lobster Place, which is a huge fresh shellfish and seafood store selling all-American lobster, shrimp and every kind of smoked salmon on crushed ice. It does a roaring trade with special lunchboxes for enjoying the High Line nearby. Pick up the bagels and cream cheese from other stores here and create breakfast in your hotel room fridge.

The Chelsea Market
SUBWAY: 14th St & 8th Ave
WEBSITE: chelseamarket.com

The Grand Central Terminal dining concourse

New Yorkers come to Grand Central to catch the train to Poughkeepsie, which we can't pronounce. Holiday Goddess editors come here to ignore the train timetable and dine downstairs. We head straight for the Oyster Bar, to sit underneath beautiful vaulted ceilings and faint at the menu.

How many things can one chef do with seafood? Well, how about appetisers, soups, cold buffets and a category just headed 'Shrimp and Scallops.' Or try the smokehouse section, the stews and panroasts section – or the raw bar.

Not enough for you? Try shellfish platters, cooked shellfish, lobster and (deep breath) poached New Bedford Sea Scallops and New Zealand Greenlip Mussels in Mustard Vinaigrette with Jumbo Asparagus.

Then there is dessert. Rum and raisin apple pie with walnut crust; lemon honey apricot tart; peanut butter and white chocolate profiteroles ...

Flip the enormous menu and the wine list will take you from France to Australia via California. There are around 800 choices.

It would be madness to actually catch a train after all this. Just sit in the sweet gloom and marvel at the poetry of the handwritten oyster menu: Arcadia, Cuttyhunk, Duckabush, Moonstone, Sister Point and Watch Hill.

TOP TEN

Oyster Bar Selections

1. Caviar Sandwich
2. Manhattan Clam Chowder
3. Point Judith Squid Salad
4. Coquille St Jacques
5. Lobster Stew
6. Blackberry Point Oysters
7. Florida Key Lime Pie
8. Brooklyn Lager
9. New York Cheesecake
10. Billecart-Salmon Brut Reserve NV

Nobu: Robert de Niro's Japanese restaurant

Book months ahead to get into the original Nobu, or just turn up at Nobu Next Door, which is alongside its more famous sister. New York's hippest restaurants change all the time (see *holidaygoddess.com* for constant updates) but Nobu is an old faithful, where the black cod miso is always fishy, sweet and sinfully rich.

Nobu Next Door is the far more casual sister restaurant that we prefer. Just turn up between 7pm and 9pm and if there's table, you're in.

**Nobu and Nobu Next Door,
105 Hudston St, Tribeca**

SUBWAY: Canal St

WEBSITE: noburestaurants.com

Deli on Madison: $10 heaven on Madison Avenue

In New York a deli is where hard-working locals go for lunch. They choose from vast steel trays of home-made gourmet food, lightly pack their plastic containers, weigh them, then dine inside for under $10. The Deli on Madison is close to Saks Fifth Avenue. It also opens from 6am with oatmeal, bagels and pancakes on the menu.

The Deli on Madison really stars at lunch, though. Create your own salad and choose from 18 dressings. Or try the perfectly cooked pink salmon and mashed potato.

**Deli on Madison, 420
Madison Ave, between
W 48th & 49th St**

SUBWAY: Fifth Ave

Chinatown: Bubble tea and baby clams

Chinatown lacks glamour but when it comes to mystique, it has oodles. And also noodles. With fresh baby clams.

This is where Chinese New Yorkers go to order hot ginger tea on a cold day, or a honeydew bubble milk tea with tapioca pearls on a warm day.

Holiday Goddess editors recently discovered a great place called King of Casserole at 21 Division Street with fish tanks in the window. Don't worry too much about maps in Chinatown though; it's a place to explore and muddle through. If you are lucky enough to actually *find* Division Street (crossing Catherine Street and Market Street) then we promise, the King of Casserole will not disappoint. But fear not if you get lost (it's easy to do). There are many such restaurants here and we've tried many of them.

The King of Casserole has zilch glamour, it's true – but it also offers a big selection of $7 cuisine – often priced well below that.

First, choose your type of noodle (vermicelli, rice, ho fun, pull, instant or udon) then select from the main event: roast duck, baby clam, ox tail or bitter melon with beef. Vegetarians will be happy to know they are well looked after at King of Casserole. Try a Lychee Green Tea Slush with Special Hometown Style Tofu. There is no muzak. The decor is forgettable. The tanks of live fish in the window may not be your favourite thing – but this is nourishing food.

Afterwards try a foot massage or pick up some Chinese slippers. Holiday Goddess editors think there is at least an hour of fun in Chinatown, lying in the fresh seafood shops and greengrocers around you. They sell buckets of live frogs and turtles here, it's true. But also feng shui charms, sweet parasols and temple fortunes.

King of Casserole
21 Division St, New York

SUBWAY: Canal St

Sylvia's: Queen of Soul Food, Harlem

Sylvia's of Harlem has been around since the 1960s, when Jimi Hendrix was playing up the road. Sylvia was born in South Carolina and met her husband, Herbert, when she was eleven and he was twelve. When they moved here, she borrowed money from her mother to buy a luncheonette. This is the place, still owned by her family.

Coming here is like time-travelling. It's dark inside, but it preserves the low-key sixties interior beautifully. The menu is strictly Southern. Carolina grilled catfish. Smothered chicken. And plates of okra (sometimes known as 'Okrah Winfrey' to local comedians).

The portions are huge, so consider sharing a stack of appetisers – like the Coconut Shrimp and Chicken Livers with Sylvia's Brown Gravy. The Collard Greens and Candied Yams are fantastic and vegetarian-friendly. And the Margaritas? Whoa, mama. We like the portrait of Aretha Franklin on the wall too. We say, R.E.S.P.E.C.T. to Sylvia's and her chilled, but always friendly, staff.

Sylvia's
328 Lenox Ave, Harlem
SUBWAY: 125th St
WEBSITE: sylviasrestaurant.com

Taking New York home

They say the Doggy Bag was invented in New York. It makes sense.
The food portions here are far too large to finish – and the dogs are
honorary human beings anyway. This must be the only place in the
world where you'll see a King Charles spaniel snuffling his way through
a silver-foil container of lobster thermidor. If only Richard Branson
would fly New York Doggy Bags all over the world! That way, the
pastrami on rye sandwiches could come home with you. And the Key
Lime Pie. There's other ways to take New York home, though ...

Let's do brunch

In Sydney, they sit outside in the sun having business meetings at 8am,
ploughing through scrambled eggs, spinach and freshly-squeezed
orange juice. In London, they stay in bed, shivering. In New York, they
down a strong coffee first thing, then combine breakfast and lunch into
that delicious, time-saving device known as brunch. And I have to
admit – I've become a brunch convert.

Traditionally, a Manhattan brunch consists of bacon and eggs,
pancakes, French toast or muffins. If you're no-carbs you'll have an
omelette, if you're yes, yes, yes-carbs then you'll have crisp home-made
waffles with cold butter whisked into warm maple syrup. Brunch is a
savvy New York habit to take home with you long after the holiday is
over. Try this cookbook – *Clinton St. Baking Company Cookbook*.
It's based on the legendary brunch palace on the Lower East Side.
We hear the omelette technique is patented.

Flowers with everything

Okay, so New Yorkers borrowed this idea from Parisiennes – but the
rule for lunch at the best Manhattan restaurants is – flowers with
everything. Downtown, you'll see single stems in 1950s chipped
teacups, plonked on window ledges.

Uptown, expect spectacular displays of the most beautiful roses, lilies, hyacinths and peonies you have ever seen. I must confess, I'm no Martha Stewart. But if you want to take a little bit of New York's botanical style home with you, her magazines and books are a great place to start. If you're serious about your flowers, though, you'll opt for this book: *The Flowers of La Grenouille* by Charles Masson. La Grenouille is probably the original *Mad Men* restaurant.

It was the place to dine in the 1960s, partly because of its magnificent bouquets. Proprietor Charles Masson shows you how to duplicate Grenouille's bouquets inside his book. Well, I learned how to keep a rose fresh ...

Gourmet soup

Nobody knew about New York's gourmet soup cult until 'The Soup Nazi' episode ran on Seinfeld. But it's another great Manhattan habit to take home with you. Until I went to New York, I used to think of soup in terms of packets and cans. It was the entrée I never wanted to have. Many people feel the same way – just the word 'soup' conjures up an image of some horrible, chalky, dehydrated packet mix with reconstituted noodles. Trust New Yorkers to turn soup into a sacred science, though. My hands-down favourite soup joint is **Veselka** at **144 Second Avenue**. They make 5000 gallons of borscht every week. As a child I never ate my beetroot, but I could live on Veselka borscht. You might find TV host Jon Stewart here at 3am (it's 24-hour). I have the soup habit for life now, but also the Veselka cookbook: funnily enough, it's called *The Veselka Cookbook* and the authors are Tom Birchard and Natalie Danford. It's almost as good as a Veselka doggy bag.

Jessica Adams

Made in New York: Cult local brands

It's easy to assume that America took over the world years ago, and that you already know the brands New Yorkers love. One peek inside a supermarket or drugstore, though, and you will realise you have landed on another shopping planet. Fred Flintstone vitamins. Pubic hair dye. Need we continue? Even if you have found some of our favourite famous names elsewhere (like Victoria's Secret lingerie or Bond NYC perfume) their New York flagship stores offer more for less.

The scent of New York

These two fragrances occasionally make their way to the rest of the world, but we associate the witty scents at **Bond NYC** and **Demeter** with unique gift-buying sprees for friends, lovers or relatives. Unless they live here, they've probably never come across the joys of a perfume in honour of Andy Warhol – or indeed, a scent dedicated to chocolate brownies. These two unusual perfume houses represent a loud Noo Yawk sniff at the overly-serious and grand, historic French brands. They are upstarts, but honestly reflect life in the city today – and fulfill our dual requirements of looking fabulous and smelling lovely. Can you bottle the scent of fresh-mown grass in Central Park? Demeter has tried. What about filtering Wall Street or Chinatown?

Bond No.9 has attempted it. Our tip: buy online from Bond No.9 and pick up their famous $15 samples. If you love it, you can buy more at the source when you land.

Bond NYC, 9 Bond St
(near Lafayette St)
SUBWAY: **Broadway & Lafayette**
WEBSITE: **bondno9.com**

Demeter, Wholefoods Market,
10 Columbus Circle
SUBWAY: **59th St & Columbus Circle**
WEBSITE: **demeterfragrance.com**

Victoria's Secret

This legendary lingerie chain had us at *'Dim The Lights'*. This is the gentle instruction, engraved in pink copperplate, on every Victoria's Secret light switch, inside her many lavish change rooms. It's a feminine touch, typical of this uber-girlie New York store. Play with the dimmer switch, and you will see yourself just as your lover will, in the bedroom.

This is Bra Nirvana, also known as Bravarna. Assistants will troop off and find you any size, any colour, any shape. Part of the fun is that husbands and boyfriends are made to sit outside the change rooms, perched on faux Louis XIV chairs, pretending to read the *New York Times* while they salivate.

Beyond the bras and pants, this is also the place to find soft cotton yoga leggings, delicious silky pyjamas, chic dressing gowns, honeymoon negligees and chic, simple singlets. Victoria's Secret can do pure white waffle-weave or tarty lime leopardskin – whatever you want, honey.

Victoria's Secret
2333 Broadway
SUBWAY: 86th St
WEBSITE: victoriassecret.com

C.O.Bigelow aromatherapy and scented oils

Founded in 1838 in Greenwich Village, C.O.Bigelow sells the most beautifully packaged aromatherapy and fragrance oils in America. The oils are sold in small, chunky, shiny brown glass bottles with old-timey engraved labels and droppers in the lid. The fragrance oils are old-fashioned and earthy: amber, rose, cinnamon and orange.

Bigelow oils will last for six months if you patiently use the dropper. Holiday Goddess editors have found that a comforting way to feel at home, anywhere, is to select one fragrance and use it everywhere you sleep, at home or abroad. Run a shallow hot bath when you check into your hotel room and put some drops in and scented steam will soon alter the atmosphere in even the most sterile home.

If you love the scent, it becomes your own, and follows you around the world, personalising the most impersonal spaces so that they feel like home. The Bigelow lip balm is also pretty good: choose from ginger, violet and plum mint.

C.O.Bigelow, 414 Avenue of the Americas

NEAREST SUBWAY:
West 4th Street – Washington Square

WEBSITE: bigelowchemists.com

The best New York gifts

What are the best, archetypically New York gifts to take home?
Tiffany's turquoise passport covers, luggage tags and keyrings are hard
to beat. We know you can find Tiffany all over the world. However,
there is something about having Tiffany's gifts, blessed by the spirit of
Audrey Hepburn from *that* famous store that is very special. We've
found men love two things from New York – Hanes T-Shirts
(American's sexy, indestructible, number one brand) or proper New
York Mets baseball caps. Prince Harry, the Royals' most dedicated
baseball cap fan, wore one on a US trip. The classic 'NY' design.
If someone you know is dedicated to chocolate, it's hard to go past a
bag of Hershey's favourites. The Fifth Avenue bar, Mr Goodbar and
the strangely named Oh Henry!, said to be an homage to O.Henry,
the American writer.

TOP TEN

New York Brands

1. Tiffany
2. C.O.Bigelow fragrance oils
3. HUE Pantyhose
4. Hershey's Fifth Avenue bar
5. New York Mets baseball cap
6. Demeter perfume
7. Bond NYC perfume
8. Henri Bendel cosmetic bags
9. Bumble and Bumble hair care
10. Dean & DeLuca
    confectionery

We love the nightlife

If you have jetlag after flying into New York, don't worry. You can wake up at 3am and go straight out in your pyjamas, with a coat over the top – a surprisingly high number of New York door bitches will let you in. This is the city that invented strange wardrobes and anti-social hours. It's where The Ramones, Andy Warhol, Lou Reed, Madonna and Lady Gaga became famous.

There is no question about going home early in New York because, as frequent visitors know, you just don't have to. The cabs run all night and the food and drink never stops. Even the pigeons don't sleep.

You can happily destroy your hearing with live music. You can go clubbing. You can find a cinema showing an old Woody Allen classic (there is always one). And then there's Broadway – your best chance to see your favourite film and television actors live on stage.

For Broadway, do your research at *villagevoice.com* and *timeout.com*. And join the Playbill Club at *playbill.com* for generous discounts and inside information.

Alternative New York indie, punk and hip hop

If you happen to be in New York for the festival dubbed All Tomorrow's Parties, then just go there and forget any other gig. It's Indie Guitar Heaven and has been blessed by Lord Iggy Pop himself. (To organise your New York holiday around it, see *atpfestival.com*.)

Missing the festival? It would be hard to go wrong with almost any act put on by the Bowery Presents at *bowerypresents.com*. Their venues include Brooklyn Bowl, Terminal 5, The Bowery Ballroom, Musical Hall of Williamsburg and The Mercury Lounge. They put on gigs from hot acts like Two Door Cinema Club, and cult favourites like Wanda Jackson, Liz Phair, Wire, Neneh Cherry and Gang of Four.

The Brooklyn Bowl at **61 Wythe Avenue, Williamsburg, Brooklyn** is part of the Bowery Presents group. Snoop Dogg has played here. Afterwards, eat, drink or go bowling on one of several open lanes.

The mighty **Music Hall of Williamsburg** is in Williamsburg, Brooklyn – the hipster capital of America. People there are passionate about their guitars, and as a general rule, if it's playing in Williamsburg, it will be huge in 2015, or it *was* big in 1977.

The other great thing about Williamsburg is its convenience. It's right on the Bedford Avenue subway stop, ten minutes from Manhattan. The trains run late in Williamsburg, the taxis are plentiful and around $20 back to Manhattan, and the coffee and bagels are 24/7.

Holiday Goddess editors also love **The Greene Space** at **44 Charlton Street**, on the corner of Varick Street. It's where Elvis Costello played his entire last album. Expect intelligent artists, excellent wine, passionate fans and brilliant repartee. The Greene Space stages everything from Chinese toy piano superstars to excellent Pop + Politics nights. See *thegreenespace.org*.

A night at The Algonquin Hotel

Jessica Adams has worked on Bloomingdale's magazine as their fashion psychic and spends part of every year in New York.

If your favourite thing in the world is to stay up all night talking and drinking, then book a room at Dorothy Parker's favourite hotel. That way, you'll have full access to the Oak Room, the lobby lounge and the Blue Bar. You will also have full access to the Algonquin Hotel cat, Matilda.

I was actually dumped here, by my travel writer boyfriend. But I still love the place. It's where I corrected the proofs of my second novel, over a Bloody Mary. Everyone in the bar helped out – it's that kind of hotel. The Algonquin is always heaving with the chattiest writers, agents, editors and publishers, bewitched by the knowledge that this is where Miss Parker once held court.

I love everything about this hotel: the sweet little 'Do Not Disturb' signs; the old-fashioned all-American soap and shampoo; the fact that the boyfriend who dumped me ended up with my spectacular credit card bill (I blame Dorothy Parker's mischievous spirit for that).

It's quite a place. But if you're going to do The Algonquin the way Dorothy did it, check in for just one night so you can be carried upstairs afterwards, kicking your heels.

Jessica Adams

The Algonquin Hotel
59 West 44th St
SUBWAY: 42nd St & Bryant Park
WEBSITE: algonquinhotel.com

The Top of the Tower Bar: The Beekman Tower Hotel

From the outside, **The Beekman Tower Hotel** looks like a place which was glamorous thirty years ago, then forgotten. Inside, on the top floor, it's a revelation. Take a deep breath, push the elevator button, then walk into one of Manhattan's most intimate bars with stunning views over lit-up skyscrapers. A stylish literary agent we know has been taking her friends and clients here for years. The Top of the Tower makes you feel as if you are landing over New York in an extremely low-flying aircraft.

Even if the views might make you faint, though, the bill won't. That's why we always go back.

The Beekman Tower Hotel
49th & First Ave
SUBWAY: **Lexington Avenue & 53rd**
WEBSITE: **thebeekmanhotel.com**

The Apollo Theater

James Brown, Ella Fitzgerald, Billie Holiday, Stevie Wonder, Jimi Hendrix and Michael Jackson all launched their careers at The Apollo Theater. There are stars bearing their names on the pavement outside. Inside you'll find a lobby and staircase, which is wonderfully retro – all red carpet, mirrors and chandeliers.

To see a special performer here (like Smokey Robinson, who was recently in town) go on the mailing list at the website and book well ahead. To dine close by, visit Sylvia's Soul Food Restaurant (see page 221).

The Apollo Theater
253 West 125th Street, Harlem
SUBWAY: **125th Street**
WEBSITE: **apollotheater.org**

NEW YORK
231

The Campbell Apartment, Grand Central Station

Are you seeing a Broadway play? Walk to The Campbell Apartment for drinks. It's easy to find, because the entrance is on one side of Grand Central Station, facing Vanderbilt Avenue. It's pretend 13th century, which is what the owner requested. Somehow, though, it's totally New York, circa 1920. Once you're up the stairs, you'll find yourself in a softly lit, beautiful, old-fashioned space which was once the office of the eccentric trains tycoon John W. Campbell. Mr Campbell had a huge steel safe hidden behind one wall, which is now in the fireplace. Look up and you will see various coats of arms painted on the interior. Look across and you'll see lots of suits from Wall Street and a few locals on their first dates.

Dress nicely, even though it's gloomy in here; if you're too casual you won't fit in. The cocktails are retro, strong and delicious: try the Prohibition Punch.

When New York banned smoking indoors, some years ago, The Campbell Apartment was one of the only places in town where you could puff a cigar. That, too, has changed. But it's an enchanting place for a gossip.

The Campbell Apartment,
15 Vanderbilt Ave
Grand Central Station

SUBWAY: Grand Central

WEBSITE: hospitalityholdings.com

A New York story

It's amazing how many people are still frightened of going to New York. My grandmother never wanted to go. I blame bad 1980s cop shows for putting people off. But even on my first trip, aged 25, I have to admit I developed a dread of tomato ketchup. Muggers used it as a shock tactic before they took your bag, squirting you in the eyes with a spray of deadly Heinz. There were ketchup warning signs in every bank I walked into. I lived in constant fear of the red splat.

Even the locals were scared in the bad old days. My American agent bought her first apartment in Chelsea around that time and told me she used to line every window ledge with empty jam jars and bottles, so that she would be woken by the rattling the second a burglar tried to climb in. Now my agent has an apartment that has soared in value. And, thank god, the ketchup stays on the burgers.

I was here on 9/11 and saw the second plane hit the second tower. My apartment was two kilometres away. In the old New York there probably would have been anarchy. In the new New York there was stoic efficiency. The city has a calm heart these days.

I still remember my friend Emma (who saw the attacks with me) jumping straight on her bicycle and riding across town to give blood.

By the afternoon, there were hand-drawn posters on every shop window offering free back rubs for relief workers and cookies for rescue teams. The radio stations were urging people to check on pets who were home alone, in case their owners had been in the towers. Fundraising calendars kicked off.

The Mayor was shooing us back into the restaurants, the bars, the theatres. All of this within 24 hours of the biggest shock the city has ever experienced.

Did the terrorists terrify New York? Not in the least. It's a can-do city. They are scared of nothing.

This is what makes New York so different to Paris, London and Rome. In Paris, when something goes wrong, they roll their eyes. In London, they swear a lot. In Rome, their hands go up in the air. In New York, they already started working on the problem five minutes before you asked.

Got an issue, as the locals say? Then New Yorkers will sort it out for you. Test it yourself. Ask a local a question and no matter how busy they are (and they are always busy) the typical New Yorker will stop and give you a detailed answer, possibly with a hand-drawn diagram on the back of an envelope. There are a few exceptions, but those people won't be from New York.

On my last trip I asked my Brooklyn friend Felicity, a *Vogue* writer, about the thriftiest way to get from JFK airport to the city – as opposed to the eye-wateringly expensive cab I always seem to catch.

It took her a New York minute to respond: 'Hmm. Well – when you arrive at JFK, follow the signs to the AirTrain. This monorail costs $5 and you can add the fare to a Metrocard so you can start your public transport adventure early. From your JFK terminal, catch the AirTrain to Jamaica (which is actually in Queens). At the Jamaica station, transfer to the LIRR (Long Island Rail Road). The LIRR is not a part of the subway so you won't easily spot it on maps. At Jamaica catch a Penn Station-bound LIRR train to Manhattan. This is a 20-minute journey and costs $8.75. It's way quicker than the subway and cheaper than the Super Shuttle.'

She knew. And she saved me a fortune. But then, all New York women are in the know about everything. Taxi drivers tremble when they see them coming, because they know they are about to be ordered around, like Eisenhower's troops before D Day.

Some people think New Yorkers are too bossy by half. They know too much. Care too much. And also say too much. I really like it.

I once had dinner uptown with a woman who was in her 50s but looked about 30. After the waiter had cleared the plates she gave me the number of her cosmetic surgeon. I hadn't asked for it. And no, I wasn't offended. She was just being can-do.

New York is a fix-it city. It's where you can fix your hair, your teeth, or your soul (nearly every neighbourhood has a Tibetan Buddhist store or centre these days). Part of the native ingenuity comes from the ongoing battle for a good apartment. And a good man. Friends learn how to help friends. Everyone rolls her sleeves up and gets involved. In New York, initiative is queen. The famous impatience that characterises the city also makes people reluctant to wait for a problem to fix itself. It's the home of people power. It's where speed dating was invented.

I think my grandmother would like New York the way it is today. It's not exactly cuddly. There are too many guns for that. But it's a city that likes to help. It's the home of super-rich philanthropists and, thus, the best free art galleries, gardens, parks and museums in the world. On a street level, it's populated with people who just can't stop trying to make things better.

On my last trip there was an unexpected snowstorm. I was visiting a woman I hardly knew, gathering research for this book. Before I could protest, she had gone into her closet and dressed me. Burberry scarf. Big fake-fur hat. Thick gloves. Then she pushed me out of the door.

That's why I always go back.

Jessica Adams

Our seven wonders of New York

We're not going to force you up the Empire State Building (Those steps! Those crowds!). And we're not about to insist you visit Times Square. Instead, Holiday Goddess editors around the world have handpicked seven special experiences – our own seven wonders of New York. These are the things we love most about our city or remember fondly from our stays there years after.

Appearing on American television

The great thing about collecting free audience tickets for the TV shows taped in New York is the immortality it bestows. Somewhere in the world, at some point in time, you will always be on TV, as your live-taped show loops around the worldwide cable TV circuit.

Holiday Goddess editors and their friends have turned up on everything from David Letterman to Donahue this way and still see themselves, years later, wearing very old clothes, on obscure cable channels.

As with Broadway theatre tickets, you need to apply online months before you fly. And we know this is heinous, but we don't think it matters which show you actually get tickets for.

It's just that being part of a live studio audience is the cheesiest, most fun, most *American* thing you can do.

Ed Sullivan Theatre, 1697 Broadway, between W 53rd & 54th

SUBWAY: 7th Avenue & 53rd St

WEBSITE: cbs.com/late_night/late_show/tickets/

Walking Brooklyn Bridge

Karen Moline is the bestselling author of *Lunch* and *Belladonna* and is a longtime New York journalist, novelist, writer and editor.

Summer is always a wonderful time to visit New York with all sorts of outdoor fun, freed from the burden of heavy winter coats and boots. But there is one huge downside – the weather stinks! The air-conditioning may be blasting everywhere, but you still have to go to your destinations when the humidity curls the straightest hair and the pollution is so rank you can barely breathe.

On such days, there is one place to go (apart from the Penguin House at the Central Park Zoo). It's the exact mid-point of the footpath on the Brooklyn Bridge. One of the Seven Wonders of New York.

The main span of the bridge is 486.3 metres, but as you wipe the sweat away during your walk there, feel free to console yourself about the effect on your quads and glutes.

It's worth it once you reach the middle of the span. Face south and you'll have the stunning vista of lower Manhattan to your right, Brooklyn Heights to your left, and the Statue of Liberty and the Verrazano-Narrows Bridge shimmering in the distance.

The sound of the cars and East River below you and the wind whipping above you melt into a sort of instantly soothing white noise. It is one of those perfect spots where you can be surrounded by throngs of people in the city, yet feel utterly, blissfully serene. And cooler.

Karen Moline

The Brooklyn Bridge promenade begins in City Hall Park.

SUBWAY: Brooklyn Bridge – City Hall

Dog watching

A well-known New York bank ran posters showing a sweet Boston terrier with the legend: 'Bark if you love your bank'. The idea being that you were free to take your dog inside (perhaps as long as you were borrowing scads of money). This is a case of In Dog We Trust, you might say, as pooches humanise the place. In Manhattan, they pop out of handbags and can also be found being fluffed with towels at special spas. In a city which is short on children, they often act as substitutes. Monthly Bagel Barks bring dog owners together in Central Park which is also the best place for dog watching.

There are hundreds of them here, often leashed in large groups, strapped to the hands of pro dog walkers. It's worth stopping by to check out the action at the many fenced-in 'corrals' where dogs of all shapes, sizes, breeds and social groups and their owners hang out.

Central Park

SUBWAY: 5th Ave & 59th St

Professional makeovers

New York is the city of cosmetic surgery (try not to do a double-take as you see all the plastic fantastics walking past). It is, however, also the world capital of cosmetics. Professional make-up artists who normally work with models, big beauty houses and Hollywood are hired by major department stores here (like Saks Fifth Avenue) to promote brands like Nars, Bobbi Brown, MAC and Laura Mercier.

Don't feel self-conscious as you perch on a stool while the magic happens – this is New York and you're anonymous. And the guru who transforms you may also have worked with Julia Roberts.

Saks, 611 Fifth Ave

SUBWAY: 47th–50th St & Rockefeller Center

WEBSITE: saksfifthavenue.com

The New York Public Library lions

Two things you might not know about the huge stone lions outside the New York Public Library. One, they are nicknamed Patience and Fortitude, names they acquired in the Great Depression. (Patience is on the left, Fortitude is on the right.) Two, this is the best meeting spot ever, because even the most clueless person can find it – and because there is so much to read inside, should anyone be late.

Seinfeld fans will remember that this is where Cosmo Kramer once dated a librarian and Jerry had a long-overdue book. And of course where Audrey Hepburn and George Peppard misbehaved in *Breakfast at Tiffany's*.

New York Public Library
5th Ave & 42nd St
SUBWAY: 42nd St & Bryant Park

The Mini Madonna Museum of Manhattan

Several Holiday Goddess editors have been fortunate enough to see what we've nicknamed the Mini Madonna Museum of Manhattan.

It lies inside tour guide Karolyn Ford's private apartment. She was Madonna's neighbour – and when Madge moved out, Karolyn inherited her possessions.

When Madonna left Karolyn's building, she gave her old friend a selection of ornaments, furniture – and even a half-empty bottle of Guerlain perfume.

The rest Karolyn sold at Sotheby's, with Madonna's blessing. All that remains lies in her sitting room, which we believe is truly the Seventh Wonder of New York. Especially if you are blessed with a quick spray of the historic perfume on the way out.

If you are very lucky, Karolyn will organise a private New York tour for you and your friends, which includes the best of NYC shopping. To book a tour with Karolyn Ford, visit *newyorkcitytourguides.com*.

Inside the Statue of Liberty's head

For the first time in history the Statue of Liberty closed interior access after the 9/11 terrorist attacks of 2001. On 4 July 2009, the crown reopened, but only for 15% of the park's 14,000 daily visitors. You have a better chance of being struck by lightning.

Despite terrible odds, I got lucky, although it was during peak tourist season. When my daughter and I joined the long ticket line at Battery Park ferries to Liberty depart, a miracle occurred:

A tourist behind us stopped a security guard. 'Can I get a refund for two tickets?'

'No, sorry.' Seeing the man's voucher, the guard's eyes widened. 'Those tickets are worth their weight in gold.'

Eureka! Reserve Crown Tickets! The crown jewels of Statue of Liberty tours ... and with a reserve time in 20 minutes! I thrust $40 at the man before someone could beat me to it, then ran past the huddled masses to the dock. After a one-mile cruise we stepped onto Liberty Island and into the maximum security checkpoint for golden ticket holders.

Outside it was a zoo, but inside it was bliss. The pedestal museum holds treasures: the original torch, sculptor Frédéric Auguste Bartholdi's tools, and giant models of Lady Liberty's lips, feet and ears.

The 360-degree observation deck – with only a few other VIP Willy Wonkas around – provides spectacular views of the harbour, skyline, and general admission sardines below. The grand finale? Climbing inside Liberty's head to peer through the crown's 25 windows – we did it during a storm, while nature composed a soundtrack of thunderstorm crackles and booms. 'Does the Statue ever get struck by lightning?' I wondered aloud. 'Several times a year,' nodded a Park Ranger. 'It's steel and copper, tall as a 22-storey building, sitting alone on an island. It's the perfect lighting rod.'

Suddenly realising our Reserve Crown tickets also include the bonus Reserve Electrocution Experience, we dashed down 354 steps, and got rain-drenched sloshing to the refuge of our return ferry. On second thought ... 'Lighting ever strike these ferries?' 'Yeah,' the boatman shrugged. 'Some light show though, ain't it? No extra charge.'

Vicki Arkoff

To secure a ticket (without Vicki Arkoff's luck) book months ahead, online, for Reserve with Crown or Reserve with Pedestal Museum tickets at *statuecruises.com*.

Spas, sanctuaries, sacred spaces

Far away from the long *beeeeee* of New York traffic, with a little help from us you can find many hidden gardens, beautiful waterfalls, huge cathedrals and simple meditation spaces. New York is also home to some of the most luxurious spas in the world. You can find bliss here, or you can find Bliss here. We call it She Time.

Wondrous New York waterfalls

I have lived in New York for years, but **Greenacre Park** still took me by surprise. The park is a tiny, privately endowed oasis. It is astonishingly lush, full of honey locust trees, and often empty when it's not lunchtime. Sit by the immense waterfall and you will not believe you are still in Manhattan.

After that magical discovery, I became determined to find more waterfalls in the city. Although the entire city is surrounded by water, seeing a waterfall while bustling around in the concrete jungle is something out of the ordinary.

Paley Park is between Madison and Fifth Avenues. It's almost as lovely as Greenacre Park but better known. The waterfall here is 20-feet high, across the entire back wall. It cools the air and provides just enough white noise to drown out the honking taxis.

Karen Moline

Greenacre Park, 217 East 51st St

SUBWAY: 51st St

Paley Park, 3 E 53rd St, between Madison & 5th Ave

SUBWAY: 5th Ave & 53rd St

New York's secret children's water park

Here is a special place for children. **Teardrop Park** lies in the middle of an apartment complex in Battery Park City. It is one of my young son's favourite hidey-holes and he dubbed it the coolest water park in Manhattan. The water features are turned on every summer, and there's a long, straight slide for children.

Parents can sit with their feet dangling in the water to cool off while the kids run around – it's heaven.

Karen Moline

Teardrop Park
Battery Park City,
between Murray & Warren St

SUBWAY: Chambers Street

Perfect for picnic hampers

Taking a picnic? Central Park Waterfalls lie on the northwest corner of Central Park. Look for a stream called the Loch. There is no sea monster, but there are two lovely waterfalls.

The first is in the area called the Ravine, close to the West 102nd Street Transverse road, and is the steepest cascade in the Park. The second is a few blocks away in the North Woods, and tumbles 14 feet down into a pool.

Central Park Waterfalls Between West 101st & 105th St

SUBWAY: **103rd St**

Sushi in a Japanese garden

Buying sushi-to-go? The Japanese Hill-and-Pond Garden Waterfalls lie in the Brooklyn Botanic Garden. It is exquisite in the spring when the cherry trees are in blossom, but almost as spectacular on a foggy, gloomy day when its serene beauty will transport you right out of the city.

Brooklyn Botanic Garden 1000 Washington Avenue, Brooklyn

SUBWAY: **Botanic Garden**

Three luxurious $100 spas

The Spa at Chelsea Piers

The Spa at Chelsea Piers is on the water, with stunning views of the boats on the Hudson River. It is steps away from the subway and the foodies' favourite, Chelsea Market (see page 217). Try the Tibetan Foot Revival or Salt Body Polish. Bring photo ID to get in.

Pier 60, Chelsea Piers, West Side Highway near 23rd St
SUBWAY: **14th St & 8th Ave**
WEBSITE: **chelseapiers.com**

Bliss Soho

Bliss is the funky, modern spa which made the oxygen facial famous. (They trademarked it – ask for the Oxygen Blast and see for yourself.) The Shopper's Delight Leg Massage is fantastic if you have been pounding Fifth Avenue.

Bliss, 568 Broadway
SUBWAY: **Prince St**
WEBSITE: **blissworld.com**

The Pensinula Spa by Espa

The 30-Minute Express Treatment involves a neck, shoulder and back massage, or a scalp massage at the luxurious Pensinula Hotel overlooking Fifth Avenue. Enjoy this sample of what The Pensinula offers: a few hours in a private suite is nearly $2000.

Peninsula Hotel
700 5th Ave at 55th St
SUBWAY: **5th Ave**
WEBSITE: **peninsula.com**

Five favourite retreats in NYC

Pip Cummings lives in New York, and her career adventures include time at the *Sydney Morning Herald* and *Mindfood* magazine. These are her favourite NYC retreats.

The Lotus Garden at **West 97th Street (between Broadway & West End Avenue):** Established in 1983, this community garden on the roof of an Upper West Side garage is a unique urban oasis, with plots and fish ponds maintained by 28 families and other volunteers. You can visit on Sunday afternoons from April until November. Visit *thelotusgarden.org*.

New York Earth Room at **141 Wooster Street:** Take in the smell of earth, the simplicity and the quiet, at this indoor installation by Walter De Maria of 127,300 kilos of soil, installed in 1977. Bill Dilworth, who has cared for the room for more than 20 years, says its unchanging nature is 'a great solace' in Manhattan. Visit *diaart.org*.

St Luke in the Fields' gardens at **487 Hudson St:** In the heart of Greenwich Village, St Luke's (1821) has cultivated a walled sanctuary; more than three acres of sun-soaked walks, lawns and flora. Visit *stlukeinthefields.org*.

The Elevated Acre at **55 Water Street (between Old Slip & Broad Streets):** Visit this hidden garden in the financial district to watch the sun rise or enjoy a quiet bag lunch, and views of the East River, Ellis Island, Brooklyn Bridge, South Street Seaport and Brooklyn Heights. Visit *elevatedacre.com*.

The Open Center Meditation Room at **22 East 30th Street (between Madison Avenue & Fifth Avenue):** Take 20 minutes out of the madness of midtown to enjoy the still and quiet of this free meditation room, housed in a healing centre. Visit *opencenter.org*.

St Patrick's Cathedral

St Patrick's is one of the largest Catholic cathedrals in the US. It's also one of New York's most sacred spaces, but anyone can walk in. On my first visit, I found myself at a burial service for the woman who founded La MaMa theatre company. It felt wrong, but it also felt right: I lit a candle and paid my respects along with everyone else.

The cathedral tells you everything you need to know about New York life. Andy Warhol was honoured here, but so was baseball great Joe DiMaggio. The Saint Michael and Saint Louis altar was designed by Tiffany & Co. It's hard to think of another place in the city which combines that classic Manhattan mix of art, baseball and shopping. It's not holy-holy inside St Patrick's. But it's very special, and it reflects the city and its people as authentically as Westminster Abbey reflects London.

Everyone knows about the 9/11 memorial at Ground Zero. But few people know that one of its biggest heroes was also honoured here.

His name was Patrick too – Captain Patrick J. Brown. On September 11, 2001, he and eleven of his men from Ladder 3 on East 13th Street, in the East Village, were among the first firefighters to arrive at the Twin Towers.

He was an unusual man. Not only famously brave and much-awarded, but also a fan of yoga. He was often written up in the press as one of Manhattan's most eligible bachelors, and even dated one of our own Holiday Goddess editors.

I'm pretty sure that when I was downtown on 9/11, I saw Patrick Brown's fire truck driving straight towards the towers. At the time I paid it no attention. I didn't realise that he and eleven other firefighters were undoubtedly going to their death.

It's almost impossible to visit Manhattan without thinking about the attacks on the Twin Towers – just going through airport security at JFK will remind you of just how much that incident shook New York to its core. I'm not sure I will ever go to the Ground Zero memorial. But I always stop by at St Patrick's Cathedral to remember the firefighters when I'm here. It's believed Patrick was working on the 40th floor of the North Tower when it fell. His ashes are scattered in Central Park. If you're close by, light a candle.

Jessica Adams

St Patrick's Cathedral
5th Avenue & 50th Street

We heart New York art

If you only see one painting in New York, make it a painting at the Metropolitan Museum of Art – and go at night. Editor, journalist and author **Susan Wyndham** lived in Manhattan for years. This is her insider advice.

Friday night viewing at the Met is no secret, but when I lived in New York, so few people seemed to know, that it felt like a private club. I would meet my husband in the softly lit lobby with its extravagant flower arrangements while music cascaded from a chamber orchestra or jazz band on the balcony. As well as wine and beer the bar served Metropolitan Martinis and Museum Mojitos.

In summer we climbed to the rooftop sculpture garden for a drink looking over the trees of Central Park. Soothed and proprietorial, we explored a new exhibition or strolled through our most-loved rooms. Often we headed for the small, dim alcoves lined with Renaissance paintings from Siena. We are not the only tourists in love with the Tuscan town but we had the distinctive gold- and pink-tinted art to ourselves. Emerging later from the Medieval or Egyptian halls back into the lobby was like being ejected from a time machine.

The Met shop sold postcards and treasures such as Minoan-style earrings. While I shopped, my husband scoured the ground outside for coloured metal entry badges to add to his collection.

After that, we often walked down Fifth Avenue to Quatorze Bis, a French bistro on East 79th Street, where the steak-frites is another dependable work of art.

Susan Wyndham

By day, **Pip Cummings** finds the Wrightsman Galleries inside the Metropolitan Museum of Art hard to leave.

Every woman needs to find her quiet place in New York.

My own oasis of calm in central New York is an 18th century bedroom, deep inside a 19th century building on sophisticated Fifth Avenue, where it's deeply tempting to climb up on the high bed, pull the heavy coverlet over me, draw the curtains around and close my eyes against the demands of the day for an hour or so.

In the heart of the Metropolitan Museum of Art, at 1000 Fifth Avenue, you will find the Wrightsman Galleries for French Decorative Arts. It is a sexy space, in an unhurried fashion. Furnishings from this period, during the reigns of Louis XV and XVI, were designed to arouse and seduce.

The hushed and instant calm of these rooms owes a great deal to their lighting (or lack of it). Some are so dimly lit it will take a moment for your eyes to adjust. When they eventually do, wonders are revealed: intricately hand-worked textiles; fine, polished furniture; exquisite tiny objects that might have just been absentmindedly placed there moments before by the room's ghostly inhabitants – all as if by candlelight.

Pip Cummings

The Metropolitan Museum of Art, 5th Ave at 82nd St

SUBWAY: 5th Ave

WEBSITE: metmuseum.org

NEW YORK
249

It's personal: heartfelt New York art

It's easy to visit New York in search of the famous artists – from Andy
Warhol to Jackson Pollock. The legends of 2050 are working hard in
Manhattan today, though. Theresa Byrnes is one of them. She paints
from her wheelchair, and goes almost-naked for her performance art
in the city. She has big opinions on everything from the War on Terror
to Wall Street. She also paints sparrows, cats and children quite
beautifully. Hollywood collects her and you can too – she is a most
accessible artist. She was named Young Australian of the Year (she is
originally from Sydney) for helping to raise $1 million for research into
her condition. Saatchi & Saatchi love her too. If you're in NY and she's
exhibiting or performing, go see!

Watch our video postcard of Theresa Byrnes, created by Holiday
Goddess TV editor Peter Clarke, at *holidaygoddess.com*.

Jessica Adams

The unforgettable Guggenheim

Holiday Goddess editor **Anneli Knight** is a newspaper journalist and the author of *Flirting with Finance*. This is her personal encounter with the Guggenheim.

'I only spent two days in New York on holiday – wandering through, with a friend of a friend, both on our way to other places. Our adventures took us to the Guggenheim – The Solomon R. Guggenheim Museum – a place that spirals into your memory. It was ten years later that I received this message from him:

> August 20: *When random people ask me what my favourite day was – it is a hard question to answer (probably because as an accountant and psychologist, my first inclination is to lie). However, the first thing I think of is the Guggenheim on Fifth Avenue, and somehow making you laugh and hold my hand.*

I felt such a stirring of memories at his message. This was my reply:

> August 21: *New York, New York. I feel like I'm watching our day on a cinema screen. It's amazing how memory and imagination can play. Here's a toast to the Guggenheim – I've never been back to New York since!*

In the year that followed this electronic exchange, we had no other. And last month I went to his funeral: a mysterious failure of his heart. Amid a city of spinning insomnia, it is those quixotic images at the Guggenheim – the soft spiral staircase, a window to the sky, an imprint of cream on shadow on white on light – that evoke a wistful epitaph.'

The Guggenheim, 1071 5th Ave
SUBWAY: 86th Street
WEBSITE: guggenheim.org

Yoko Ono's New York

Alana Hunt is an artist and writer based in India and Australia.

When I first visited New York City, Yoko Ono (now over 70 years of age) was everywhere! And she still is.

Yoko is one of the most complex public figures of the last 60 years. As a migrant, classical musician, aristocratic daughter, rebel, pioneering conceptual artist, lover, poet, widow, rocker, peace activist and mother, any visit to New York would be incomplete without Yoko on the agenda.

Her work pops up frequently here, at the Whitney, Guggenheim and MoMA but it can also be seen at some of the smaller contemporary art spaces around the city.

I was lucky enough to place a personal wish on Yoko's Wish Tree as part of the Garden Party exhibition and performance project that took place at Deitch Projects in Soho. At Printed Matter in Chelsea, you can pick up a Yoko piece to suit any budget. Try 'imagine peace' buttons for $1 or the $3000 limited-edition *Fly* box set containing artificial flies with cards inscribed, 'I found this fly and thought of you'.

Across from the Dakota apartments in Central Park, where Yoko, John Lennon and their son Sean used to walk, 2.5 acres of land in the shape of a tear drop has been designated as an official 'quiet zone' in memory of Yoko's late husband, and former Beatle, John. Known as Strawberry Fields, the area is blossoming with plants contributed by 121 different countries, an Italian mosaic spelling out the word 'imagine', and an unofficial mayor. His name is Gary and he leads visitors through a unique, if eccentric, tour of the site.

Yoko is a woman who moves with the times, effortlessly. She has a regular Friday twinterview session on Twitter and in 2010 her Plastic Ono Band jammed with, among others, Iggy Pop, Perry Farrell, Vincent Gallo – and Lady Gaga on top of a grand piano.

Alana Hunt

WEBSITE:
imaginepeace.com
printedmatter.org

Vintage and markets

Lily Evans has worked on shoots for international editions of *Vogue* and as an assistant on catwalk shows for Victoria's Secret, which makes her our go-to person for the best inside information on New York's vintage stores and markets.

Wearing vintage means never walking into a party wearing the same dress as somebody else. Vintage clothing is fun, fashionable and often very cheap.

Living in New York there is so much choice but I have two favorite vintage shops.

Malin's is in the heart of Brooklyn's hipster hotspot, Williamsburg. The owner and buyer, Malin Landaeus, has superb taste and is often in the store to style you.

When she's not, however, she has a troop of salesgirls who look more like stunning European models and add to the beautiful aesthetic of the place.

Often wearing stock from the shop floor, they act as moving mannequins – friendly ones, who will invite you to sit on the couch and chat for hours or suggest looks for you to try when you're stuck. And all the while you're thinking, 'I want to look like you.'

It's a very good sales strategy.

This boutique is cosily cramped, but comfortable, with Nick Cave's voice seducing from a hidden speaker. On Sundays they serve tea and cakes to help you mull over the '90s swing dress or '80s high-rise swimsuit.

The stock is divided into 'trends' – 'circus' and 'goth' are two of my favourites – which transforms the boutique into a huge dressing-up box and the easy atmosphere encourages you to play dress-ups all day. The clothes are mid-priced but they are all in good condition.

Although you can imagine the history of the garment and who wore it, you won't find the smell to match its past. My best find from Malin's is a floor-length black dress with sheer black arms, very Morticia Addams, for $70.

The second store is the opposite end of the vintage-shopping spectrum. **Urban Jungle** is a Brooklyn warehouse, far out in Bushwick but well worth the trip. Here, you don't shop; you dig, scoop, shovel and sift through mounds of clothes, hung in loose categories.

You may have to hold your nose at times and you might discover an ominous stain or slight rip here or there, but the selection is incredible. This is *the* vintage source: buyers from every elite Manhattan vintage boutiques come here to sift through the unedited second-hand stock. So you'll feel extra smug when you find that perfect-fitting '50s dress for $5 – because if a buyer had found it first they would have slapped a price tag on it for twenty times that price before rushing it across the East River and into their store.

This warehouse is usually uncomfortably humid with loud reggaeton blasting overhead but the treasures I have found are worth it – from a pretty embroidered prairie dress, to a black mohair oversized cardigan with pink paisley swirls, to a white lace wedding dress (just in case), all under $10. A pair of perfect Ferragamo pumps were half that.

It's the kind of secret no one wants to let out, but if you love vintage as much as I do, you deserve to know.

Lily Evans

The Brooklyn Flea

The Brooklyn Flea is a huge vintage and retro market held all year round, with no fleas whatsoever. Spend the morning here, then enjoy a lobster roll from the Red Hook Lobster Pound for lunch.

There are genuine collectors' bargains here, like the black-and-white 1970s Hollywood film stills we found for $5 which had come straight from someone's filing cabinet.

The usual suspects are here, if you are passionate about vintage clothing. Quirky 1950s tourist scarves, decorated with lovely old prints of Paris or even Australia. Crocodile-skin handbags. Beautiful 1970s loafers. What we really wanted, though, were the old red Hunter wellies, the chosen cult footwear of any hipster at a music festival.

Around half the stock is well under $50, including the Fez hat we saw. You'll pay more for second-hand Tiffany's jewellery, 1960s spectacles or the occasional leopardskin coat.

The Brooklyn Flea
176 Lafayette Ave

SUBWAY: **Clinton & Washington Ave**

WEBSITE: **brooklynflea.com**

Beacon's Closet, Williamsburg

Holiday Goddess editors agree – Beacon's Closet has the largest selection of beautiful second-hand clothes, shoes and bags in New York, at the lowest prices, in the best condition.

Beacon's Closet buys, sells and trades vintage and modern clothing. When you walk in, you'll see locals dragging wheelie suitcases behind them into the back section, where some extremely fussy buyers pick and choose.

This choosiness means there is no rubbish at Beacon's Closet. Instead, you'll find wonderful one-off shoes in almost every colour and style, from the towering heels of 2005 to the two-tone funky loafers of 1973 that Linda McCartney would have worn on tour with Wings, and Stella McCartney would probably love now.

Beacon's Closet also makes room for 1960s dress shoes, stitched in faux leopardskin silk – and solid 1990s Yves St Laurent heels. The prices vary accordingly but you can easily walk out of here with change from $50.

The best buys are American labels because they are so plentiful – like Donna Karan. There are plenty of unknown labels under $25, though. We found a 100% cashmere cardigan at that price, and a beautiful hand-beaded chinoiserie jacket. We *purred*.

Beacon's Closet
88 North 11th St, Williamsburg
SUBWAY: Bedford Ave
WEBSITE: beaconscloset.com

Our favourite daycation: Connecticut

One of our favourite daycations away from the madness of Manhattan is Connecticut, which has something for every woman. Holiday Goddess editor and US-based travel writer **Julie Moline** suggests you begin by catching the train to Fairfield County. At the very least, go here for the Glass House, one of the world's strangest and most stunning buildings. The house is almost wholly transparent and completely public: its architect Philip Johnson, although undoubtedly a genius, is not someone we would have ever wanted to spend the night with.

Visiting The Glass House, Connecticut

The Glass House offers tours between May and December, but you need to book months ahead online at *philipjohnsonglasshouse.org*.

It was declared a National Trust Historic site in 1997, almost 50 years after Philip Johnson created it. Catch the train to the Metro North stop in New Canaan, on the New Haven line, from Grand Central Terminal in Manhattan.

Fairfield County

Fairfield County, in southwestern Connecticut, has long been a haven for artists, tycoons, and celebrities seeking serenity over scrutiny. It is quintessential New England here, with listed buildings that date back to the colonial era, and all the accoutrements you'd expect from a place that caters to the uberwealthy: estates galore, fabulous shopping, superb restaurants and all sorts of interesting ways – cultural, sportive and otherwise – to amuse oneself.

But for day trippers, the biggest draw might be the jaw-dropping beauty. There are sandy beaches and salt marshes here, rolling hills and forest preserves. Fairfield County is in stark contrast to the vertical drama of Manhattan. Here the aesthetic is all about open spaces, the lush countryside, and the wide swathe of coastline.

If the white clapboard churches and pristine village greens look familiar, it may be because you've seen them in a film – many major motion pictures have been shot in the towns and villages here. This is also an easy getaway, between 35–75 miles (or 55–120 kms) from New York City and served by a frequent rail service. A few of the attractions listed below are within walking distance of the train station although you may also need to use the local taxi service to travel between them. The great thing about Fairfield is that it has something for every woman.

The water lover's escape

In summer, take a cruise from Norwalk to Sheffield Island (accessible only by boat) for a traditional lobster bake and a tour of the historic lighthouse. In any season, check out South Norwalk's historic maritime district, which is filled with foundries and factories converted into coffeehouses, galleries and restaurants.

The beachcombing is lovely at Short Beach, Long Beach or Point No Point, all in Stratford. In Westport, Sherwood Island State Park has wooded nature trails and a wide strand with the Manhattan skyline as a backdrop.

The horse lover's day out
Darien's week-long Ox Ridge Hunt Club's Charity Horse Show is held every June and is recognised as one of the top five horse shows in the nation. If you are in New York then, catch the train and come over. It's a fashion event as well as an equestrian one.

The foodie's fantasy
The villages of Easton and Monroe are ringed with farms; go for hayrides, corn mazes, pick-your-own produce, maple sugaring and strawberry and apple festivals in May and October, respectively.

The nature lover's nirvana
The Connecticut Audubon Society's Birdcraft Museum and Sanctuary in Fairfield is wonderful. And if you do go to Fairfield, you can't miss a local treasure: the Super Duper Weenie stand, where the hot dogs and condiments are made by a chef trained at the Culinary Institute of America. Even fast food is almost natural here.

The historian's holiday
The New Canaan Historical Society runs a cluster of five mini-museums inside restored buildings; the Bush-Holley House, a listed building in Cos Cob, is one of the first American Impressionist colonies. My personal favorite is the 62-room Lockwood-Mathews Mansion in Norwalk, for the Victoriana run amok.

Music lovers

If you are in New York in July, the perfect way to celebrate Independence Day in America is to head to Bridgeport's Seaside Park, where the local symphony performs Tchaikovsky's *1812 Overture* after dark, and fireworks and cannon blasts are timed to the music.

Architecture fans

If I only had a single afternoon in Connecticut, my number one pick would be the Glass House, the former residence and modernist masterpiece of architect Philip Johnson. Tours of the property, which also includes an underground painting gallery, begin and end at the New Canaan Visitor Center, conveniently adjacent to the train station.

Julie Moline

Playlists and downloads

When we think of New York, we always picture the city with a jazz soundtrack from Woody Allen. If you're in Manhattan on a Monday night, you can still see Allen playing at the Carlyle Hotel. Can't make the gig? Download our NYC jazz podcast instead. **James Williams** and **Justin Tabari** have created a complimentary jazz sampler for your flight at *lifestylejazz.com/nyc*.

James and Justin are Holiday Goddess editors who have also created one of the fastest-growing podcast websites in the world: Lifestyle PodNetwork at *lifestylepodnetwork.com*. This is their selection of the best free New York podcasts.

The Bowery Boys

theboweryboys.blogspot.com

The Bowery Boys are Greg Young and Tom Meyers, who have lived in New York for over fifteen years. As you listen, they will tell you about the landscapes, the buildings and the landmarks of the city, now and then. One of the best features of this podcast is the enhanced function which allows you to split the episode into chapters. That way you can jump through any episode and flick back to your favourites.

Revel in New York

revelinnewyork.com/blog

Think New York City meets *Twin Peaks* for this vodcast (video podcast). Revel In New York gives you a different view of Manhattan, Brooklyn and beyond – through the eyes of the locals. Listen and you will be introduced to writers, artists, chefs, musicians and other intriguing individuals who exist on the fringes in New York City.

Made in New York

nyc.gov/html/film/html/news/podcast_main.shtml

Seinfeld or *Sex and the City*? Woody Allen or *Friends*? The Made in New York podcast from the Mayor's Office of Film, Theatre and Broadcasting is something else. This podcast consists of two hour-long tours that walk you through key film and television locations in lower Manhattan. The tours are designed to flow together so you can enjoy them back-to-back if you wish.

The New York Times Popcast

nytimes.com/ref/multimedia/podcasts.htm

The New York Times Popcast is a weekly report on new music. Host Ben Sisario is joined by *New York Times* music critics delivering news and reviews. It's a great way to discover new tracks to download on iTunes, or to buy in-store. The Popcast will give you a big shot of in-flight entertainment for your iPod on the flight and maybe a shopping list for when you touch down.

New York Insider TV

newyorkinsider.tv

Hosted by ex-*Town and Country* reporter Thomas P Farley, New York Insider TV is a great vodcast that reports from exclusive events in Manhattan and The Hamptons. You'll be given an insider's glimpse of black-tie galas, film festivals, fashion shows and private parties. You can even settle back with a cocktail to watch the show and the recipes are all on the website! Holiday Goddess editors' favourite episode? The vodcast featuring Prince Harry playing a charity polo match at Governor's Island.

Valence
Die
Montlimart
Embrun
Gap
Oranges
Auignon
Aix
Toulon
Nice
R DE FRANCE
MER DE
Florence
Pisa
Bologne
Destroit
hele de .40. grandes
ues de france de 3000.
s geo. Chacune
P Cento

Rome

Ciao Bella! Welcome to Rome.
It was built for romantics ...

There are three different kinds of Rome. One belongs to Julius Caesar. Another is all about the popes. The third version revolves around cappuccino, Pucci and Vespas and stopped in the 1960s. All three kinds of Rome are within walking distance of each other. Thus, you can stroll 200 metres and skip 2000 years. Rome is where the clocks stopped. The underwear still hangs on washing lines above balconies and the nuns still wear sandals. The noses on the statues may be missing, but everything else remains intact.

Before you go

Rome looks like a lot of very old stone, unless you do some holiday homework. Without some leisurely background reading on the plane, it can seem like meaningless grandeur. You have to know Rome's soul to love her. And her soul is either pagan (the gods and goddesses of Ancient Rome) or Catholic (angels and saints).

- The eternal religion in Rome is style. Leave your trainers at home. Do as the Romans do – they wear endless variations on the classic Gucci loafer or J.P. Tod car shoe. It has to be leather, polished and flat. Be warned – the locals will look you up and down.
- To avoid the classic overwhelm that affects all visitors, single out small aspects of something vast (like the Sistine Chapel) to focus on when you arrive. Or find your favourite angel, saint, god or goddess, then pursue them through the city.
- For a fast update and brilliant practical advice before you go, the best Rome blogs are *roninrome.com* and *blogdolcevita.com*.

When in Rome ... expect miracles

Romans from pagan times to the Vatican have always believed in an invisible world where miracles are a perfectly normal part of life. Before you go, expect your own miracle, because the city is entirely built on them. This is not a place for tourists – it's for converts. It's for anyone who longs to be changed, on some level, by the most powerful and mysterious city in the world. You can't walk one mile in Rome without seeing a fervent request for a blessing, or heartfelt thanks for a blessing bestowed. It's where men kiss the cross before leaving church – and where an entire empire was built on a devout faith in a god called Jupiter. One of our favourite actors and writers, **Noah Taylor**, believes he was changed just by being in Rome too:

To say Rome saved my life is a bit of an exaggeration, but only a bit of one. It certainly changed me, instantly and forever; my chemical wedding by the banks of the Tiber; my miraculous transformation from sullen joyless nihilist dirtbag to ... er ... joyful ... nihilist dirtbag? It changed me okay? Geez ...

Some fragmentary memories:
- Clinging for dear life to the warm fleshy body of a belladonna, on her clapped-out Vespa, as we sped through three lanes of traffic – all of it Italian!
- Being slapped in the face by the man mountain manager of the pensione for smoking (after being warned not to), then having the other cheek tenderly pinched.
- Jumping into the Fontana di Trevi (a bit of a no-no apparently) in a pathetically gallant attempt to retrieve a girl's ring. I did – just before the Cabeneri told me to hop it.

Despite this, they seemed to understand it was pathetic gallantry, not just splashing around like a dickhead. I am a gallant dickhead, if nothing else …

- Nuns looking at some very plain brown tights in the window of a department store for nuns and priests. It made me a little sad. Nuns are kind of considered bad luck in Rome, and my more superstitious local friends had warned me to touch metal if I saw one. So I did. The love/hate relationship with the Vatican in Italy is a mind-bender.

- Complaining to the concierge at the (charming beyond words) Hotel Locarno about the mosquitoes – and being given a rolled-up newspaper and a deadpan stare.

- Watching women on scooters and girls walking by, and old ladies shuffling along. Oh them belladonnas.

- Discovering the rather humble Basilica Di Santa Cecilia in Trastevere (my local as it were) actually contained a bejewelled crypt, so beautiful it could make you cry blood! (Although it was just tears really.)

- Listening to nuns singing something ancient and beautiful. Cecilia, an early Christian, is the patron saint of music. She was beheaded by the Romans for refusing to renounce her faith and kept on singing after the blade severed her head from neck … I think.

- I also remember couples fucking here and there in the hills and parks on summer evenings. The young mostly live at home so it's a necessity rather than the 'vice anglais' as it's known on the continent.

- Sitting on the Isle di Tiberini staring at the swollen waters and thinking of nice ankles I have known.

- Watching my friend try to chat up some poor innocent donna on the very spot poor old Caesar got it in the back.

In a way that's Rome in a nutshell too. Blood, sex, friendship, birth, death, life ... but mostly life.

Walk the streets of Rome, just walk. Leave your maps (if anyone uses maps anymore) and just get lost ... lose yourself. Let yourself dissolve into the soft light, the gentle breeze, the sensual darkness. Let the shouting and laughter that is everywhere vibrate within you. Walk down the darkest alley and fear no one. Watch the children play late into the night, watched over by plaster Madonnas and grannies in widows' black.

Sit on the steps of the Tempio di Vesta, with the warm wine in your blood and think of all the things you have burnt, and not in Vesta's name. Realise that the films of Fellini are not in anyway, er, Felliniesque, but out-and-out documentary.

As well as being ancient, Rome is gloriously old fashioned. One day, very suddenly, Campo de' Fiori becomes filled with scruffy anarchists, commies and puppeteers. If it's all beards, slogans, bad folk songs and chaos, it must be 1973!

In Rome, you can wear your fur coat and drink Cinzano as you puff away regally on your ciggie. Bring your dog, bring your kids, bring your mistress, relax, enjoy, eat!

Pop into your local cafe too. It will be nice there 'cause they still think it's 1959 and haven't felt the need to change anything since. Not the decor, the menu, the staff, the music ... nothing.

Rome is a glorious and winning combination of ultra chic and hilarious uncool. See, I'm smiling now thinking about it. It makes you smile Rome, it does.

It makes you smile and laugh and feeds you lovely simple food that beats all the culture and hipster druggy nonsense of Paris, New York, London, Berlin, hands down.

But – 'Surely you mean it's the people of Rome and not the city, who provoke these sickening displays of light-heartedness in you?' I hear you ask.

Well, yes of course ... but in writing what amounts to a travel piece, I'm determined to use the term psychogeography, a term with its origins in the Situationist International, and now de rigueur for any post-anything travelogue. There, I've used it, and not only that but also de rigueur and a mention of the SI in one sentence. Pretentious? Moi? *Ceci n'est pas une pipe!*

Er ... where was I? Oh right.

People used to be happy to talk about the 'feel' of a place and for me, Rome has always felt loving and kind. Its people and streets, curses and smells have changed my very DNA, I'm sure of it.

I can feel it in my soul.

I'm still a nihilist dirtbag, but a happier one all the same.

Thank you Rome, I love you for it.

Noah Taylor

Where to stay

Convent stays

American Holiday Goddesses are huge fans of Rome's best secret – convent or monastery accommodation. One of our favourites is Casa Il Rosario, expertly managed by Dominican nuns. There is an 11pm curfew but don't worry, you won't be required to take holy orders. The nuns welcome polite foreign visitors (but don't roll home after too many Bellinis).

If you don't speak Italian, finding your way around the selection of local monasteries and convents can be a maze, but American Catholics in Rome have created an excellent website for English-speaking visitors at *santasusanna.org*.

Expect simple accommodation, with a continental breakfast included, at incredibly low prices. Knowing basic Italian helps – please, sorry and thank you will go a long way. Just remember that if you are booking a room in a convent or monastery, the church has its own peak times too, and if you want to visit Rome during special papal events, your first choice should be booked months ahead.

Casa Il Rosario is the first choice for most visitors because it is a short walk from the Colosseum, which means you can try our illustrator Anna Johnson's lovely night walk (see page 322). Ask for a room overlooking the courtyard too. Just make sure you're home by 11pm or you may be locked out.

We hear many women are given free rosary beads by the nuns when they check out. That never happens at The Ritz. Enquire first at *monasterystays.com*.

Hollywood's Roman home

Hotel Eden had us at the honey and golden raisin ice-cream (high above Rome, in their wonderful sixth-floor terrace restaurant, La Terrazza dell'Eden). When we found out that this was where Fellini gave all his interviews, though, we were sold. The Hotel Eden is Hollywood's Roman home, which is why Nicole Kidman and Gwyneth Paltrow have both checked in.

The Spanish Steps and some of Jane de Teliga's favourite boutiques (see page 288) are ten minutes away. Try to book a front room for the best views, or enquire about a bathroom with windows. It's eye-wateringly expensive, but once you are over your flight, you will be in marble bathroom heaven, with fluffy robes and Hermès products on the shelves. After your bath it's time for feather pillows and linen sheets. The curtains make us want to do a Scarlett O'Hara in *Gone with the Wind* and make frocks out of them.

If you're a single traveller, you'll like the occasional deals here – like the hundreds of loyalty points on offer. Whenever offers appear, you will also find them at *holidaygoddess.com* – just use our hotel booking box to key in your dates. If you go during one of Rome's sunny winters (and book months ahead) you can save one-third off the usual price, just by using our magic booking box. Just saying.

Your first day

Be prepared to fall in love with Rome on your first day. It's the most romantic place on earth. As in Rome-antic. Sceptics and cynics need not apply. This is the city where Keats spent his final dying hours, in a bedroom with a convenient view of all the sexy artists' models on the Spanish Steps. It's where the women of Ancient Rome were prepared to be executed for love. And, of course, it's where Claudia Schiffer famously got wet in a Valentino photo shoot in Fontana di Trevi. The best way to take it all in? Believe it or not, it's by bus.

The heart-starting coffee

Romans start the day with a cappuccino, a caffè latte or a caffè lungo. They repeat the ritual throughout the morning, according to personal preference. An espresso is the real heart-starter; a caffè lungo is kinder: it contains espresso, but it's not the giant black caffeine pill that the locals drink. It's almost impossible to get a bad coffee in Rome. If you've been indoctrinated by Starbucks, though, prepare yourself: it doesn't come in three sizes. Do as the locals do and drink it standing up. Within minutes, your eyes will be wide open (wide, wide open) ready for everything Michelangelo and Bernini can throw at them. The best coffee in the city can be found at **Sant'Eustachio Il Caffè** in **Via della Palombella**, near the Pantheon.

All aboard!

Don't be shocked, but the most blissful way to spend your first day in Rome is on top of a garish, touristy, open-topped bus. We wouldn't make you do this in London, Paris or New York – but in Rome it is completely worth the fare (and the mild embarrassment of sitting upstairs in your sunglasses, for all the world to see).

Why the big neon-bright bus? Because you won't have to cross any roads. Roman traffic is crazy. This is the only city we know where motorcyclists will actually accelerate and aim at you. There is a reason why some Catholics here make the sign of the cross before crossing the road.

Tourist buses will take you to all three madly romantic versions of Rome – pagan, Catholic and 1950s. You are free to walk off, wander around, then reboard as you wish. Yes it's cheesy. But oh, it's easy-peasy.

You'll see these buses all around the city, and you can board anywhere. The bus also allows you to see Rome from above, which is the way she was originally viewed (and dreamed up), from the top of her famous seven hills.

The other great advantage? You can peer up and see architectural details never seen from the street. Roman stonemasons loved creating tiny clam shells and starfish under window ledges.

Looking up also gives you a chance to see small altars, built above archways, containing statues of the Virgin Mary, waiting for prayers to be heard. There is no other clear way of seeing these icons, except from the top of the bus.

For the best, most up to date list of hop-on and hop-off buses, see *holidaygoddess.com*.

Roman romance

Along with the heart-starting coffee, the best way to spend your first day in Rome is in the company of a heart-starting Italian man. Even one really good eye-meet on the street can restore your lust for life. It happens like this: on your first day in Rome you will be walking along the street (in good leather shoes, of course) doing nothing much in particular, when – *wham*. You will receive a long and passionate stare from a handsome Italian. The first time it happened to me I thought I was Sophia Loren, but then I compared notes with other Holiday Goddess editors and discovered it happens to everybody. At least if they're wearing lipstick and a skirt.

Perhaps the famous Roman eye-flirting happens because men here have always admired the female form through statues and sculptures of goddesses (busty Venus is everywhere in the city, along with voluptuous Juno and sexy Minerva).

For some reason, it never feels sleazy. Oh, I know that Italian men can go to seed and turn into podgy old Berlusconis (like Roman versions of Benny Hill). But when young and handsome, their X-ray eyes can make your day.

Quite a few Holiday Goddess editors have dated Italians or even married them, either before or after the trip to Rome. I'm on the list too – I will never entirely forget my Italian ex. But what it is about these men? One Roman businesswoman explained it to me this way: 'Men here are passionately interested in women. In London or New York, the female of the species is pretty low down on the list of priorities. They care more about their football or their sharemarket prices. In Rome, you are a goddess. The men give you their full and absolute attention.'

Order a drink in a Roman bar on your first day and put the theory to the test. See the serious, lingering, dark-eyed stare? The respectful, intense interest in what you have to say? *Mamma mia!* It's extremely seductive. Rome has always been R-rated, which is why she is so interesting.

When I studied ancient Latin texts at university, I was amazed at the huge range of saucy classical euphemisms for male and female bits.

Roman men had corn cobs, crowbars, boat poles, batons and, inevitably, swords. Women in the old city had seashells, roses, figs, bushes, gardens and (my favourite) mouse holes.

With or without mouse holes, even the buildings are sexy. The Forum Augustum floorplan looks like a phallus, with its two semi-circular galleries and long projecting forecourt. Some historians believe its rude architecture was quite deliberate.

Wander into any museum and you will find schoolgirls giggling at Priapus, the old god with the enormous ... crowbar. In Pompeii, which is one of Holiday Goddess editor Karen Moline's favourite places, you may still see a huge flying penis, complete with wings, dating from 79AD.

It was a good luck charm, hung in a Pompeii doorway. Don't bang your head, madam!

Rome also has the world's sexiest food, well worth exploring on your first day. The fierce sucking of spaghetti and asparagus over dinner completes the experience. Which nation invented the word 'fellatio' and the phrase 'in flagrante delicto'? No, don't even guess.

Jessica Adams

Chiconomical secrets

The cheapest way to reach Rome is to book a winter sale fare to London, then fly from there using Irish airline Ryanair. The sun will be shining in Roma and you'll also save a fortune. Expect your return fare to cost about the same as a pair of shoes. Not expensive shoes. Just okay shoes. That's a small price to pay to visit a legendary city.

Fly from Gatwick Airport, which is a mere half-hour train ride from Victoria Station in central London. Don't take the expensive Gatwick Express, though. Just get the Southern Express trains to Brighton, (book online for less) and you'll stop at Gatwick Airport anyway, for far less money. The trick with Ryanair is to arrive two hours before departure. That way, if there are any cancellations or delays (or other confusion) you can just sit down with a cup of tea and a magazine.

This is not Qantas. Staff announcements to passengers are not necessarily made over a PA system. They may be made by someone at the check-in counter yelling at you over the top of the queue. Once on board, you may also be sold lottery tickets. To say Ryanair is eccentric is like saying the Irish like Guinness. Luggage costs, so to get the cheap advertised fare, take a large, squashy shoulder bag (the kind that stuffs under the seat in front). Pay just a little extra, and you'll print out a special ticket that allows you to board first. Stand next to the ground staff at the barrier with the others in your elite group, then as soon as the flight is called, march firmly towards the aircraft door. That's how you can end up in the front row, there and back. It's fake first class, Ryanair style. (See *moneysavingexpert.com* for more details.)

The Terravision bus will be waiting for you in the car park when your plane lands, and for a few euros, it will take you straight to the cheap hotel district around Termini train station. If you can afford two pairs of shoes, you can afford two days in Roma. Run, don't walk.

TOP TEN

Rome bargainista rules

1. Check Holiday Goddess on Twitter for deals
2. Go in autumn/winter
3. Go midweek
4. Fly very early or late
5. Avoid public/school holidays
6. Arrive early in case of check-in chaos
7. Pay more for fast boarding
8. Take under-seat luggage
9. Take the Terravision bus on arrival
10. Stay near Termini Station

$10 picnics

Rome is the place to join a friend and shop at delis, supermarkets and markets for picnic ingredients, then walk to lush, historic parkland for million-dollar views. It all begins with the salami ...

Salame Felino is the most delicate salami, made near Parma, low on fat, flavoured with wine. *Salame Toscano* is a strong-flavoured salami with a lot of garlic and fennel added. *Salame di Fabriano* is the best salami of central Italy, flavoured with garlic and peppercorns. *Salame di Napoli* is flavoured with chilli.

The city also has plenty of packets of *salatini* on the supermarket shelves, as an alternative to bread. These are crackers flavoured with cheese, cumin seeds, fennel or herbs.

Roman cooks buy antipasto to eat before the meal, and in restaurants you will traditionally see an antipasto counter, groaning with delicious morsels, as you walk in the door. For a woman on a budget, though, antipasto is lunch.

Shop for *Gaeta* olives (round and black), prosciutto, stuffed mussels, raw anchovies marinated in olive oil and lemon juice and seafood salad.

One bargainista we know keeps her hotel fridge stocked like this and, after buying some plastic picnic accessories, dines al fresco every day, grapes in hand, admiring Roman history.

Rome's best delicatessen:

Antica Caciara Trasteverina
Via di San Francesco a Ripa 140a/b

WEBSITE: anticacaciara.it

Peasant food

Bargainistas are blessed by the prevalence of peasant food on Roman menus. Simple, delicious and ... cheap. As you might expect, it lies in trattorias away from the main attractions.

Riso in Cagnone is a traditional dish made in Milan and Piedmont. Boiled rice is dressed with melted butter, sage leaves, a clove of garlic and Parmesan or fontina cheese.

Mozzarella in Carrozza or 'mozzarella in a carriage' (the bread is the carriage) is a fried mozzarella sandwich, created in Campania.

Linguine all'Aglio, Olio e Peperoncino is linguine or spaghetti with salt, virgin olive oil, garlic and dried chillis.

Spaghetti alla Puttanesca actually translates as 'spaghetti of the prostitutes' but who cares? The sauce was invented in the Italian slums. It's spaghetti in a chilli and anchovy sauce with olives, capers and flat-leaf parsley.

Spaghetti Cacio e Pepe is a traditional Roman recipe, where spaghetti is smothered in grated pecorino cheese, and a great deal of spicy black pepper.

Beans (*fagiolo*) are another chiconomical and delicious menu option. In Italy they call beans '*la carne dei poveri*' (poor man's meat). Roman chefs turn them into luxurious main courses by adding them to soups and salads or pasta.

Chiconomical dining

San Lorenzo is east of Termini Station, and home to plenty of cheap pizzerias and trattorias, thanks to the nearby university. A trattoria is a family-run establishment, cheaper than a restaurant, but with the added bonus of an Italian grandmother's cookbook.

If you wander San Lorenzo with the students on a budget, you're bound to get lucky. Or try:

Arancia Blu at Via dei Latini 55/65, for brilliant vegetarian food.

Il Dito e la Luna at Via dei Sabelli 51, for delicious Sicilian dining.

The joy of cold pizza

Roman pizza is crisp, with a thin crust, and is delicious hot or cold. It is perfect for a bargainista picnic, so invest in a lunchbox when you land in Rome. Try the original pizza, *Pizza alla Marinara*, which is covered in tomatoes, extra virgin olive oil, garlic, oregano, salt and pepper.

Another old recipe is *Pizza Margherita*, created to honour the visit of Queen Margherita to Naples in the 19th century. It has the three colours of the Italian flag – green (basil), white (mozzarella) and red (tomato). The two best wow-factor picnic locations are the Palatine Hill and Circus Maximus.

Circus Maximus

It's pretty hard to beat cold pizza and Circus Maximus on a sunny day. Joggers have replaced the chariot racers, but it's easy to find a tree, lie back on the grass and imagine the past. Nothing remains (not even one of Kirk Douglas' gladiator sandals) but the basic structure of the circus is still there. Close to half a million Romans used to watch wild beast fights and mock sea-battles here.

The Palatine Hill

This is where Romulus and Remus (the twins raised by a she-wolf) founded Rome. Cicero had a house here, Caligula had a palace, and Emperor Augustus was born here. What a place to have a $10 lunch! Reach the hill by walking up from the Roman Forum, for which you will need a ticket. Once there, you may want to spend the afternoon exploring the House of Livia, with a copy of *I, Claudius*.

The secret diaries of several shopaholics

Rome is the place to find Pucci, Gucci and Fiorucci. But is there an identifiable Roman style? Holiday Goddess editors and their friends gathered around a tray of Bellinis to try and work it out, with a pile of e-mails from readers to assist.

Retro Roma chic

This is a sweet spring/summer look that came up from the streets of Rome in the 1950s and is still reinterpreted today by indie rock chicks and women who dislike fashion. It was agreed that the Retro Roma look really begins with a sleek ponytail, and ends in a basket over the arm. 'The great thing about this look is that you can pull it together from the markets or whip it up from Benetton,' one of our informants said. Another aspect of Retro Roma chic? Tight Capri pants and a knotted shirt – either by itself, or over a camisole. Big straw hat optional. Summer frocks (not corporate dresses, *frocks*, one editor emphasised) also rocked many Roman wardrobes. In a perfect world, we would wear them with pre-war Salvatore Ferragamo sandals. But any flat sandal (not gladiators!) will do. Add Ray-Bans.

Shouty accessories

'Shouty accessories' was one fashionista's fantastic description of all those loud, proud handbags that Roman women have worn and loved since the 1960s. The fruity-coloured geometric designs of Emilio Pucci lead the pack in this regard. 'Good luck if you can find the real thing from forty years ago,' our insider said.

'But in the meantime, there are some fantastic copies of his silk scarves doing the rounds. And that's a very shouty accessory, just waiting to happen all over again.' The shoutiest accessory of all, it was agreed, was the It Bag, taken to extremes by Euro millionaires. 'Flat boots over tight jeans with an It Bag sums it up,' one said.

Very, very Versace

If there is one Italian designer who some women love, and some women just don't love at all, it just has to be Versace. Born in the south of Italy, Gianni Versace founded the label in the show-off 1970s and brought in his sister Donatella. Today she is the media face of the label, which is loved by both Elton John and Jennifer Lopez. After Gianni was murdered in 1997, Donatella took his sexy-diva aesthetic and ran with it. Elizabeth Hurley's 1994 safety-pin dress is a good example of the Versace vibe that some of us queue in the sales for, and others run a mile from. If you want to see Versace worn by real women, though, Via Condotti is the place.

Rocking Via Condotti

Holiday Goddess editor **Jane de Teliga** has some shopping suggestions for Rome's most famous shopping destination.

Bulgari

'I introduced her to beer, she introduced me to Bulgari,' said Richard Burton about his wife Elizabeth Taylor. What an introduction it was; his engagement and wedding gifts included sumptuous Bulgari emerald and diamond pieces.

Nowadays, the divine Julianne Moore graces Bulgari campaigns, wearing nothing much but the odd jewel.

Founded in Rome in 1884, the grand Via Condotti store has long been the place to buy a stupendous jewel or glamorous bauble. Aside from serious bling, bag yourself a divine evening clutch, movie star sunnies or an elegant leather tote.

TOP TEN

Iconic Italian designers

1. Pucci
2. Gucci
3. Versace
4. Moschino
5. Armani
6. Valentino
7. Schiaparelli
8. Bulgari
9. Prada
10. Gianfranco Ferré

Bulgari
Via Condotti 10
WEBSITE: **bulgari.com**

Dolce & Gabbana

The sexy glamour of Italian design duo, Domenico Dolce and Stefano Gabbana, has long been a celebrity favourite. Madonna does their sunglasses campaign, while pint-size songstress Kylie Minogue struts her stuff in their designs on tour. Scarlett Johansson and Monica Bellucci smoulder in their curvaceous creations.

The lingerie-inspired dresses of Dolce & Gabbana reflect *la dolce vita*, that quintessential Italian notion of 'the good life'. Virginal white lace, corsetry, leopard print and black 'widows weeds' are all elements in their mythic recreation of Italian life in dress.

Dolce & Gabbana
Via Condotti 51/52
WEBSITE: dolcegabbana.com

Gucci

With a name like Guccio Gucci, it was a foregone conclusion that in 1921 the purveyor of leather goods named his company as he did.

Since 1938 the rich and famous fashionistas, Jackie Kennedy and Grace Kelly amongst them, have flocked to the Gucci boutique at the foot of the picturesque Spanish steps.

The brand was originally known for its leather goods, in particular its trademark horsebit-trimmed loafers.

But it had a fashion makeover at the hands of master marketer Tom Ford and recently by Roman born designer Frida Giannini. Gucci is now the go-to label for sharp Italian modernity with heritage elements.

Gucci
Via Condotti 8
WEBSITE: gucci.com

Prada

The quirky vision of Miuccia Prada is a fashion phenomenon that defies the normal rules of giving people fashion they want. Somehow, in her fashion line, she makes the seemingly ugly and unfeasible look alluring and covetable.

The leather goods empire, built first by her grandfather, was given a contemporary shot in the arm when Miuccia introduced black nylon as a material for bags, which has now become a signature Prada look.

A Prada bag is the definitive mark of a dedicated fashionista, hence the book and film title *The Devil Wears Prada*.

Prada
Via Condotti 92/95
WEBSITE: prada.com

Valentino

The jetsetter's ultimate fashion house was set up by the perma-tanned Valentino Garavani on the Via Condotti in 1960.

His wedding gowns were worn by both Jacqueline Onassis and Jennifer Lopez, and his red carpet dresses have been donned by countless movie stars, including Julia Roberts, who wore vintage Valentino to pick up her Oscar in 2001.

Since the maestro's retirement, the designers have modernised his vision so successfully that a Valentino delicious lace and organza confection is once again the height of desirability for a whole new generation.

Valentino
Via Condotti 15
WEBSITE: valentino.com

Sephora

I first met Alicia Richardson and Marina Go working on *Elle* magazine. Alicia is presently one of the global editors of *The Knot*, the world's most successful online bridal magazine, and Marina is the publisher of the cult beauty site *Primped*, among other titles. I take their opinions about fashion and beauty very seriously, as they are so experienced with glossy magazines. And guess what? They both adore Sephora.

Sephora is a luxurious beauty superstore which is loved all over the world, but there is something particularly nice about shopping at the Rome branch as Italian brands are so well-represented. If you're going to try fragrances from Gucci, Dolce & Gabbana or Acqua di Parma, you may as well try them on Italy's Planet Beauty. Swing that little wire basket on your arm and go.

Sephora is the place to find Tocca candle travel sets – one of several hip brands on the shelves. You are encouraged to try all the make-up on too, with cotton buds and cotton wool balls in plentiful supply, and properly lit mirrors.

Everyone's big secret is the Sephora own-brand cosmetic counter. It looks like the control desk of the Star Trek ship, but covered in make-up.

Jessica Adams

Sephora
Via del Corso 480
WEBSITE: sephora.com

Zara

This is a Spanish chain, worshipped all over the world, but it is huge in Rome, where you can shop without the heaving New York crowds or mass of Oxford Street bag women in London. Zara in Italy is just a joy. If one store doesn't have your size, the next will.

The shop has made its name by adapting high fashion for low, low prices. Roman women love the beautiful fabrics, razor-sharp cuts and delicious colour combinations. Some of it is reminiscent of Prada, McCartney or Dior. Only a fashion insider would know.

New stock comes in every week, and as soon as it arrives, it disappears. Some *Vogue* staffers cheerfully admit that 70% of their wardrobe comes from Zara.

Jessica Adams

Zara

Via Del Corso 129-135

Via Del Corso 189

Porta Di Roma

Di Tor Vergata

Galleria Alberto Sordi

WEBSITE: **zara.com**

Audrey Hepburn's Rome

There is a seldom seen photograph of Audrey Hepburn in Rome at a Givenchy fitting in 1959, where she has her back turned to the camera in one of his amazing, floor-sweeping, strapless gowns. She looks completely at home in Roma, even though she never made it her home. (Though her second husband was an Italian.) She also understood the ancient Roman idea of the muse particularly well.

Audrey was Givenchy's muse from 1953, when he created her spectacular wardrobe for the film *Sabrina*, including the showstopping evening gown she wore in one of the film's most famous scenes. *Sabrina* would go on to win an Oscar for its costume design.

The two became close friends as well as lifelong collaborators. Audrey summed up Givenchy's magic: 'Balenciaga once said that the secret of elegance is elimination. I believe that. That's why I love Hubert Givenchy ... They're clothes without ornament, with everything stripped away.'

The look we know so well from most of her films and photo shoots is pure Givenchy. The black sheath dress she wore in *Breakfast at Tiffany's* is his, along with outfits for *Charade* and *Funny Face*.

He also created the pink dress and matching scarf she wore for her second wedding.

Givenchy even created a perfume for Audrey's own personal use – L'Interdit – which eventually went on sale to the public.

The Givenchy label still lives on in Rome, where the fashion faithful continue to call. Hepburn's Givenchy clothes went on auction, partly in aid of her foundation, a few years ago.

The couture lace cocktail dress by Givenchy that she wore in *How to Steal a Million* sold for £60,000. For us, a bottle of L'Interdit in our bag on the way home feels as good.

Well, *almost*.

Hotel Hassler

The luxurious Hotel Hassler, at Piazza Trinità dei Monti, was one of Audrey Hepburn's favourite places in Rome. The roof was the place to be in the 1950s and 1960s, when the restaurant (with its incredible views) attracted not only Audrey but also Grace Kelly and John F Kennedy. Today the restaurant has been reborn as Imago, but the views are still there. For more information, visit *imagorestaurant.com*.

The Fontana Sisters

The wedding dress Audrey Hepburn ordered, but never wore, was created by the Fontana sisters – Zoe, Micol and Giovanna. Today Micol helps the name live on – see her website *micolfontana.it* for news of Fontana fashion exhibitions. Sorelle Fontana also remains at Via San Sebastianello 6. If you can find vintage Fontana in Roma, then snap it up. Audrey's wedding dress (for the nixed nuptials with James Hanson) was given away, at her request, to the most beautiful poor Italian girl the Fontanas could find. It went to one Amabile Altobella, who kept it in the family until it was auctioned for £13,800.

Salvatore Ferragamo

There is a famous photograph of the shoe designer Ferragamo surrounded by wooden shoe lasts, all in different sizes and widths, daubed with the names of his celebrity clients. Sophia Loren is there, and Greta Garbo too. But typically, someone has put Audrey Hepburn's lasts at the front. Salvatore Ferragamo is at Via Condotti 66.

Louis Vuitton

ROMA

Oh how we long to travel like
Audrey Hepburn in headscarf,
gloves, coat – unafraid of customs
officials. Part of her style was the
Louis Vuitton Speedy 25 – a
squashy, smaller version of the
classic LV carry-on bag created
especially for her. Vuitton is at
Via Condotti 13, near the Spanish
Steps, in a part of Roma which
is a target for Hepburnistas.

Audrey secret

Bestselling novelist, columnist and Holiday Goddess editor **Rebecca
Sparrow** is a confirmed Audrey Hepburn and *Roman Holiday* fan.
'Did you know Gregory Peck ad-libbed the part where he pretends
his hand has been bitten off?' She asks. 'So Audrey's look of horror is
genuine!' Rebecca's extended fabulous guide to Audrey's Rome can
be found at *holidaygoddess.com*

Rome in books and film

Some Holiday Goddess editors and readers are firm Fellini fans. Others love the idea of Russell Crowe in sandals. Still more are enslaved to *Spartacus* and *Quo Vadis*. There is nothing like the sight of Hollywood actors with fake tan, fake blood and what appears to be Johnson's Baby Oil all over their manly torsos to prepare us for a trip to Italy. Alternatively we can never get enough of Monty Python's *Life of Brian* and its stuttering Romans. Our favourite translation of Ancient Rome onto screen, though, is a legendary 1970s BBC television series called *I, Claudius*. It is based on Robert Graves' brilliant novels, *I, Claudius* and *Claudius the God*.

'I first saw *I, Claudius* on television as a teenager and never really got over it. The scene where an irritating fat boy has a coughing fit and is beheaded by Caligula has to be seen to be believed (even if the head does look like something the *Doctor Who* props department threw into a BBC skip). I love everything about this classic series, from the mosaic title sequence, to the deadly snake which slithers across the opening credits.

Derek Jacobi's interpretation of Claudius, the stuttering Roman emperor who conquered Britain, has never been bettered. And John Hurt as Caligula is unforgettably creepy. When they tried to steer me in the direction of Latin at university, I quickly steered myself over to the video box-set. I've seen this so many times; I last downloaded it for the flight from London to Rome and fell in love with it all over again. *I, Claudius* (the book or DVD set) will truly make all those crumbling old busts of emperors come alive for you.'

Jessica Adams

Wendy Holden is a comic novelist with eleven bestsellers under her belt, and an occasional travel writer. Her latest book is *Marrying Up*. Wendy's books skewer British society perfectly, so we were not surprised to find out that she is also a dedicated fan of *I, Claudius*, which does much the same thing to the Romans.

'*I, Claudius* is the ultimate mood-setter for any trip to Rome. Few people, including me, have the classical education required to bring the Forum to any sort of life. For the likes of us, Graves' book is a crash course in Roman history, and one that sticks in the mind infinitely more than guidebooks do. Probably because of all the rude bits. There's also plenty of gore, people falling on their swords and dying in any number of horrid ways. C-C-Claudius lives through the reigns of the likes of Caligula and Nero, escaping with his life only because everyone thinks he is stupid. Which makes *I, Claudius* the ultimate Roman survival guide in more ways than one.'

Wendy Holden

Who's who in *I, Claudius*

The cast of characters in *I, Claudius* is vast, but here are the superstars –
get to know *them*, and you will get to know Rome, even before you land.

Augustus: Augustus was the adopted son of Julius Caesar. With his
pudding-bowl haircut, Augustus was an unlikely hero, but after he
died, the people made him a god. Augustus made adultery a crime, so
when his own daughter Julia committed it, he was forced to send her
into exile. Nobody could blame Julia for her adultery, though, as
Augustus continually forced her into arranged marriages she hated –
including one to his own nephew. He had a huge ego. Any smug-
looking statue will be him.

Livia: The unfortunate third wife of Augustus. Surviving sculptures
show a pointy nose and steely, determined gaze. She was the power
behind Augustus' throne, but strangely, also found the time to sew her
husband's clothes. She was allegedly a murderess, removing anyone
who stood in the way of her ambition. She is supposed to have killed
Augustus with poisoned figs but the people still loved her. After she
died, they dragged her likeness (by elephant) to all the games in Rome.

Claudius: Claudius limped, stammered and dribbled, and was nearly
50 when they made him emperor. After his insane nephew Caligula
(see next page) had been murdered, Claudius was next in line. He is
most famous for successfully invading Britain. He had four wives,
including Messalina, 30 years his junior, who was notoriously unfaithful.
She plotted to make one of her lovers the next emperor, and was
executed by Claudius when he found out. His last marriage was to
Agrippina, who apparently poisoned him.

Caligula: Caligula was a sweet child who wore boots all the time, thus giving him his nickname (which translates as 'little boots'). After a serious illness he became insane. He made his horse, Incitatus, a senator. Then he built a two-mile bridge of boats and drove a chariot across it. A Roman invasion of Britain failed because once the troops had landed, Caligula ordered them to collect seashells. He was murdered by his couriers and officers. You may want to fast-forward his sex scenes in the DVD.

Nero: Nero became emperor at the age of 17. He really wanted to be an actor and singer, though, and horrified the upper classes by appearing on stage. His sex life was notorious. He had a boy, Sporus, castrated and then married him in a mock wedding ceremony. When he finally persuaded another woman to marry him, he kicked her to death in a rage. You may hear that he fiddled as Rome burned. He didn't. But he did burn Christians. He gives his name to Risotto Nero, made with cuttlefish and ink.

Professor **Jane Pirkis** not only loves Rome, but she is also related to Max Pirkis, one of the stars of the BBC-TV epic *Rome* (he played the young Octavian). Naturally, she's a fan – but she likes *I, Claudius* too.

'Like Wendy Holden, my entire knowledge of Roman history came from *I, Claudius*. Or at least it did until I watched *Rome*, which dispelled some myths and confirmed some facts for me:

1. Everything in Roman history happened inside, except for the bits that happened in Augustus's courtyard (e.g. the bit where an overhead eagle dropped a wolf cub on Claudius, or Livia tampered with all the fruit on the trees to trick Augustus into eating poison). This is a myth. In fact there was a lot of outside space where Romans liked to hold markets and public floggings.

2. All Romans were capable of evil and debauchery, even the nice ones. This is a fact. In *I, Claudius*, the fine and upstanding Claudius did a few bad things once he overcame his stutter and began writing his memoirs on long scrolls of parchment. In *Rome*, Octavian, who is described as 'a boy gifted with uncommon intelligence and clarity of vision' was not above a bit of brutality. He had no compunction about ordering his soldier mate to cut their captive's thumbs off when he couldn't answer a few simple questions. Oh, and he slept with his sister.

3. Roman women were presciently influenced by 1970s fashion. I was pleasantly surprised when *Rome* confirmed this was partially true, because I remember being troubled by all the blue eye shadow when I first watched *I, Claudius* on television at the age of 12. Roman women were quite subtle in their application of make-up, favouring a small amount of kohl and a bit of mascara over great smearings of eye shadow, so that bit's not right. However, they did all go to the same hairdresser and long, ringletty, Kate Bush perms were quite popular.

If you do find yourself in Rome, don't forget to visit some of the local artisans. Fortune tellers, old women who prepare toxic potions for bumping your relatives off, and men who perform neurosurgery with corkscrews are particular favourites.'

Jane Pirkis

Jane Pirkis' brilliant guide to the walk around the Spanish Steps can be found at *holidaygoddess.com*.

Eat, Pray, Love by Elizabeth Gilbert

Holiday Goddess editors were not surprised to hear there is now an *Eat, Pray, Love* tour of Rome – which you can book at *romaround.it*. If you haven't read the book, then all you need to know is that Rome supplies the 'eat' part of the title. It's where our heroine learns about *spaghetti cacio e pepe* (spaghetti with pecorino cheese and black pepper). And also where she gorges on gelato three times a day.

If you have read the book, and loved it – as millions of women have – then the flight to Rome is the perfect time to reacquaint yourself with it. The San Crispino gelato on arrival (honey and hazelnut, grapefruit and melon, and cinnamon ginger) will taste better for it.

If you haven't read the book, then maybe it should be on your hotel bedside table.

Our favourite San Crispino gelato flavour is white fig and cream, for the record. To live the book (and feel the love) you can find Elizabeth Gilbert's favourite gelato at these locations. Just try not to stain too many pages.

San Crispino gelato

Via della Panetteria, 42
Piazza della Maddalena, 3

Retro Roma on Film

After all the poisoning and perversion of *I, Claudius* and *Rome* it is refreshing to turn to lovely Audrey Hepburn and charming Gregory Peck, who star in every woman's favourite piece of retro Roma on film, *Roman Holiday*. Italian friends and readers also tipped us off about a wonderful Vespa tour of all the locations. Vintage Tours of Rome take visitors out twice a day, for a four-hour guided trip (at a safe 30 kph) which begins at your hotel. It's just one big photo opportunity, which you can book at *happyrent.com*. But how can you resist chugging past the classic locations from *Roman Holiday*: **Piazza Della Repubblica** (the drinks truck scene), **The Spanish Steps** (the gelato scene) and **La Bocca Della Verità** (the unconfessable secret scene).

La Dolce Vita

You can recreate this classic 1960 film from the moment you arrive at the (rather low-budget) Ciampino Airport, which is where the blonde and beautiful Anita Ekberg flies in at the beginning of the film, stunning the locals. Swing that hand luggage, bella!

This film was achingly hip in 1960 and remains so today, with all its jukeboxes, bikinis, cigarettes, pillow fights and barefoot dancing. Fellini filmed the Trevi Fountain scene in winter, when all the tourists were away, which is also our favourite time to see this sacred location. Apparently brave Anita Ekberg didn't mind the freezing water during the shoot.

But her shivering co-star Marcello Mastroianni had to wear a wetsuit underneath his clothes. Some Italians insist he drank an entire bottle of vodka, just to get through the scene.

The Trevi Fountain

The greatest Retro Roma location of all just has to be the Trevi Fountain, where the famous hair-cutting scene in *Roman Holiday* can be found – but it is also the site of Anita Ekberg's illegal shower in *La Dolce Vita*, and the coin-tossing ritual in *Three Coins in the Fountain*. Few film directors can resist Fontana di Trevi and you, too, may be gripped by a strange urge to make a two-minute holiday video here.

La Fontana di Trevi

Just one thing – go at dawn, or at night. At every other time, there is precious little atmosphere here, and the spirit of Audrey Hepburn and Anita Ekberg has all but gone. Why? Flying coins. Sometimes it seems like there are a thousand tourists here, all pelting euros into the water over your head.

Part of the thrill of the Trevi Fountain is the build-up. It is notoriously hard to find. The last time a goddess visited there were just two signposts in dull brown, rather like municipal signs to the nearest public lavatory.

Persist, though, and you will wander up a narrow alleyway and find yourself in what appears to be a huge 1960s movie set – it's the most fantastic surprise.

No, you can't put on a black evening gown and plunge into the water. But you can be captured for posterity posing against a backdrop of sea-horses, gushing water, clam shells and tritons. All you need to do is kidnap the nearest Gregory Peck or Marcello Mastroianni lookalike and make him film you. Throw a coin into the fountain and you will come back. Truly, you'll want to.

Eat, love, eat more

Roman history is measured, as everyone knows, by BC (Before Christ) and AD (After Christ, Anno Domini). Holiday Goddess editors and their friends measure Roman history this way: BFP and AFP. That's Before Fresh Pasta and After Fresh Pasta. Because once you've been to Rome, you will never buy rock-hard, dried spaghetti and leave it in the cupboard again.

The foodies among us become so addicted to the fresh stuff in Rome that, once home, they end up buying gleaming machines to make their own. Even if you're not a foodie, you will still bless the day you walked into a trattoria and ordered fresh egg tagliatelle with (just) olive oil, black pepper and grated Parmigiano Reggiano.

It's a very long way from your ex-flatmate's mince spaghetti bolognese with the canned tomatoes, and the cheddar that smelled like old football boots. Remember that? We're sure you'd like to forget it, but that was BFP. Before Fresh Pasta. We know that Romans don't consider fresh pasta in any way superior to the dried stuff. But they do have exacting standards for their dried, packet spaghetti, which don't exist outside Italy. It's tightly controlled by law.

Balsamic vinegar is also under legal control, believe it or not. But when you finally taste the real thing after years of cheap supermarket imitations elsewhere, you will understand why Romans are so passionate about the stuff. Foodies tell us it is properly made from Trebbiano grapes. It's aged in kegs made of oak, cherry, chestnut, mulberry and ash. If the label says '*aceto balsamico tradizionale*' then it's twelve years old, and may even be *decades* old in some restaurants. Try it on strawberries – delicious.

Travelling with children? They absolutely love the pasta in *minestrina* (soup). It's shaped like stars, butterflies, alphabet letters and ... Hail Marys. Expect much slurping.

Rome typically supplies a conversion experience for lovers of pizza and ice-cream. In other parts of the world it can seem cheap and junky. In Rome it's fabulous and funky.

A lot of our readers also convert to artichokes in Rome. The rich volcanic soil in the local countryside produces the very best. Try them as part of *pinzimonio*, where a variety of delicious raw vegetables are eaten with a dip of olive oil, lemon juice, salt and pepper.

Other conversion experiences? Raw meat, or *carpaccio* (thinly sliced beef), is at the top of our list. It was created in 1961 by Giuseppe Capriani of Harry's Bar in Venice. (He also invented the Bellini.) Carpaccio is named after the painter Vittore Carpaccio. Capriani made it for an aristocratic lady who was on a strict diet. It's tenderloin beef, almost thin enough to see through, dressed with mayonnaise, mustard, brandy, Tabasco and cream.

Do skip the eels immersed in Vernaccia wine, though. Pope Martino IV loved it but as much as we love a bottle of white, it's an awful thing to do to an eel.

The best breakfast in Rome

Holiday Goddess contributor **Eleonora Baldwin** has one of the most wonderful jobs in the world. She is a food docent and leads walking tours of Rome, every day of the week. She also knows exactly where to find Rome's most pedigreed cappuccino, the flakiest warm pastries stuffed with Nutella, the best brunch scene, and the widest smiles in the city.

Bar del Cappuccino di Santoro at **Via Arenula 50** is a hole in the wall that serves the finest cappuccino in town. Luigi works the foam pitcher like no one else, and the flavour, texture and aroma of his frothy, cacao-laced creations are truly unfailing. Pair with a warm croissant and, *voilà!* Italian breakfast is served.

In the heart of the San Lorenzo university area, **Bar Marani** at **Via dei Volsci 57**, a bohemian century-old coffee house, draws students, families, lost travellers, shopkeepers, artists, intellectuals, pickpockets, and rock stars. Grab a table on the vine-covered terrace and bring a book.

Caffè della Pace at **Piazza delle Pace 4** is known for its show business clientele and aficionado sophisticates. Most of the espresso knocking-back action takes place outside, against draped ivy and glinting cobblestones. Website: *caffedellapace.it*.

Bernasconi at **Piazza Benedetto Cairoli 16**, is a family-run pasticceria bakery, where the freshly made croissants, tartlets and kosher pastries lure devotees in hordes. Come early in the morning to avoid fighting over the few outside tables.

The Perfect Bun at **Largo del Teatro Valle 4** is famed for its friendly staff and stellar Sunday brunch buffet. For a flat €25 the all-you-can-eat fares feature a constant supply of pancakes, French toast and waffles, a wide selection of eggs and omelettes, salads, sausages, bacon and hash browns. Just when you thought the heap on your plate was scandalous, you spot the desserts: a cornucopia of muffins, carrot cakes, cupcakes, plum cakes, and cheesecakes, plus bagels, fruit juices and freshly brewed caffè Americano.
Website: *the perfectbun.it*

Eleonora Baldwin

Our favourite market: Campo de' Fiori

Romans nickname this fabulous market 'Il Campo'. It's open from 6am to lunchtime, when you can depart to a nearby restaurant (there are dozens) to see what the local chefs have done with the tomatoes you just saw on a stall. Or, *mamma mia*, the artichokes. You will see the magic words *carciofi alla giudia* inscribed on restaurant menus near the market: these are delicious twice-fried artichokes.

Campo de' Fiori market is also the place to buy the ingredients for a DIY Roman banquet. Eat like an emperor: buy grapes to drop into your mouth as you sprawl sideways on the grass, or invest in some figs, honey or dates.

Quite apart from the stunning market food, this is a great area to walk and wander in: there are plenty of old palaces nearby Campo de' Fiori.
Bus: Corso Vittorio Emanuele

TOP TEN
Market Classics

1. Olives
2. Ciabatta
3. Prosciutto
4. Figs
5. Dates
6. Black grapes
7. Pecorino cheese
8. Melon
9. Honey
10. Artichokes

Rome's best breakfast juice

Freshly-squeezed orange juice (*spremuta d'arancia*) is always on the menu at **Caffè Farnese**, next to the food market, Campo de' Fiori. Find a table, then shop the market for a picnic.

**Caffè Farnese,
Via dei Baullari 106.**

Ghetto food

Claudia Roden's meticulously researched cookbooks are a bodily way to revisit the criss-crossed history of the Mediterranean. It was her recipes that first led me to Rome's Jewish Ghetto, whose community predates the city's Christian era. Here I found a potent blend of simple cooking – this was one of Italy's most tightly regulated ghettos and, hence, poorest – religious mandate and flavours that reflect a history of immigration and influence that's as rich as it is long. Dishes might be drawn from Sicily, Al-Andalus, North Africa, and, of course, the Levant itself.

Fritto misto – fried baccalà and zucchini flowers or artichokes, depending on the season, harks back to the local, the ghetto's street vendors, while fat anchovies served with dark and bitter olive-oil doused chicory uses what was always the cheapest catch. Pasta and chickpeas screams the south, as does the forerunner to the world's cheesecakes, ricotta tart. The ghetto centres on Via del Portico d'Ottavia, a tight knot of quiet, and now very affluent, streets. The most famous dish of all, deep-fried artichokes, resemble one of Van Gogh's sunflowers, and can be had here at Nonna Betta's, or at a laneway table at La Matricianella.

Donna Wheeler

Obika Mozzarella Bar

Every day in the Paestum and Agro Pontino areas of Italy, the local dairy farmers milk the buffalo. Then they shape the resulting cheese with their hands and send it to Obika Mozzarella Bar, where you will shortly die and go to heaven. This particular kind of cheese is so important to Italians that in 1993 the government actually protected its good name – *mozzarella di bufala* – to stop the cheap imitations. There is nothing cheap about the cheese at the Obika Mozzarella Bar, but then you are paying for the ears.

The ears are the little peaks at either edge of the ball – so you can tell a machine didn't make it. At Obika, you may choose prosciutto, tomatoes, pesto, anchovies or salami on the side. The mozzarella comes in four flavours: *paestum* (delicate), *pontina* (strong), *affumicata* (smoked) and *straccietella di burrata* (creamy). If there are six of you, then you can even order a kilo.

Obika Roma Campo de' Fiori

Piazza Campo de' Fiori
Corner of Via dei Baullari

WEBSITE: obika.it

Aperitivo haunts

Romans really know their pre-dinner drinks, as does **Eleonora Baldwin**. To the resourceful, socially inclined and thrifty bar-hoppers, *aperitivo* provides both faux dinner and social recourse. By definition, aperitivo is a flûte of Prosecco (sparkling wine), Spritz, Negroni and Bellini – or simply a glass of wine or beer – accompanied by *stuzzichini* (tapas-like appetisers). Rome's 'happy hour' scene is living a renaissance. Folks rush out of offices and workplaces in droves to meet, drink, flirt and mingle around buffet tables spilling with seafood paella, hearty pastas, risottos, cold cuts and baskets of bread and pizza. At sundown, come Campari o'clock, here's where it's all happening:

With its dimly lit, rustic Roman character, **Société Lutèce** at **Piazza Montevecchio 17** is a great starting point for a romantic evening. The buffet spread offers pasta and veggie couscous dishes, bruschette and homemade dips. The arty crowd brims with trendy Romans who take their drinks and food outside, balancing tumblers and plates on their Vespas.

Sexy bohemian cafe-cocktail bar **Salotto 42** at **Piazza di Pietra 42** is thronged with hot intellectuals leafing through art, fashion, film and music books. In the evening espresso gives way to wine, cocktails and hip clientele, who recline seductively on stylish armchairs, nibbling off plates of Swedish hors d'oeuvres.

The minimalist Provence-style ambiance at **Etablì** at **Vicolo delle Vacche 9** is so well decorated you may feel you've landed in a plush living room with comfortable sofas and armchairs, rather than in a cocktail bar. With its blazing fireplace in winter, the atmosphere is romantic, inviting, and packed with yummy-looking locals. Wines, drinks and free Wi-Fi usher the delicious finger food menu.

One of the top 10 bars in the world, **Freni e Frizioni** at **Via del Politeama 4/6** has tables and sofas inside, but people mostly pour out onto the charming cobblestone piazza outside. Heaped pastas, salumi and vegetarian dishes grace the buffet. But it's the droolworthy bartenders that attract the biggest crowds.

It should be noted that for these particularly Roman pre-dinner drinks and feasties, prices are normally raised to include the 'free' food, and range from €4 to €10 per drink.

But Romans aren't shy about going back to the buffet for seconds on the strength of one drink.

Cin cin!

Tea or coffee, madam?

Caffè Grecco and **Babington's Tea Rooms** are the two rival big sisters in Rome's cafe culture, and about five minutes' walk from each other. One is deeply Italian. The other is very, very British. Both have done a roaring trade for the last 100 years, and can be rather crowded. So why do people line up at Caffè Grecco? To stand in the same space as Lord Byron and John Keats, who both drank their coffee here. You can choose to sit on tables in the back room, or stand up at the counter, like the Italians, near the front window. One shot and they're off!

Babington's Tea Rooms, not far away, was originally set up by the Babington sisters to serve tea and scones to homesick British visitors. They wisely set it up at the bottom of the Spanish Steps, grabbing some of Rome's best real estate. The Tea Rooms were an instant success in 1896 and remain today, offering an alternative to espresso and pizza. Proper tea can be hard to find in Rome. This is the place.

Babington's Tea Rooms
Piazza di Spagna,
METRO: Spagna

Caffè Greco, 86 Via Condotti,
METRO: Spagna

Ova sfongia ex lacte (Pancakes and milk)

8 eggs
600ml milk
100ml oil
A little bit of honey
A little bit of ground pepper

Mix eggs, milk and oil until you have a pancake dough. Fry in a pan and serve topped with honey and a pinch of pepper.

Taking Rome home

Here are our favourite ways to take Rome home.

Bellini cocktails

There is a good reason why Asti Spumante used to be known as Asti Spew-Often, in the bad old days, fifty years ago. Before 1960 it was sweet, it was sparkling and it was dangerous. It also used to get confused with Prosecco, which is why so many of us are still terrified of the P-word on a drinks menu and order champagne instead. One visit to Rome may change your mind, though, as Prosecco these days has transformed itself into heavenly, chiconomical, crisp and light faux champagne. Prosecco is also the main ingredient in our favourite Italian drink – the Bellini Cocktail, invented in Venice.

The Bellini was dreamed up during the Second World War by the man who created Harry's Bar, Giuseppe Cipriani. Its rosy pink colour reminded him of a saint's toga in a painting by Giovanni Bellini, so he christened his new cocktail after the artist. It is always made with Prosecco and fresh peach puree. You can also add fresh raspberry or cherry juice. Divine! All it takes is a blender for the peach.
Not ready to go home yet? The best three places to order a Bellini in Rome are **Hotel Russie** at **Via del Babuino, 9**, **Hotel Hassler** at **Piazza Trinita dei Monti, 6** and **Harry's Bar** at **Via Vittorio Veneto, 150**.

First century pancakes

This recipe is from an old Roman cookbook dating from the 1st century AD, by a cook named Marcus Gavius Apicius. We discovered it through a Holiday Goddess fan at the BBC who told us about their amazing program, *The Roman Way*. It's the only 2000-year-old recipe we know. And yes, the pepper and honey topping works! We say *grazie*, Marcus Gavius Apicius.

Made in Italy: Cult local brands

Milano has the fashion, and Firenze has the fragrance. But Rome has it all, at prices that may be lower than you expect. Italians are fiercely loyal to their favourite cult brands, no matter if it's a stylish scooter or a pair of gloves. One of our favourite things about Italian brands? They're often covered in angels. Just look at the labels of local bath salts or mineral water next time you shop.

Ortigia

Ortigia make the most unusual and beautiful soap and bath oil in Italy. It smells clean, strong and beautiful, just like fresh lemon juice or a garden full of red roses. I found boxes of Ortigia Florio guest soap in a sale a few years ago, and whenever people come to stay they always want to take their bar home! Each piece of soap is sculpted like a precious egg, and stamped with the trademark leopards of the brand. The packaging uses images from ancient Greek and Roman woodcuts, and is stamped with silver. The Sicilian Lime bath oil is so beautiful I can't actually bring myself to use it. The great thing about Ortigia is that both men and women love it equally.

I can imagine Richard Burton and Elizabeth Taylor using this, on the set of *Cleopatra*. Or maybe Cleopatra and Mark Antony. Don't blame me if the man in your life tries to sneak the bath oil, though.

Jessica Adams

All hail the Vespa

Travel writer and author **Anneli Knight** is our very own Thelma (and Louise) at Holiday Goddess. While most of us fly on our travels, she is happy to drive overland. Anneli also happens to adore the Vespa, one of the very coolest Italian cult brands.

Vespa is a global symbol of style, freedom, youth and romance – and exudes a playful egalitarianism those Italian four-wheelers might only dream of. Immortalised in the 1953 film *Roman Holiday*, *Forbes* magazine declared in 2000 that the Oscar should have gone to the film's metallic-green Vespa that year, rather than to Audrey Hepburn. The Vespa is such a starlet that an exhibition was held in 2011 dedicated to the stylish Italian motor scooter's appearance in the movies, which includes more than 100 titles – and even a Walt Disney animation – to her credit. But, in the Italian way, this cult brand is much more than a pretty face – those timeless aeronautical curves have also been celebrated as a triumph in industrial design.

Anneli Knight

Vespa

Brave enough to brave Roman traffic? Try Bici and Baci (Bikes and Kisses) at bicibaci.com or Scooteroma at scooteroma.com

Baci chocolate

Baci chocolates famously come with a romantic quote inside. Like these:

'There is no instinct like that of the heart' Byron

'The ideal husband is unmarried' Oscar Wilde

The original 'love notes', as the Italians call them, date from the 1930s when they were dreamed up by Frederico Seneca.

The love notes are printed in English, Italian, French and Spanish – so it's quite nice to take home Italian chocolates with Rome-antic romantic messages inside.

They are now collectors' items (although the chocolate has long since been eaten). Baci is on sale on almost every major shopping street in Rome, often displayed in the windows of foodie shops and corner stores.

Most importantly, there is a whole hazelnut inside every chocolate.

Moriondo e Gariglio chocolate

Put down that Ferrero Rocher. Rome's most famous chocolate and confectionery shop has other ideas for you. Moriondo e Gariglio, the city's oldest and best chocolate emporium, is suitably cherry-red inside. The red heart-shaped boxes are a wonderful present to take home, but the little bags of fruit jellies (wrapped in ribbon) can also be personally dedicated if you are looking for a one-off present. Try the strawberry or lemon jellies, or that ancient Roman favourite, fig.

The chocolate comes in a huge range of flavours, but also Italian favourites like pistachio and zabaglione. Tastings are available so you may try before you buy. This is where the cognoscenti buy their pale sugared almonds, traditionally given at weddings or Holy Communion. The old King of Italy ordered his chocolates here too. Find the shop in Via del Piè di Marmo, which translates as 'street of the marble foot'.
Confetteria Moriondo e Gariglio
Via del Piè di Marmo 21-22

Lorenzo Villoresi fragrance

Lorenzo is the most famous Italian super-nose on the planet. He studied psychology at the University of Florence, then travelled in North Africa and the Middle East, where he developed a passion for exotic scents.

In true Italian style Lorenzo has also been known to use olive oil and tomato leaf notes in his perfumes. At home in Florence, Lorenzo creates tailor-made fragrances for the rich and famous.

Perfumistas from all over the world have been known to make the pilgrimage to the Lorenzo Villoresi studio just to track down hard-to-find blends. Madonna and Sting are just two of his many fans.

The best place to buy a precious bottle of the divine Lorenzo Villoresi fragrance in Rome is **Profumeria Materozzoli** at Piazza San Lorenzo in Lucina 5, Piazza di Spagna.

TOP TEN

Roman Chocolates

1. Pistachio
2. Zabaglione
3. Fig
4. Almond
5. Lemon
6. Strawberry
7. Chestnut
8. Hazelnut
9. Espresso
10. Cherry

Carthusia fragrance

This beautiful old-school Italian fragrance was created in Capri in 1380 when a priest from the Carthusian monastery created a bouquet for Queen Giovanna d'Angio. After three days, the water in the vase was scented so beautifully that it formed the basis for a new perfume. In 1948 some of the ancient formulas from the monastery were found again. With the Pope's permission, these were then given to a chemist in Turin and the rest ... is on your wrist. The wild carnations of Capri are used in the perfume today. The best place to buy Carthusia eau de toilette and perfume is **Castelli Profumerie** at Via Frattina 54, Piazza di Spagna.

We love the nightlife

Holiday Goddesses don't necessarily want to go clubbing when they hit Rome. Many of us are steadfast romantics who want to spend the night strolling around the city's ruins. If you do want to go out and stay out, though, tell your taxi driver to drop you at Monte Testaccio. This is actually a famous hill, but with clubs, bars and restaurants built into its base. The hill used to be the site of the old Carnevale of the Middle Ages, when drunk locals would put squealing pigs on carts and send them careering down the side. These days, you do the squealing. Choose from Caffè Latino, Radio Londra, Coyote, Akab, Joia, Ketumbar and Hulalà. If you only have a few nights in Rome, though, don't miss churches lit by candles, or ancient monuments lying in pools of floodlighting. You can go clubbing anywhere, but seeing Rome's most stunning buildings with the moon overhead is unforgettable.

Ponte Milvio bridge

Roman romantics (of which there are many) love to flirt around Ponte Milvio bridge in the evening. And it's all because of a book called *Ho Voglia di Te* (I Want You), which is still in huge demand years after publication.

It turned a little-known ritual on Ponte Milvio into a city-wide obsession. The story is about great passion between two young Romans who swear eternal love to each other by locking themselves together to a lamp post on the Milvio bridge. The key then gets thrown into the Tiber River. Of course.

Before the book, there were just a few mad lovers' padlocks near the bridge. After the book, two lamp posts began to collapse with the strain. There is even a website where you can use a virtual padlock at *lucchettipontemilvio.com*.

Come here at night and you'll feel the buzz. The Met Bar is not far away, and in warm weather you can dine al fresco on sushi (and the inevitable pizza). Come dressed for the occasion and if you've padlocked yourself to a Roman, try to take it off before the bouncer sees your chain. Visit *met-roma.it*.

Anna Johnson

Churches by candlelight

I make a point of seeing churches one hour before closing time. The first time I did this it was an accident: I arrived at a cathedral very late, and wasn't sure if the doors would still be open. They were, and the cathedral was lit by candles, and virtually empty. Then evensong began, and a choir lifted their voices up to the angels. After that, I realised that the only way to really experience these sacred spaces is to slip in just before the gates are locked. It's your chance to get up close and personal with some of the most stunning sculpture and painting in Europe. Nobody obstructs your view and silence reigns, except for (if you are lucky) a heavenly choir. All traces of modern life disappear and for a precious hour, you're back in the 16th century or earlier.

My favourite 5 to 6pm experience is the church of Santi Giovanni e Paolo, dedicated to two Roman officers who nobly refused to fight for the pagan emperor, Julian. They were beheaded here, where their house once stood – their relics are under the altar. The only British pope, Adrian IV, added the bell tower a few centuries later. It is lit by thirty enormous chandeliers in the evening, when the whole place glitters and gleams with gold. I particularly love the lions on the doorway.

Don't be surprised if you see a few young lovers wandering around. This is Rome's most sought-after wedding church. The urns you see leading up to the altar are there to hold vast wedding bouquets.

Jessica Adams

A Roman night walk

Piranesi's etching of the Colosseum (executed in 1757) has a grimy density and sense of potent decay that would be obliterated by a blue sky. Yet that is how most people experience the oldest monuments in the world under a baking sun, deafened by clicking cameras, feeling harried and profoundly disconnected from the past.

I think the very best time to visit ruins is at night. Go in the day for historical facts and functions, then go in the moonlight for the intimate darkness that enfolds the voices and the ghosts.

I once walked to the Colosseum though the Forum at one in the morning. My guide was my southern Italian husband but we didn't talk much. Grass and broken stone underfoot that night made us imagine moving within the biblical throng. You could feel it, that strange mix of the pastoral and the violently urban that Tacitus and Virgil captured so well.

Rome has unpredictable pockets of silence. You find them in shuttered courtyards that peel off from lesser known streets and you find them well outside of herded touring hours. Everyone deserves a moment of personal mystery.

Tourists in the late 18th century insisted on visiting Roman ruins at night and today walking night tours for smaller groups in Rome are becoming more popular, especially in the summer months of June through early September when the monuments are illuminated and free concerts and music are on offer (go to *estateromana.comune.roma.it* for event details).

For a pretty penny (about €250) it is possible to visit the Vatican museums at night (including the Sistine Chapel) and I think this would be a far better investment than a pair of Fendi shoes (visit *italywithus.com*).

I have only ever spent one night in Rome and my expectations were fuelled by the Fellini epic *Roma*. His famous quote – 'There is no end. There is no beginning. There is only the infinite passion of life.' – describes this fantastic movie perfectly. In it, Fellini used the night like a big black canvas to unite the extremes of history. Rome, at midnight, still feels like his fantasy.

A woman screaming in high heels or a centaur playing a flute – I half expected either to trample us in an unguarded moment walking past a decaying temple built for the Vestals.

When we reached the Colosseum it was late. There were no students strumming guitars or idling on scooters. I pressed my face and both my hands against the stone, and I listened. It felt so good to be humbled by the scale of the building, not to 'master' it by taking a photograph.

In that darkness it was easy to imagine the roar of 5000 spectators, or the stench of animals and blood, and deep fried artichokes eaten as snacks in the blazing sun. It was a relief not to see anyone impersonating Russell Crowe at this moment.

And it was a relief to simply be able to feel a profound encounter with history, almost alone. Afterwards we went to the Colosseo subway across the street and zoomed back to the Trevi Fountain for a gelato. I kept my eyes open for women who looked like sacred prostitutes or Vestal Virgins and men who looked like gods. One of them made me a coffee.

Today, the Colosseum is permanently lit in the evening. The walk from Piazza Venezia is through the forum of Trajan at street level.

Anna Johnson

Our seven wonders of Rome

Popes or cats, popes or cats? Holiday Goddess editors were engaged in hot debate over the choice for Rome's seven wonders. Some of us like the black and white kittens which roam Rome. And some of us are Catholics. But in the end, we realised it was all part of the experience. The homeless cats have their own patron saint (Francis of Assisi) just as the papacy has its patron: St Peter, Prince of the Apostles.

The Popes

Pope translates as 'papa' in Latin. The famous keys, which you will see everywhere, come from the story that Jesus gave the keys to the kingdom of heaven to St Peter. Every pope is Peter's successor. New popes are voted by secret ballot. When the ballots are counted, they are burned and smoke rises from the chimney of the Sistine Chapel, letting the faithful know the old order has changed.

The old popes have poetic names – Boniface, Celestine and Leo. Some of them ruled for days, some for decades.

The gold ring you see the current pope wearing is the Ring of the Fisherman. It shows St Peter, the fisherman, in his boat. Followers kneel to kiss this ring. It is always crushed upon the death of any pope, and a new one made.

To be part of a general audience with the Pope, book several months ahead at viator.com

The Pantheon

I first saw the Pantheon circa 1982. My parents had taken me to the Colosseum and the Forum, which I loved, but they looked like ruins that had long ago been abandoned. The Pantheon didn't.

It was already about 2000 years old and I was only 12, but what struck me was the Pantheon's symmetry and perfection when it was clearly so very old. After walking through the precise rows of columns at the front, the inside blew my little mind. From the carved grid pattern on the ceiling that got smaller as the dome got higher, to the marble floor with a similarly spectacular geometric pattern, and then, most astoundingly, this ancient and beautiful building had a big hole in the top. So opulent (and yet so dry). I was stunned and obsessed, asking 'How did they do that? And that? And what about that?'

I now know some of the answers. The inside is so appealing to the senses because it is as wide as it is high (43 metres, if you were wondering); the 'hole at the top' is called an oculus, and the Pantheon can still be fancy inside because they had clever people a couple of thousand years ago who devised subtle but effective drainage.

When I returned to Rome as a teenager, I had to see it again. Since then I've visited so many buildings that look like Rome's Pantheon. This architectural marvel has been an inspiration to many since Hadrian ordered it to be rebuilt in its current form (from Florence's Santa Maria del Fiora, to Paris' Pantheon, to Istanbul's Hagia Sophia, and DC's Jefferson Memorial). But sometimes there's nothing like seeing the original.

Emma Killick

The Pantheon
Piazza della Rotonda

Bus 116

The Vatican post office

The Vatican post office is a real, working post office and sells postcards of the Pope. It is just steps away from St Peter's, making it the most beautifully situated post office in the world, lying within that odd Roman mini-country known as The Vatican. The shops nearby sell saints' cards (everyone from St Francis to the new Australian saint, Mary MacKillop, is represented) and rosary beads.

Look above the post office, and you will see the statues of 140 saints encircling the piazza. The postbox is yellow so you can't miss it.

The Vatican post office
Piazza San Pietro

METRO: Ottaviano San Pietro

Barberini bees

The Barberini family are Rome's oldest fashionistas. They made their fortune trading in fabric in the 16th century, and later achieved fame when one of them became Pope. Today the Prince of Palestrina carries on the Barberini family name. The family's coat of arms is represented by three chic bees, known as Barberini bees.

The distinctive Barberini bees turn up on every library, painting, altar, palace or other great building paid for by the family. And as they did a lot of building, Rome buzzes with dozens of them.

You can see the most beautiful bees at Palazzo Barberini and Piazza Barberini in Rione Trevi.

Palazzo Barberini & Piazza Barberini
Via delle Quattro Fontane

METRO: Barberini

The Sistine Chapel ceiling

The Sistine Chapel ceiling, painted by Michelangelo, at The Vatican, is worth the queue. Everyone sees something different in it. As an astrologer, I was amazed to find Aries, the sign of the ram, tucked away in a section devoted to the creation of the planets. Michelangelo's horoscope is dominated by Aries.

Michelangelo didn't want to do the job because he was a sculptor, not a painter – in fact, he imagined his rivals had orchestrated the commission, with the help of Pope Julius, in order to see him fail. He began the work on May 10, 1508 and wrote a memo to himself, noting the fee (500 ducats).

The sexy male nudes on the ceiling of this biblical work are extremely saucy.

And the question is still asked. Was Michelangelo gay? There is no documentary proof of this at all.

There are many more mysteries in the ceiling of the Sistine Chapel itself.

How on earth did Michelangelo manage it, standing up, with all his cramps, spasms and headaches?

He even wrote a poem about it for his friend Giovanni, moaning 'I've got myself a goitre from this strain.'

Perhaps the work really was an act of God. But the artist didn't see God as previous painters had visualised him. Instead of being a disembodied hand in a cloud, or just an old man with a beard, Michelangelo's God flew through the air by his fingertips.

The best way to see the Sistine Chapel is on a VIP Vatican Tour at 8am. No queue, no heaving crowd. It costs €50, or about AUD$65. Visit *italywithus.com*.

Jessica Adams

The Sistine Chapel
Citta del Vaticano
Entrance in Viale Vaticano

METRO: **Ciprio Musei Vaticani**

WEBSITE: **vatican.va**

Keats-Shelley House

The English poet John Keats died of consumption (tuberculosis) in a house next to the Spanish Steps, which has now been turned into a museum honouring him, Shelley, Byron and other Romantic poets. Amazingly, the man who nursed him here, in his final hours, hardly knew him. His name was Joseph Severn, and he was a British artist. He was also the only person who volunteered to see Keats through to the end – tuberculosis was infectious and deadly. After Keats died, Severn wrote to a friend, 'I am broken down from four nights' watching, and no sleep since, and my poor Keats gone ... the police have been. The furniture, the walls, the floor, everything must be destroyed ...' Well, not quite. The original fireplace and beautifully tiled ceilings are intact, and you can gaze through the window and see the same view as the dying Keats. Women working as artists' models used to drape themselves over the Spanish Steps, opposite, hoping to catch the eye of a painter and get work.

So at least Keats had something interesting to look at in his final days. It made up for the fact that his doctor refused to give him opium. But it was his doctor who planted daisies on his grave. This is a sad place, but a fascinating space. Lord Byron rented a flat over the road.

Jessica Adams

Keats-Shelley House
26 Piazza di Spagna
METRO: **Spagna**

The cats of Rome

If only cats could wear condoms. But even then, the popes of old may have frowned upon kitty contraception. Rome is filled with dumped kittens, who become streetwise moggies living among the ruins where Julius Caesar was murdered. The Cat Sanctuary at Torre Argentina saves them. The cats are cared for by the *gattare*, or cat ladies of Rome.

Italian film star Anna Magnani, the Roman Brigitte Bardot, was one of them. Drop in to say ciao/meow or volunteer to work there on your holidays.

**Torre Argentina Cat Sanctuary
Corner of Via Florida and
Via di Torre Argentina**

WEBSITE: romancats.com

Spas, sanctuaries, sacred spaces

If there is one place in the world where you need a sacred space, it is Rome. In New York they have crosstown traffic, just like the Jimi Hendrix song, but in Rome they have Toytown traffic and it's much crazier. Thousands of tiny cars in primary colours – red, yellow and blue – pack the streets, so finding a quiet place becomes essential. The Temple of Venus and the Temple of Vesta are great places to start.

Know your goddess

To find the Temple of Venus and Temple of Vesta, head for the Via Sacra (Sacred Way) through the Forum. First, though, know your goddess. It will make a huge difference to your Roman holiday as you wander around the galleries, museums and ruins. Minerva, Diana, Juno and all the rest were quite real to Roman women.

- Minerva is the goddess of wisdom. She is often pictured with an owl.
- Diana, goddess of the hunt, is always accompanied by a dog or a deer.
- Juno was Jupiter's wife – the patron of wives and mothers.
- Vesta was worshipped by the famous Vestal Virgins. She was Rome's guardian.
- Ceres was goddess of the harvest. She is often pictured with wheat.
- Proserpina was her daughter – kidnapped by Pluto, god of the underworld.

- Flora was the goddess of flowers and trees. Good for gardeners.
- Psyche was represented by a butterfly – Cupid fell in love with her.
- Venus was the goddess of love – usually shown semi-naked.
- Iris was the messenger goddess, symbolised by a rainbow.

TOP TEN

Roman Goddesses

1. Minerva
2. Diana
3. Juno
4. Vesta
5. Ceres
6. Proserpina
7. Flora
8. Psyche
9. Venus
10. Fortuna

Our favourite spa: AcquaMadre

The AcquaMadre Hammam (Turkish Bath) has women-only access every Monday and Friday. It's minimalist and BC-retro. Thus, there is a tepidarium section (heated to the temperature of a hot summer's day on the beach) a calidarium, with steam, and a frigidarium, or cold bath. The vaulted ceilings and mosaics would have made any ancient Roman goddess feel at home. One of our readers loves the black soap with olive oil in particular.

You can wear your bikini or one-piece, or go naked. Treatments use Dead Sea salt and shea butter, and prices range from €15 for a face-mask to full packages. Holiday Goddesses love the tea room to rehydrate after all the steaming and pummelling.

The AcquaMadre
Via di Sant'Ambrogio 17
WEBSITE: **acquamadre.it**

When in Rome, do your yoga

Holiday Goddess editor, yoga teacher and host of *Yoga TV* Kris McIntyre asked local Kundalini Yoga teacher Uttamjit Kaur to recommend Rome's best yoga spaces. Close to the Vatican, **Budokan In** (Via Properzio 4, *budokanin.com*) offers drop-in yoga and meditation classes as well as interesting workshops and courses with local and international teachers including renowned teacher, trainer and author, **Sadhana Singh**. At Budokan In you can also experience Shakti Dance lessons with **Sara Avtar**. **Guru Dev Singh**, acclaimed in the Americas and Europe as 'one of the greatest healers of our time' also calls Rome home. His teachings combine the ancient Mayan, Totanac and Curandero traditions of Mexico with Kundalini Yoga, yogic healing and Re Man meditation practices. His yoga centre in Rome (Via F. Corridoni, 15 – 00195, *satnamrasayan.it*) is renowned for producing some of the finest healers in Europe.

If Kundalini Yoga is not your thing, **Instituto Samantabhadra** (Via de Genrosa 24, *samantabhadra.org*) teaches Tibetan Buddhism; **Essere Pace** (*esserepace.org*) offers Zen meditation with Vietnamese master Thich Nhat Hanh; and **Nives Yoga** (Via S. Onofrio, *nivesyoga.it*) offers classes in Jivamukti Yoga and meditation.

For updates on classes and workshops in Rome, visit **Italian Yoga Journal** at *yogajournal.it*.

The Janiculum: sacred space

Climb the hill known as **The Janiculum** at sunrise to offer your Salute to the Sun, or go at sunset for an amazing view of Rome's domes. American Holiday Goddess readers are particularly fond of this ancient hill, so you may make some new friends once you all climb down. The Janiculum was home to the god Janus, who had two faces – one gazing at the past, the other at the future. This is also where the soothsayers of Ancient Rome used to sit and watch for signs, or omens. Janus is the god of beginnings and transitions, and it's uncanny how many women we know end up in Rome at the start of something – or during a time of change. You will find images of Janus all over the city, but this is the god's special place. It's a wonderful place to stretch, or sit, knowing that for hundreds of years, others have contemplated their own beginnings and transitions before you.

And Venus was her name

Venus is the most famous Roman goddess. She's been the subject of the Velvet Underground song 'Venus in Furs', the Bananarama hit 'Venus' and Uma Thurman played her (naked) in *The Adventures of Baron Munchausen*. And everyone knows the famous Botticelli painting of her being born in a clam shell. Where do you find her in Rome today, though?

The answer is, everywhere. But her most sacred space is the Temple of Venus and Roma. Like so many other ancient and beautiful Roman places, it's best seen at night, by floodlight, under the stars. Roma is '*amor*' (love) spelled backwards so the twinning of Venus, goddess of love, with the city is one of the best 2000-year-old puns in the world.

This was the largest temple in Ancient Rome, which gives you some idea of how important Venus was to the city.

Her husband Mars, the god of war, and her son Cupid – the naughty cherub with the bow and arrow – also dominate the city. You might call them Rome's first family.

Venus was known as Aphrodite to the Greeks and to Woody Allen as *Mighty Aphrodite*. Unbelievably, the old temple was used as a car park in the 1980s. When it was finally restored, traces of gold leaf were found in the ruins.

A Roma Pass, which gives you use of the city's public transportation network, and free entry to two museums, is the easiest way to gain access.

The Temple of Venus and Roma, The Forum

Roma Pass website: **romapass.it**

Looking for the real Madonna

There are many Madonna fans at Holiday Goddess. Several of us have made the pilgrimage to the Mini Madonna Museum of Manhattan (see page 239) in New York. If you are seeking sacred space in Roma, though, you have to turn to the real thing. The most famous Madonna in the city is at Sant'Agostino church. She is the subject of a staggeringly realistic painting by Caravaggio, *Madonna di Loreto*. The Loreto is the place where the Madonna's house was said to have been miraculously transported to in the 13th century, carried by angels.

The painting shows Madonna in Loreto, holding the infant Jesus and receiving peasants at the front door, who are on their knees with dirty feet. Also in the church is the *Madonna del Parto*, where pregnant mums leave their prayers. The *Madonna della Rosa*, also inside, shows her with roses on the bed.

Basilica di Sant'Agostino

Piazza di Sant' Agostino

We heart Roman art

Ancient mosaics

Holiday Goddess editors have divided opinions on Italian art. Some think the Futurists are still where it's at. Others prefer the Pietà of Michelangelo. One thing everyone loves about Rome, though, is the charm of the ancient mosaics.

Our favourite mosaic of all time shows women in leather bikinis throwing what appear to be pizzas at each other. The mosaic tiles on the floors of the Roman baths are now safely on museum walls, carefully restored after heavy gladiator sandal impact and the dust of time. As you wander around Rome's preserved mosaics you will notice plenty of aquatic themes. Sea creatures were great favourites in Roman baths. We have to admire the way they pieced together the tiniest tiles to create gigantic squid, and frolicking fish.

As you walk around the Baths of Caracalla today you will have to close your eyes and imagine the beautiful tiling around the swimming pool, the plunge baths, the steam room, the hot room, warm room and cold room. Your boyfriend may have fun closing his eyes and imagining the women in leather bikinis throwing pizza.

Cupid, the toddler god of desire, is a firm favourite in many Roman mosaics. He is always naughty, even when he is not holding his notorious bow and arrow.

It all makes your hotel bathroom look pretty ordinary. Two thousand years ago, they thought nothing of creating the most complicated scenes using mosaic (a man bending over, bottom in the air, picking olives) or the most ambitious panoramas (ships which look almost 3D today).

Perhaps it was the ancient Roman equivalent of today's *Magic Eye* books. One of our editors, who has two small children, took them to see the mosaics in the church of Santa Pudenziana, then inspired them to make their own mosaic back home, using crushed-up cornflakes and coloured paint. Don't do that in the hotel.

Our favourite Roman mosaic collections (easiest to get to, easiest to see) are in Palazzo Massimo alla Terme, near Termini train station. The mosaics are on the top floors, faded by time, but somehow even more beautiful for it. The soothing palette of washed-out sea blue and pale white suits the mesmerising underwater scenes, displayed on the walls. It's the most beautiful interior decoration in the world.

Palazzo Massimo alla Terme
Largo di Villa Peretti 1

METRO: Repubblica

Livia's wall paintings

If you're going to see the mosaics at Palazzo Massimo alla Terme, then don't miss Livia's wall paintings on the top floors.

But first, a word on the museum. A huge statue of Minerva, the ancient Roman goddess of wisdom, greets you at the entrance to Rome's most female-friendly museum and gallery. Downstairs you'll see stone heads of all the beastly Roman emperors, from Nero to Caligula. Bronzes from Caligula's villa lie upstairs: the heads of lions and wolves with rings in their mouths look alternately cruel or sad. A bit like Caligula himself.

Of all the gods here, Apollo is the biggest rock star. With his firm, peachy buttocks and permed pubic hair, he is like the Roman version of our fantasy of Robert Plant, circa 1970. Apollo was the god of music, too.

Livia, wife of the filthy-rich Emperor Augustus, ordered a fresco for the dining room of her villa which is still intact, upstairs. The fresco shows herbs and plants you can still grow today: the ilex (which Romans used for fortune-telling), the laurel (sacred to sexy Apollo), the myrtle (sacred to Venus, the goddess of love) and the opium poppy too. The fresco is stunning and takes up all four walls of a large upstairs room. In the absence of a flat-screen TV, Livia had this in her life instead.

Caravaggio in Rome

My first fleeting visit to Rome was spent tending to a fractious toddler. Late on our last afternoon, not long before we were due to head to Fiumicino, I regretted all the art I hadn't seen. My husband proposed a detour, leading me to the steps of Santa Maria del Popolo. 'In you go,' he gestured, 'you've got fifteen minutes.' Fifteen minutes, plus a conversion and a crucifixion (Paul and Peter's): Caravaggio at his queasily vertiginous best.

The painter skipped Rome on a murder rap, never to return. I came back asap – for the unmissable *Judith Beheading Holofernes* at Galleria Nazionale d'Arte Antica; *David with the Head of Goliath* at Galleria Borghese; and also for *John in the Wilderness*. Caravaggio created several paintings with this title, the most notable of which are in Galleria Nazionale d'Arte Antica and Galleria Borghese.

Donna Wheeler

Italian Moderns: the Futurists

As the 20th century arrived, the British had the Bloomsbury Group, who sat around drinking tea, chatting about Picasso, fancying each other rotten and choosing curtains. The Italians, in contrast, had a mad poet named Filippo Tommaso Marinetti, who created a manifesto and printed it on the front page of *Le Figaro* in Paris. It declared in part that art could be nothing but 'violence, cruelty and injustice'. Not only did Marinetti have one of the worst moustaches known to womankind, he was also a boy racer, and crashed his car in a ditch early on in the movement.

If you're a lady fan of Marinetti and his wild colleagues, then you're called a Futurista. They were into fashion too. Ernesto Michahelles (known as 'Thayaht') designed unisex overalls for men and women as part of the revolution. Eek.

The best Futurist work is at The Galleria Nazionale D'Arte Moderna at Viale delle Belle Arti 131.

Enzo Cucchi

Although he was born in Ancona (and is now exclusively represented by Galerie Bruno Bischofberger, Zurich), Enzo Cucchi is a Roman artist through and through. He came to Rome as a poet in the 1970s, coming to painting after encountering Italy's then flowering Transavantgarde. His expressionist canvases skirt chaos with a very classical sense of form.

They are riven with poetic, figurative symbolism, a not-so-subliminal rendering of the city's many layers, its innate theatre, and its restless, carousing ghosts. Look for his work at the Galleria Nazionale d'Arte Moderna, and MACRO, plus mosaics gracing Stazione Termini's l'ala Mazzoniana.

Donna Wheeler

Beautiful Bernini

Bernini was the 17th century sculptor and architect who worked on St Peter's – and practically everything else in Rome. He was all about drama. Even hundreds of years ago, his fountains in Piazza Barberini must have stopped crowds. Today, people still stop and stare.

There is passion and sensuality in everything Bernini created. His statues don't stand still, they often pose as if they are between the sheets. His famous sculpture of Saint Teresa has been interpreted by some people as a rendition of a woman in mid-orgasm. Well, it is called *The Ecstasy of St Teresa*.

Whatever you might think of that, Bernini manages to make marble look succulent, fleshy, warm and real. It's very hard not to reach out and stroke his work, even when signs forbid it. He was inspired by mythological creatures, like the triton (a kind of male mermaid) as much as he was by religion, but everything gets the Bernini touch: it's all R-rated.

Bernini is about the climaxes in life, no matter if he is supposed to be sculpting a saint at the time. He was passionate in real life too, although not a lover you would want to mess with: his mistress suffered horribly when he caught her out.

Imagine being on the other side of the grille in the confessional box with Bernini. Some poor priest must have done the honours. What a visionary, though. He helped magic up Rome.

Jessica Adams

Bernini's Fountains

Fontana del Tritone, Piazza Barberini

Fontana delle Api, Via Vittorio Veneto

Vintage and markets

Holiday Goddess editors' and readers' favourite Rome market is Porta Portese held every Sunday. **Daria La Valle** is an Italian conference producer who knows the city (and its second-hand bargains) well.

On Sunday mornings, between Trastevere and Ostiense, you can find a market that's a little like Portobello Road in London. This is the famous Porta Portese Sunday market. It's huge – you need at least two or three hours to visit it. It's like an open-air thrift store where people bring out telephones, books, furniture, clothes – anything that can be sold.

Rome's best retro treasures

The Trastevere neighbourhood has lots of traditional trattorias, so you can come here for lunch after the market. The hipster bar Freni e Frizioni is here too, if you want to stay for dinner – they have fantastic aperitifs (visit *freniefrizioni.com*).

Via del Governo Vecchio is the best street to look for Rome's ever-changing vintage and second-hand clothing ranges. In all cases, here are the biggest Italian names or designs to dive for:

Olivetti typewriters Those funky old orange and red Olivetti typewriters may be tricky to ship home (or even get through customs) but they are also tomorrow's antiques – especially if in working order.

Valentino The menswear can be surprisingly cheap and a well-cut Valentino jacket looks great with jeans. What you're really after, though, are the white couture frocks from circa 1968.

Elsa Schiaparelli Her handbags are in fashion museums all over the world, but you may see some old perfume boxes – in which case, pounce. Even an empty bottle of Shocking is valuable.

***Bellezza* magazine** Old copies of *Bellezza* or Italian *Vogue* are extremely collectable (if you can fight the designers off at the trestle tables). The 1950s editions are worth framing.

Emilio Pucci Sometimes Pucci can be cheap. One of our Holiday Goddess editors found a slightly grubby cosmetics bag (recent) for an okay price. The '60s evening bags are very precious.

Brioni suits Cary Grant wore this immaculately-cut Italian label and so did Pierce Brosnan as James Bond. Thrill the man in your life if you spot the magic Brioni brand, or alter for yourself!

1960s Mod jackets Colin MacInnes' 1959 novel about British youth, *Absolute Beginners* (which later inspired the film, which produced the David Bowie song), was a hymn to 1960s Italian Mod clothing. The jackets were produced by plenty of no-name labels but are still collectable. MacInnes said the jacket had to have 'two little vents, three buttons'.

Missoni Missoni knitwear with its signature zigzag and wavy stripes can be surprisingly cheap if recent. The 1970s sweater sets are in fashion museums around the world.

Fiorucci If it's the colour of neon fruit then it's probably Fiorucci, which was massive in the 1970s, and isn't too hard to find in Roma. Lauren Bacall used to wear it too.

Giorgio Armani What you're seeking is 1980s Giorgio, and preferably one of his famous unstructured jackets. Totally yuppie and in 2020, probably your eBay delight.

Gianni Versace cosmetics Here's something else Roman women seem to regularly deposit at market stalls – partly used Versace cosmetics. Bargainista!

Moschino One Holiday Goddess reader picked up a Moschino denim jacket for €10 and says she has worn it endlessly. Anything from his 'Stop the Fashion System!' period is worth buying.

Gianfranco Ferré The vintage gods will be beaming down upon you if you can find Ferré, but his sculptured, dramatic pieces are easy to spot. They'll take up half the stall or rack.

Laura Biagiotti The Queen of Cashmere, and also surprisingly chiconomical when found second-hand. She dared to make cashmere coats, which you may not find – but the tops are out there.

La Perla underwear Would you wear someone else's underwear? Maybe, if it was a black mesh bustier from La Perla. Founded in 1954, La Perla creates *La Dolce Vita* undies.

Gucci handbags These beautifully made bags can be seriously cheap in Rome, depending on the design. You won't find the bamboo-handled bags from the 1960s at a good price, but the logo-printed, heavy fabric clutches can be found for around €25.

Fendi baguettes 'Buy! Buy!' one of our fashionista insiders shrieked. They're totally over, and that's why they're totally worth investing in, should you find them in a vintage store.

Salvatore Ferragamo scarves The 1940s 'invisible sandals' with Perspex heels may be beyond you, but the 1980s scarves turn up with surprising regularity in Italy.

Prada nylon rucksacks Prada shoes (if a bit battered) can be had for a song in Rome, but it's the nylon rucksacks that are tomorrow's collectors' items. Iconic, and rumoured to be making a comeback.

Daria La Valle

Our favourite daycations

Pompeii for beginners

When Vesuvius exploded with the force of 10 atom bombs on 24 August 79AD, it buried Pompeii under 30 feet of ash, pumice, and mud. Ironically, the ash that killed the over 20,000 inhabitants preserved many of their outlines for posterity, so when plaster was poured in centuries later, moulds of the actual people were made, startling in their detail and heartrending in their desperation.

These figures are only one of the highlights of Pompeii, which is a must-see if you're travelling near Rome or Naples. Once a resort city for rich Romans, with 118 bars, open-air amphitheatres for plays and gladiator bouts, gorgeous bathhouses, and brothels with frescoes that leave little to the imagination, Pompeii has been astonishingly well-preserved. When you're standing in the city square, looking up at the benign slope of Vesuvius, it is quite easy to imagine the terror of its inhabitants when their world was about to be shattered.

If your Italian schedule is tight, it is possible to do a day trip for those sturdy of limb – but be warned that walking on the uneven cobblestone streets worn smooth by thousands of feet and the wheels of long-gone chariots is not easy, and in the summer it is brutally hot and exhausting. Be sure to visit the sumptuous House of the Vettii, House of the Faun, the X-rated Lupanar brothel, and the glorious Villa of the Mysteries just outside the city walls. I was particularly drawn to the Garden of the Fugitives, where a grouping of 13 plaster figures lay silently where they fell, one of them stretching out his hand in supplication to the city gates.

The least stressful and most expensive day trip is to have your hotel arrange a car and driver, and hire a guide when you arrive or take a detailed guidebook.

You can also take a very early train to Naples (2½ hours), then transfer to the Pompeii Scavi commuter train (30 minutes); reverse it to get back to Rome by around 11pm.

Or, do a Google for tour groups, which normally I avoid but in this case are worthwhile, as you'll share (or have a kip in) a van with like-minded travellers, perhaps catch a bit of Naples, and have a knowledgeable guide to show you the naughtiest frescoes. Avoid any tours that make pit stops at tourist trap 'local artisans'. Dark Rome Tours (*darkrome.com*) has a day trip that takes you first to the rim of Vesuvius, a perfect way to set the mood for what lies in the valley below.

Karen Moline

Dating, mating and dining in old Pompeii

Pompeii is the most amazing time-capsule – lost for over 1700 years and only uncovered in the 18th century, it shows what Italians believed long ago, and why they believed it. They lived in a world of myth, which was far more powerful and true for them than our current mishmash of beliefs (and non-belief) today. They really did think that the goddess Venus had given birth to a cherubic son called Cupid, and that he used his bow and arrow to wound helpless humans so that they would fall helplessly in love. When Cupid was sent to trick the beautiful Psyche (Venus was jealous of her) it all went horribly wrong, though, and hot candle wax dripped on his skin. He faltered, and plunged the arrow into himself. Obsessive desire for Psyche followed, enraging his mother Venus still further. Seeing the Cupids (there is a small army of them) in Pompeii shows you how the Romans dealt with lust. They tried to laugh at it. Why? Because it could get you killed. This was something the Vestal Virgins knew to their cost. And so did high-born Roman women, who could be exiled for adultery. No wonder Cupid was associated with the pain of an arrow wound.

Today's cute Cupids owe something to this great need within the Romans to defuse and downsize desire. Cupid in Pompeii is shown as a mischievous imp. By picturing him as nothing more than a chubby toddler, they tried to downplay the utter seriousness of the 'wound'.

In the bedrooms of Pompeii (the cubiculum) the naughty frescoes that Holiday Goddess editor Karen Moline knows well are still unbelievably fresh and clear after all these years (and all that ash). It was normal for people to have erotic art painted straight onto their bedroom walls, and one scene could be straight out of *Cosmopolitan* magazine. The only thing that will probably concern you is the fact that in so many scenes, the women appear to be doing all the work.

In the changing room of the Suburban Baths at Pompeii you can still see the incredible paintings above numbered lockers (for bathers to store their clothes) sorted by sexual acts. A description of one locker fresco translates as 'woman-riding' and another as 'cunnilingus'. It's truly difficult to think of this getting past any municipal council today! (But it would probably make more people swim their daily laps.)

Of course, the other great Roman pleasure was food. The House of Julia Felix has a wall-painting only discovered in the 18th century, clearly showing eggs in a bowl, and birds ready for roasting. It's so fresh it looks as if Nigella Lawson had just left the building.

The Italian lust for life seems so strong in the ruins that it seems quite wrong that it all vanished in minutes. The bird that is perched on a thorny rose next to laurel and chamomile daisies on the walls, inside the House of the Golden Bracelet, is practically chirping.

They seemed so much like us, with their skylights and sunken pools. Even our modern chair arrangements (based on their famous triclinimum three-way seating) are based on the old Italians. But what a waste of serious interior decoration. Rather like the people on the Titanic, the people of Pompeii couldn't possibly have known the music was going to stop – and there wasn't even a chance for the band (or in their case, the women with harps) to play on.

Jupiter couldn't save them despite the fact that he had a temple there. Neither could Apollo, the brilliant, beautiful young god with the perm and the mysterious powers. The eruption, which began near lunchtime on 24 August 79AD, came from a mountain called Vesuvius that nobody had even guessed was a volcano.

Jessica Adams

To see more, visit our video tour of Pompeii at *holidaygoddess.com*

Bologna

Bologna – *la dotta, la grassa, la rossa*. So named *smart*, for its thousand year old university, *fat*, for its proud culinary heritage of pasta, cheese and ham, and *red*, for, some say, its ochre-red streetscapes, but, more often, for its fiery left politics. If cities had dating profiles, this is one that I'd want to answer. While Bologna's miles of Mediaeval colonnades have always had appeal (even Dante raved about its skyline of spindly, tilting towers), it has long suffered a stodgy reputation, playing second fiddle to its glamorous Tuscan neighbours. I came for the Casa Morandi – the studio museum of a meditative mid-century painter of quotidian *natura morta* – but found a city that was worth many repeat visits. Yes, for all its above stated attributes, including the tortellini, but also because it's an Italian anomaly – Bologna understands cool.

I've always loved the frisson of house museums, and artists' houses in particular. Casa Morandi, up a flight of dark stairs in Via Fondazza, was the apartment where Giorgio Morandi lived and worked for over fifty years. Restored and open to the public in 2009, one can peer at his atelier and various cupboards stuffed with vases, bottles, shells and such. I was particularly enchanted by the view of a little garden, glimpsed from a circular window, imagining he had similarly gazed out, between gentle, careful brushstrokes. The city has a significant collection of his work at Museo Morandi, housed in a grand palazzo on the main square. It's extraordinary to see his work en masse, encountering the gentle repetitions, variations and painterly musings that emerge over years, and years, of disciplined work.

After Morandi's calm, one is ready for the energy of Museo d'Arte Moderna di Bologna – MAMbo – one of Italy's best contemporary museums, with a strong collection of Italian art from the '60s on, and hard-hitting temporary shows. The bar is great too, stylish without being uptight, with unusually good music.

This mix – on the ball, but rarely uptight – extends to the way locals dress. In Bologna they've banished bling, swapping it for deconstruction, irony and stealth-wealth luxe. Camera con Vista, on Via Santo Stefano, drew me in when my small daughter spotted a rather dashing looking cat-headed mannequin in the window. Super-human sized, dressed in an ancient naval jacket, he also packed something of a bulge in his rather scanty skin-coloured shorts; a perfect introduction to the idiosyncratic fancy waiting inside. This is one of the world's most beautiful shops, with silk dresses, feather capes and candles by Mad et Len, and a gallery space. Best of all, the idea that they are selling goods seems secondary to visual wonder.

Bologna's restaurants don't try to fix what isn't broken: piadina, precise little pasta parcels in brodo (broth), parmesan (really from Parma, which is just up the road), or plates of prosciutto. Two hours by fast train from Rome make it perfectly possible for a day trip, though missing out on dinner and, after that, the city's cracking nightlife, would be a shame.

Donna Wheeler

Playlists and downloads

Tamara Sheward has featured in, or written, some of our favourite travel books, and is also a Holiday Goddess editor. She is based in Australia, where her career adventures include time at *triple j magazine*. Tamara is presently roaming Europe for Lonely Planet, but has some special playlist and download recommendations for Rome.

Whether you're a seasoned Trevi Fountain penny-pitcher (remember folks: three coins, right hand, left shoulder = Italian husband) or your *esperienza Italiana* stretches as far as slopping pasta over the pages of a dog-eared Dan Brown, everyone has a mental impression of the Eternal City. From pizzas to piazzas, Italy's (and once the world's) exalted capital is embedded in our psyche, so it's hardly surprising that it's been honoured repeatedly in song and screen. Treat your eyes and ears to these evocative Rome-centric hits before you go for a taste of what awaits in *La Bella Citta*!

Tamara Sheward

Rome playlist

Phoenix, *Rome*: French indie band sings about the Colosseum (apt), smoking (ditto) and a 'tropical sunset' (say what?). Atmospheric and a bit mysterious, just like its namesake.

Dean Martin, *Arrivederci Roma*: Remember those 1950s movies in which the heroine says goodnight to her suitor, closes the front door and collapses against it, eyes sparkling and hands crossed over heaving bosom? And you were always like, 'as if'? That's what I thought too. Until it was Rome standing on the other side of that door.

Peggy Lee, *Autumn in Rome*: *Romanticismo*, Roma-style. Swoony, scratchy nostalgia punctuated by breathy sighs and twittering birds. Prepare to fall in love.

The Three Tenors, *Nessun Dorma*: This is a back-of-neck-tickler no matter where it's sung, but these boys do it best belting it out live in Rome (at the Baths of Caracalla, no less). Grand, majestic and possibly prophetic, given the city's legendary nightlife: the title translates to 'None shall sleep'.

B52s, *Roam*: Yes, I know. But this song – all kick-arse, girl-on-the-road harmonies and handclaps – will have you boogeying around your (half-packed) suitcase in goosebumpy pre-travel delirium. And who says you can't pretend they *are* saying 'Rome'?

Complimentary Download: Roma Chill
Want to unwind in the hotel after a day of dodging crazy Roman traffic? Holiday Goddess editors James Williams and Justin Tabari have compiled a free, exclusive podcast of music to unwind to. Visit *lifestylechill.com/rome* to collect your download.

Meet the Holiday Goddesses

Jessica Adams worked as a team editor on *21st Century Goddess*, *Girls' Night In* and *Kids' Night In*. She is a contributing editor at *Cosmopolitan UK*, a novelist and astrologer.

Gillian Anderson-Price's cult Primrose Hill shop, Judith Michael & Daughter, features in *London Vintage*. Her clients include Helena Bonham-Carter, Kate Moss and Jude Law.

Victoria Aitken's music has topped the UK dance charts four times in a career that has taken her from Istanbul to Paris. She is a well-known freelance travel writer in Europe and the US.

Vicki Arkoff's magazine work includes *MAD*, *Daily Variety* and *Entertainment Weekly*. She is the author of authorised biographies on Paul McCartney and Frank Sinatra.

Eleonora Baldwin is an American born, Italian raised writer, gourmet connoisseur, and culinary travel enthusiast. She lives in her small Rome flat with her son and many dreams.

Helen Basini is currently studying for her PhD at the University of Limerick, Ireland. She is a team editor on the *Kids' Night In* series in aid of the children's charity War Child.

Pia Jane Bijkerk is the author and photographer of *Paris: Made by Hand* and *Amsterdam: Made by Hand*. Visit *blog.piajanebijerk.com*.

Faith Bleasdale is the author of six books and working on her seventh. She lives with her toddler in North Devon, which she reached via London and Singapore.

Janine Brown is a graphic artist and greeting card designer, who has collaborated on several books with Affirmations Publishing House. She's a seamstress and passionate about vintage.

Alison Carmichael-Rulten loves to travel and has marketed *Harper's Bazaar*, *Cosmopolitan*, *That's Life!*, *Sydney Morning Herald*, *Vogue Entertaining + Travel* and *delicious*.

Peter Clarke is a DOP and cameraman who has been smuggled into Sri Lanka, but also covered interviews with Tom and Nicole. He now runs Heaven and Earth Films.

Art and music lover and avid antique collector, **Liz Challis**, follows her passion and paints full time, living six months in Australia and six months in France every year.

Andreina Cordani is a travel-obsessed writer whose magazine career has spanned from *Cosmopolitan* to *Good Housekeeping*.

Pip Cummings is based in New York. She has worked as a deputy editor at McHugh Media and Fairfax Media, and was curator and editor at TEDx in Sydney from 2010–2011.

Jane de Teliga is a fashion writer and stylist, with a passion for travel. A contributor to the media in London and Sydney, she co-created personal styling service, *styleoncall.co.uk*.

Imogen Edwards-Jones is the author of the internationally bestselling *Babylon* series. She has travelled all over the world and is an honorary Cossack.

After fifteen years of working in fashion and photography in London, **Leonie Edwards-Jones** is now based in Delhi, bringing a bit of London to India and vice versa.

Lily Evans is a stylist and has worked on shoots for international editions of *Vogue* and runway shows including Victoria's Secret.

Sara Foster is the bestselling author of two psychological suspense novels, *Come Back to Me* and *Beneath the Shadows*, and is always on the lookout for the next travel adventure.

Mia Freedman is the editor and publisher of *mamamia.com.au*. She is a former editor-in-chief at *Cosmopolitan*, *Cleo* and *Dolly* and the author of *The New Black*, *Mama Mia* and *Mia Culpa*.

Harriet Griffey is a writer and journalist, and the author of fourteen books. She has lived in Camden, London for the last 25 years. For more visit *harrietgriffey.com*.

Louise Hawson is the Sydney-based author and photographer of the cult blog and book *52 Suburbs*. She is also an award-winning copywriter and art director.

Wendy Holden, a former journalist, is a writer of comic novels with ten top-ten bestsellers under her belt. Recent books include *Filthy Rich*, *Gallery Girl* and *Marrying Up*.

Alana Hunt is an artist and writer who works between the Sydney suburbs, the streets of New Delhi, the occupied valley of Kashmir and the East Kimberly region of Australia.

Bethea Jenner is a writer, astrologer and Londoner who left the music industry in 1990 to concentrate on esoteric disciplines. London Transport is just one of her obsessions.

Anna Johnson has written for magazines including *Vogue*, *Condé Nast Traveller* and *Vanity Fair*. She is the author of *Three Black Skirts*, *The Yummy Mummy Manifesto* and *Handbags*.

Rachel Johnson has three children, two houses, one husband, and a dog. She edits *The Lady*, and is the author of *Notting Hell*, *Shire Hell*, *The Mummy Diaries* and *A Diary of The Lady*.

Anneli Knight is author of *Flirting with Finance*, contributor to *The Age* and *Sydney Morning Herald* in Australia and has recently completed her PhD in creative writing.

Daria La Valle qualified in International Relations in Rome, then moved to Singapore to marry her long-time-long-distance love. She tries to return to Rome whenever she can.

Emma Killick is an avid gardener, California lawyer and UK solicitor. She has travelled all her life, and is now based in London, escaping often to a farmhouse in France.

Helen Lederer is well-known for *Absolutely Fabulous*, *Calendar Girls* and *The Vagina Monologues*. Her wine expertise has featured in the *Sunday Express* and on the BBC.

Valli Little trained at Le Cordon Bleu in London and is the food editor at *delicious.* magazine and the author of several cookbooks for HarperCollins.

Felicity Loughrey is the editor of *Vogue Australia* online at *vogue.com.au*. She writes for *Vogue Australia*, *Vogue Living*, *GQ*, *Men's Style*, *Sunday* and *The Australian Way*.

Kathryn McCusker has taught in many leading yoga studios throughout London, including Triyoga and Alchemy. Visit *kmyoga.com*.

Kris McIntyre is best known as the host of Australia's *Yoga TV*. She's a writer, editor and yoga teacher with a love for wellness travel. Visit her at *krismcintyre.com*.

Julie Moline's travel writer credits include *Harper's Bazaar*, *The Daily Telegraph* and *The International Herald Tribune*. She also writes speeches for travel professionals.

Karen Moline is a NYC-based novelist, journalist and ghostwriter, who has travelled the world in search of all things divinely, delectably, and deliriously Goddess.

Rosie Mullender is *Cosmopolitan*'s commissioning editor and 'Sex and the Single Girl' columnist. She blogs about single-girl life and burritos, and recently made her very first trip to New York.

Freya North is currently working on her twelfth novel. She lives on a small farm in Hertfordshire and classifies her bestselling novels as 'feisty romps'.

Justin North is one of the world's most acclaimed chefs and the author of two award-winning books *Bécasse: Inspirations and Flavours* and *French Lessons*.

Rachael Oakes-Ash is a journalist, travel writer, documentary maker, author of two books and ski writer for the *Sydney Morning Herald* and *The Age*. Visit her at *oakesash.com*.

Tyne O'Connell's thirteen novels are inhabited by British eccentrics and aristos at large. She has written features for *Vogue* and *Elle*. For more visit *clementyne.com*.

Sue Ostler runs Flirt Diva Therapy in London. She is the author of several books, and has written for *Rolling Stone*, *Metro* and *Time Out*. Visit her at *flirtdiva.com*.

Jane Pirkis is an academic psychologist based at the University of Melbourne. She has published more than 120 scientific journal articles on various aspects of mental health, and is a firm believer that travel is good for the soul.

Tamara Pitelen is the Dubai-based editor of *Wealth*. She has written for newspapers and magazines for 18 years and has lived in Asia, England, New Zealand and Australia.

Tamara Sheward is an author, travel writer, guidebook author/ occasional TV presenter for Lonely Planet and co-editor of anthologies *Your Mother Would Be Proud* and *Kids' Night In 4*.

Rebecca Sparrow is deputy editor of *mamamia.com*, an acclaimed novelist and a columnist for the *Sunday Mail*. Visit *rebeccasparrow.com*.

Justin Tabari is picture editor at Holiday Goddess and is also part of the team at Lifestyle Podnetwork. His interests include Reiki and Asian food and travel.

Noah Taylor has been tooling around with film and music for 25 years. He's smoked Turkish cigarettes with Sir John Gielgud and made some unpopular records. He lives in Brighton.

Jenny Valentish has worked as an editor on *triple j magazine* and *Your Mother Would Be Proud*. She is a writer whose freelance work includes the *Sydney Morning Herald* and *NME*.

Julian Venables is a life long traveller and astrologer. His adventures include BBC radio, podcasting on *The Astrology Show*, writing for *New Woman* and Solar Fire Gold software.

Donna Wheeler is the author of several Lonely Planet guidebooks and also writes on art, architecture and food. She divides her time between Melbourne and Europe.

James Williams is a Holiday Goddess editor based in Sydney, where he also runs Lifestyle Podnetwork, one of the world's fastest-growing podcast websites. Visit *lifestylepodnetwork.com*

Susan Wyndham is the literary editor at the *Sydney Morning Herald*, and a former editor of *Good Weekend* magazine and New York correspondent for *The Australian*.

Continue the Holiday Goddess journey online

Point your phone at this code to be transported to Holiday Goddess online. Every chapter in *The Holiday Goddess Handbag Guide to Paris, New York, London and Rome* comes with a complimentary suitcase of information on our website, including exclusive Holiday Goddess TV postcards, created by Peter Clarke from Heaven and Earth Films. You can also collect your podcasts, luggage tags and downloads from *holidaygoddess.com*.

Praise for holidaygoddess.com

'A website for women who love their holidays: it shares classified travel information, best tips and secrets and real-person tips.'

Sydney Morning Herald

'A one stop shop for anyone too busy to spend hours on the Internet looking for holiday information.'

Vogue Entertaining + Travel

'With contributions from more than thirty former journalists and editors from fashion and lifestyle magazines, the site is packed with information from all corners of the globe.'

Time Out Singapore

Acknowledgments

Every book is a journey involving many people. The Holiday Goddesses would like to thank their publisher Fiona Henderson and agent Pippa Masson for guiding them so brilliantly from departure lounge to final destination.

Every Holiday Goddess editor from New York to London would also like to acknowledge Mel 'Melticulous' Maxwell as the most dependable of co-pilots and designer Jane Waterhouse for her creative vision and inspiration.

To Natalie Costa Bir, Rachel Dennis, Kelly Fagan, Sarah Haines and Claire Wharton – after all your hard work on our book, we wish you the happiest of holidays too.

And finally, a large bottle of champagne from the drinks trolley to Maggie Alderson, John Colpo, Rita Davidson, Mark Ferguson, Joe Guario, Paula Henderson, Jackie Kavanagh, Emmanuel Moline, Miss Moneypenny, Fiona Perkins, Clair Roberts and Holly Venables.

HarperCollins*Publishers*

First published in Australia in 2011
by HarperCollins*Publishers* Australia Pty Limited
ABN 36 009 913 517
harpercollins.com.au

Compilation copyright © Jessica Adams 2011
Illustrations copyright © Anna Johnson 2011

HarperCollins*Publishers*

Level 13, 201 Elizabeth Street, Sydney, NSW 2000, Australia
31 View Road, Glenfield, Auckland 0627, New Zealand
A 53, Sector 57, NOIDA, UP, India
77–85 Fulham Palace Road, London W6 8JB, United Kingdom
2 Bloor Street East, 20th floor, Toronto, Ontario M4W 1A8, Canada
10 East 53rd Street, New York NY 10022, USA

Cataloguing-in-Publication entry is available from the National Library of Australia

ISBN: 978 0 7322 9390 1

Cover and internal design by Jane Waterhouse, HarperCollins Design Studio
Cover and internal illustrations by Anna Johnson
Colour reproduction by Graphic Print Group, South Australia
Printed and bound in China by RR Donnelley on 128gsm Matt Art

5 4 3 2 1   11 12 13 14